Chitto Harjo

The Henry Roe Cloud Series on American Indians and Modernity

SERIES EDITORS

Ned Blackhawk, Yale University
Joshua L. Reid, University of Washington
Renya K. Ramirez, University of California, Santa Cruz

*Domestic Subjects: Gender, Citizenship, and Law in Native American
Literature* (2013), by Beth H. Piatote

Hollow Justice: A History of Indigenous Claims in the United States (2013),
by David E. Wilkins

For a Love of His People: The Photography of Horace Poolaw (2014),
edited by Nancy Marie Mithlo

The Sea Is My Country: The Maritime World of the Makahs (2015),
by Joshua L. Reid

Indigenous London: Native Travelers at the Heart of Empire (2016),
by Coll Thrush

Memory Lands: King Philip's War and the Place of Violence in the Northeast
(2018), by Christine M. DeLucia

Our Beloved Kin: A New History of King Philip's War (2018), by Lisa Brooks

Indigenous Visions: Rediscovering the World of Franz Boas (2018),
edited by Ned Blackhawk and Isaiah Lorado Wilner

*A Journey to Freedom: Richard Oakes, Alcatraz, and the Red Power
Movement* (2018), by Kent Blansett

*Assembled for Use: Indigenous Compilation and the Archives of
Early Native American Literatures* (2021), by Kelly Wisecup

"Vaudeville Indians" on Global Circuits, 1880s–1930s (2022),
by Christine Bold

*The Makings and Unmakings of Americans: Indians and Immigrants in
American Literature and Culture, 1879–1924* (2022), by Cristina Stanciu

*The Rediscovery of America: Native Peoples and the Unmaking of U.S.
History* (2023), by Ned Blackhawk

Chitto Harjo: Native Patriotism and the Medicine Way (2025),
by Donald L. Fixico

CHITTO HARJO

NATIVE PATRIOTISM AND THE MEDICINE WAY

DONALD L. FIXICO

Yale
UNIVERSITY PRESS
New Haven and London

Copyright © 2025 by Donald L. Fixico.

All rights reserved.

This book may not be reproduced, in whole or in part, including illustrations, in any form (beyond that copying permitted by Sections 107 and 108 of the U.S. Copyright Law and except by reviewers for the public press), without written permission from the publishers.

Yale University Press books may be purchased in quantity for educational, business, or promotional use. For information, please email sales.press@yale.edu (U.S. office) or sales@yaleup.co.uk (U.K. office).

Set in Gotham and Adobe Garamond type by Westchester Publishing Services.

Printed in the United States of America.

Library of Congress Control Number: 2024946688
ISBN 978-0-300-27241-3 (hardcover : alk. paper)

A catalogue record for this book is available from the British Library.

This paper meets the requirements of ANSI/NISO Z39.48-1992 (Permanence of Paper).

10 9 8 7 6 5 4 3 2 1

To my Mvskoke and Semvnole relatives,
Echoille and Hockifke, and Tustennuck Hadjo
who walked the Road of Suffering to Indian Territory

May justice be done to save the original Hickory Ground
in the Old Homeland

Down with him! chain him! bind him fast!
Slam to the iron door and turn the key!
The one true Creek, perhaps the last
To dare declare, "You have wronged me!"
Defiant, stoical, silent!
Suffers imprisonment!
Such coarse black hair! such eagle eye
Such stately mien!—how arrow straight!
Such will! such courage to defy
The powerful makers of his fate!
A traitor, outlaw,—what you will
He is the noble red man still.
Condemn him and his kind to shame!
I bow to him, exalt his name!

—Alexander Lawrence Posey

Contents

Glossary	ix
Maps	xv
Preface	xix
Chitto Harjo's Testimony	xxv

Introduction	1
The Importance of the East	11
1 **The Medicine Way**	13
A Black Preacher Punished by the Creek Lighthorse	
in 1845	37
2 **Moving Fire**	38
A White Boy's First Stomp Dance	54
3 **The White Man's War**	57
The Green Peach War	74
4 **The Sands Uprising and the Green Peach War**	75
Fus Fixico's Letter to Pleasant Porter about	
Allotments, 1905	107
5 **The Snakes**	108
Chitto Harjo's Nephew	137

CONTENTS

6 **"Snake War"** 139

Redbird Smith's Grandson 158

7 **Legacy** 159

Notes 171

Acknowledgments 203

Index 209

Illustrations follow p. 98

Glossary

All spellings, pronunciations, and definitions are from Muscogee (Creek) Dictionary, https://www.webonary.org/muscogee/, an electronic edition of Jack B. Martin and Margaret McKane Mauldin, eds., *A Dictionary of Creek / Muskogee* (Lincoln: University of Nebraska Press, 2000), accessed June 11, 2024.

Mvskoke	Pronunciation	English
Aktvyahcvlke	*aktayahc-âlki*	Aktayahche clan
Botha	*both-a*	greed, evil
Cahtvlke	*ca:ht-âlki*	the Choctaw
Cehecarēs	*ci-hic-á:łi:-s*	"see you later"
Cēpvnē	*ci:pan-í:*	1 noun boy
		2 adjective young (of a boy)
Cēpvnvke	*ci:pan-áki*	boys
Culvalke	*colá-âlki*	fox clan
Ēcatēcvlke	*i:-ca:ti:c-âlki*	Red Sticks
Eccaswvlke	*icca:s-âlki*	beaver clan
Ecovlke	*(i)co-âlki*	deer clan

GLOSSARY

Ehosa	*ihosá:*	1 a mystical being who mimics people and who causes those who cross his path to get lost 2 the illness of forgetfulness and senselessness associated with this being
Ehvtkecvlke	*hvtkē:c-âlki*	White Sticks
ēkvnv	*i:kaná*	land, earth, ground
enhesse	*in-híssi*	friend
enkepayv	*in-kipá:ya*	enemy or opposition town
Epohfvnku	*e-po-fan-ca*	totality
este-cate	*(i)sti-cá:t-i*	1 Indian, Native American 2 Muscogee person (used loosely)
este-hvtke	*(i)sti-hátk-i*	white person
este-vpuekv	*isti-apóyka*	slave
Estemerketv Nene	*istimiłk-ita- niní*	the Trail of Tears (literally, "Trail of Sorrow")
Etekvlkē	*(i)ti-kálk-i:*	divided in pieces
fek-hērkv	*fik-hí:l-ka*	inner peace
fēke ofv	*fí:ki ó:fa*	in one's heart
Fuswvlke	*fosw-âlki*	bird clan

GLOSSARY

hecetv	*hic-íta*	1 to see, look at 2 to be able to see 3 to try (to do some- thing) and see
heles-hayv	*hilis-há:y-a*	medicine maker, traditional doctor
heleswv	*hilí(:)swa*	medicine
Henehv	*hiníha*	second chief of a tribal town
Hesaketvmesē	*hisa:k-ita-m- is-í:*	Maker of Breath or Life
Hesaketvmesē em vnvtvksetv	*hisa:k-ita-m-is-í: im-anataks- itá*	look up at the Maker of Breath
hotvlē	*hotal-í:*	wind, air, breeze
hotvlē-rakko	*hotal-i:-łákko*	hurricane, storm, tornado
Hotvlkvlke	*hotal-k-âlki*	wind clan
Hvlpvtv	*(h)alpatá*	alligator
Hvmmaketv	*hamma:k-itá < heyyô:m-+ ma:k-itá*	to say this
kērrv	*kíth-a*	psychic or fortune teller
Kohvsvlke	*kohas-âlki*	cane clan
Konepvlke	*konip-âlki*	skunk clan
Kowakkucvlke	*kowa:kk-oc-âlki*	wildcat clan
Lucvlke	*locá-âlki*	turtle clan
Maskoke or Mvskoke	*ma(:)skó:ki*	Muscogee

GLOSSARY

mēkko-hoyvnēcv	*mi:kko-* *hoyaní:c-a*	dwarf willow (*Salix tristis*), red root
mēkko, mēkkvke	*mí:kko,* *mi:kk-akí*	1 chief 2 lord 3 king
Momekvs!	*mó:m-ík-as*	Let it be so! / Let it happen!
Momen vculvke em maketv yvt omēs	*mo:m-ín* *acol-akí* *im-ma:k-itá ya-t* *ô:m-i:-s*	And this is the saying of the old ones.
Mvskoge iemvnicv	*a:-im-anéyc-a*	Muskogee assistant
Nokosvlke	*nokos-âlki*	bear clan
Ocē-vlke	*oci:-âlki*	hickory nut clan
Okcvnwvlke	*okcanw-âlki*	salt clan
Osvnvlke	*osan-âlki*	otter clan
Owalv	*owá:l-a*	prophet
Posketv	*posk-itá*	Green Corn Dance
poyvekcv yekcetv	*poyafíkca* *yikc-itá*	spirit strength
poyvekcv yekcetv eyoksicetv seko	*poyafíkca* *yikc-itá* *iyokseyc-itá* *seko*	spirit strength without end
Poyvfekcv	*poyafíkca*	soul, spirit, ghost
poyvfekcv em eyoksicetv seko	*poyafíkca* *im-iyokseyc-itá seko*	spirit without end
Rvro-vlke	*łało-âlki*	fish clan

GLOSSARY

Sapetv	*sa:p-itá*	to scratch (for medicinal reasons)
Sopaktvlke	*sopa:kt-âlki*	toad clan
Tàmi	*tàmi*	Tàmi clan
Totkv	*tó:tka*	fire
totkv-ētkv	*to:tk(a)-í:tka*	fireplace—area surrounding the fire at a ceremonial ground used for dancing
Tvkusvlke	*takos-âlki*	mole clan
tvlofv	*(i)taló:fa*	town
Tvstvnvkevlke	*tastanáki-âlki*	House of Warriors
uewv	*óywa, wí:-, ó:-*	water
vce	*aci*	corn
Vce lane emposketv	*aci-la-ne-im- posk-itá*	Green Corn Dance
Vce-vlke	*aci-âlki*	corn clan
Vhvlvkvlke	*ahalak-âlki*	sweet potato clan
Waksvlke	*waks-âlki*	Waksalki clan
Wotkvlke	*wo:tk-âlki*	raccoon clan
Yekcetv	*yikc-itá*	1 verb to be strong 2 noun strength, power, authority
Yvhvlke	*yah-âlki*	wolf clan

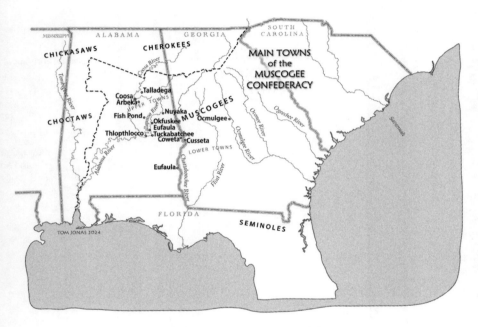

Main Towns of the Muscogee Confederacy

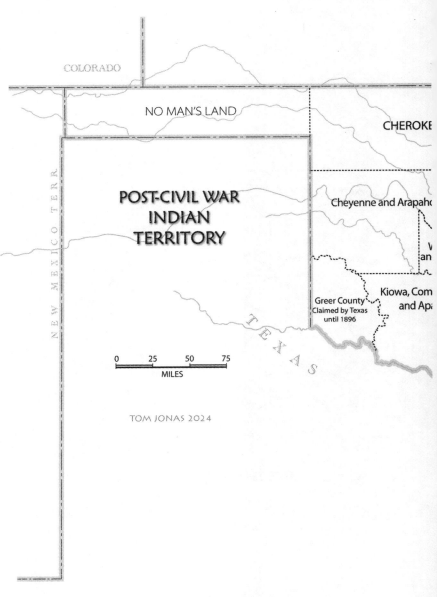

Post–Civil War Indian Territory

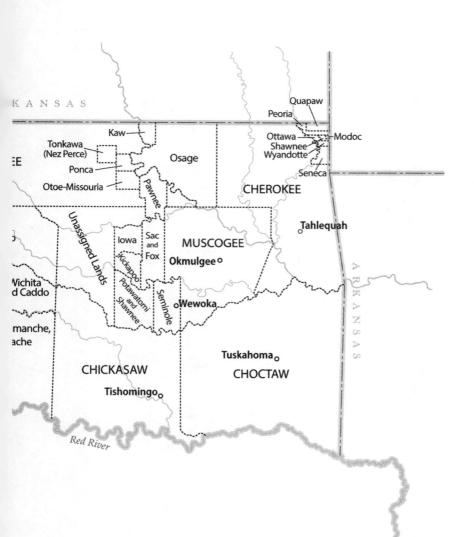

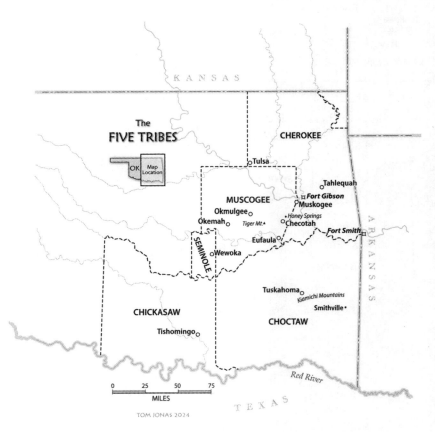

The Five Tribes

Preface

In 2001 my father, my six-year-old son Keytha, and I left Sapulpa, Oklahoma, late at night to drive to a stomp dance. Our destination was the Tallahassee Stomp Ground near Hectorville about an hour from where my parents lived. The three of us got into my dad's old Silverado pickup and headed south on I-75, known as "the beeline toward Okmulgee." When I was growing up, we visited many square grounds throughout the Mvskoke Nation and danced at Hickory Ground, Fish Pond, Arbeka, and even at Little Axe with the Shawnees, to visit my mother's relatives who were my relatives. But that night my dad could not remember the last time he had been to Tallahassee. Raindrops began to sprinkle on the windshield of the pickup. I worried that we might get wet at the dance, but my dad grinned and said everything would be fine. Coming off the interstate we turned onto a dirt road and then onto another one. A couple of times, when we ran out of road, we got lost in the moonlight, once backing up over an old wooden bridge (very carefully). Keytha was excited about the dance and as he pointed toward the full moon the clouds began to roll away, as if to unveil an invitation.

Finally, around one in the morning, we arrived and parked next to a van. To our surprise, we had parked next to my cousin Nadine Harjo King and her family. We immediately began visiting and talking as the smoke of the ceremonial fire blessed everyone. Memories flowed back to my childhood, listening and watching the people.

PREFACE

While we were sitting in our lawn chairs and watching Keytha dance, one of the two "they pick the leaders" of Tallahassee invited my father to lead a song. Naturally, he said yes. My dad had lived the Medicine Way of the Mvskokes and Semvnoles all his adult life, but he became a Southern Baptist preacher after surviving a serious auto accident. Some might say stomp dancing and Christianity do not mix, but most traditional Mvskokes do not see this as a conflict.

At a stomp dance, there is no drum (except for a hand-carried drum sometimes), and the leader of the song begins to circle the ceremonial fire to the right going sun-wise (counter clockwise), joined by the community: man woman, man woman, then the younger people, boy girl, boy girl. The song leader sings a short phrase in Mvskoke and the men respond with a phrase, in a pattern that goes back further than anyone can remember. With my father singing around the fire and leading the dancers I stood on the edge of the circle to join. I started dancing, and I looked at the large white circle in the night's sky. At that moment, with my father on the one side of the fire, and my son on the exact other side, all three of us were in alignment with the moon and the fire—three generations— my father of the potato clan, my son of the wolf clan, and me of the fox clan. Time had stopped and the past and present had become one. In sync with the moon, the fire, the earth, the wind from the singing, and a light sprinkle, the elemental powers merged together to celebrate life.

In the eighteenth century, all the *tvlofvs* were summoned once a year to the main *tvlofv* at old Ocmulgee, which hosted the largest Green Corn ceremony. Runners from Ocmulgee delivered a small bundle of sticks to each *tvlofv* for the *mēkko*, who would break a stick each day until the last remaining stick signaled the morning when it was time to leave for the central *tvlofv*. This tradition of counting was called "breaking days."[1] The Mvskoke Confederacy met annually

PREFACE

during the eighteenth century, but before then there was little need for such gatherings due to the autonomous power of the everlasting Spirit Power within each *tvlofv*. The benefits of protection and security were important enough that people identified more with their *tvlofv* than with the confederacy.[2] This changed with the arrival of European traders in the early 1700s, when clusters of three or four *tvlofvs* gathered to hold dances, thereby forming and maintaining town alliances.[3]

Presently the Green Corn Dance continues to be held every year. The Green Corn is a complex ceremony of many songs that starts about midnight and continues until dawn and lasts four days, eight days in earlier times. The events focus on the sacred fire in the middle of a circular cleaned ground twenty to thirty feet in diameter, where the people dance sun-wise. The men sing, with one of them selected to lead a song, and the women shake turtle shells laced together and filled with river gravel tied to both of their calves, as many as ten or twelve on each leg. After World War II with turtles harder to find, the shells were replaced with about twenty small stacked cans, five in a row, laced together and tied to each lower leg.[4] In this way, the women, shaking shells in unison while dancing, provided the rhythm to accompany the men's singing.

The dancing symbolizes the Mvskoke and Semvnole peoples emerging from the earth.[5] By dancing until dawn, the people paid homage to the East where the sun rose, representing the genesis of life for the Mvskokes and Semvnoles. One Mvskoke elder stressed the importance of all human and non-human life beginning "under the Rising of the Sun."[6] Of the principal directions, East figured prominently in the Medicine Way of the people. The seven principal directions are North, East, South, West, Up, Down, and Inner direction of each person.[7] The Inner direction is toward the heart of everyone. It is a lifetime journey starting on the good path, having to decide

PREFACE

between right and wrong, and making choices about how to live one's life.[8]

Everything was in balance. My heart felt light and alive. The Mvskokes and Semvnoles believe in a totality called *Epohfvnkv,* an enormous sphere of unimaginable size that contains all, known or unknown, in a flexible equilibrium where all things are included and all things are related. The stomp dance, like *Epohfvnkv,* creates harmony, welcoming visitors and strangers alike to Mvskoke-Semvnole reality. This worldview of inclusion goes back centuries, and dancing creates a feeling of balance with the four powers of this Indigenous universe—fire, water, wind, and earth.[9] This feeling of balance and inclusion extends for song after song until the birth of a new day. In those remaining minutes of dark into light, I stood hypnotized by the pink, orange, and red rays of dawn, and I felt blessed. Everything was perfect: the singing, the dancing, the fellowship of seeing old friends and relatives.

Among the Mvskokes and Semvnoles, it is important to belong to a *tvlofv* "town" or "community." It instills in you a personal identity, of belonging to a ceremonial ground and being connected culturally to an ancient past. I was born in Shawnee and grew up at Gar Creek. Our Semvnole *tvlofv* developed from the Chiaha Ground in Semvnole County in the former Indian Territory. Both of my tribes on my dad's side are matrilineal. My Mvskoke grandmother, Lena Spencer Fixico, was born on July 1, 1901, in Seminole County to Ramsey and Ludie (King) Spencer. The parents of Ramsey Spencer and Ludie King were my great-grandparents, Echoille and Hockifke (no last names). They survived the Trail of Suffering to help put down the fire in our new homeland in the Indian Territory. On my Semvnole side, my great-great-grandfather Tustennuck Hadjo walked the Path of Suffering and was listed as the fourth prisoner of war of Coe

xxii

PREFACE

Hadjo's band, removed from Florida in 1841. Coe Hadjo's stubborn patriotism meant fighting to hold onto his people's land. Resilience, survival, and pulling together helped the community to endure this forced migration. My grandfather was Jonas Fixico, Roll No. 945, Census Card No. 277; his father was Ar-ha-loc Fixeco, according to the Dawes rolls No. 7898, Census Card No. 2700; and his mother was Nelsey Fixico, Roll No. 941. My grandfather was a farmer, a Methodist preacher, and a medicine maker; he passed away when I was seven years old.[10]

My parents raised me in the Mvskoke and Semvnole tradition for the first dozen years or so of my life. On my mother's side I am Absentee Shawnee and Sac and Fox. At our ground, Gar Creek, Jack Wolfe was the *mēkko* (town leader), and my grandfather, Jonas Fixico, was the *heles hayv* (medicine maker). My grandmother, Lena Spencer Fixico, was of the potato clan and she was from New Tulsa Stomp Ground that used to be called Little River Talsi in Hughes County. My granny Lena was an Upper Mvskoke and her relatives were from Little Tallassie *tvlofv* at the confluence of the Coosa, Alabama, and Tallapossa Rivers in Alabama. Later my uncle Telmond Fixico served as the *heles hayv* for Gar Creek. A lot of members of my family were Hitchitis and included people from Ochesee, Okfuskee, and old Chiaha, plus Mvskoke Semvnoles.[11]

The Mvskokes studied nature and the heavens in order to understand life and to live it in the best way possible. Mvskoke elder Ted Isham of Hillibi Ground explained, "The placement of the sun along the horizon is very important to the timing of our ceremonial cycle. The objects of the sky are important and their behavior is closely watched. The cycles of the sun are known to control the seasons, which in turn gives us plants that help sustain us with food and also our traditional medicines." Isham concluded, "As we go from the time when we begin to gather together during the vernal equinox time, to

xxiii

PREFACE

the high time of Green Corn (*Vce lane emposketv*) during the mid-summer of the solstice, and to the east/west match games during the autumnal equinox, we become in sync with the natural world. Being in accord with this solar cycle is our greatest achievement and allows us to live in harmony with nature."[12]

This Mvskoke lifeway has persisted through the centuries. But times were changing, and they were changing perhaps too fast. The ways of the white man had influenced the Mvskokes by the early 1800s, and some Mvskokes started living like the white man. The dilemma of being caught in a changing world perplexed many Indians. Embracing change is a part of the Medicine Way, but not when it threatens the core identity of the Mvskoke people.

Chitto Harjo, who lived in the late 1800s, saw the changes happening around him and became convinced that the true Mvskokes were losing control of everything. Chitto Harjo means Crazy Snake in the Mvskoke language. He was a traditionalist and believed all Mvskokes should live the Medicine Way of life. This book is about what he experienced, what it means to stand within your traditional community and see it being changed by uncontrolled external forces, to find yourself being on the outside of your own world. Many Indians, even today, feel this estrangement of being caught between two cultural forces. It is an alien feeling that many full-bloods still experience. Sometimes I feel it too; I am a full-blood of four tribes. To be at odds with another worldview, another ideology, and a different belief system is to feel conflicting emotions.

This book is about blood, kinship relations, the Native world, and the Mvskoke Medicine Way of life; it is about how Chitto Harjo tried to cope with the white man's world in a zone of indifference. I am grateful for his strength. Chitto Harjo believed in and fought for traditionalism. His efforts tried to preserve the original cultural identity of the Mvskokes and Semvnoles in Oklahoma.

Chitto Harjo's Testimony

My ancestors and my people were the inhabitants of this great country from 1492. I mean by that from the time the white man first came to this country until now. It was my home and the home of my people from time immemorial and is today, I think, the home of my people. Away back in that time—in 1492—there was a man by the name of Columbus came from across the great ocean [Atlantic] and he discovered this country for the white man—this country which was at that time the home of my people. What did he find when he first arrived here? Did he find a white man standing on this continent then or did he find a black man standing here? Did he find either a black man or a white man standing on this continent? I stood here first and Columbus first discovered me.

I want to know what did he say to the red man at that time? He was on one of the great four roads that led to light. At that time Columbus received the information that was given to him by my people. My ancestor informed him that he was ready to accept this light he proposed to give him and walk these four roads of light and have his children under his direction. He told him it was all right. He told him, "The land is all yours; the law is all yours." He said it is all right. He told him, "I will always take care of you. If your people meet with any troubles, I will take these troubles away. I will stand before you and behind you and on each side of you and your people, and if any people come into your country I will take them away and

xxv

CHITTO HARJO'S TESTIMONY

you shall live in peace under me. My arms," he said, "are very long." He told him to come within his protecting arms and he said, "If anything comes against you for your ruin I will stand by you and preserve you and defend you and protect you."

"There is a law," he said at that time, "that is above every other law and that is away up yonder—high up—for," said he, "if any other town or nation or any other tribe come against you I will see through that law that you are protected. It does not make any difference to you," he said, "if as many as twelve other nations come against you or twelve other tribes come against you it will not make any difference for I will combine with you and protect you and overthrow them all. I will protect you in all things and take care of everything about your existence so you will live in this land that is yours and your fathers' without fear." That is what he said and we agreed upon those terms. He told me that as long as the sun shone and the sky is up yonder these agreements shall be kept. This was the first agreement that we had with the white man. He said as long as the sun rises it shall last; as long as the waters run it shall last; as long as the grass grows it shall last. That was what it was to be and we agreed upon those terms. That was what the agreement was and we signed our names to that agreement and to those terms. He said, "Just as long as you see light here; just as long as you see this light glimmering over us, shall these agreements be kept and not until all these things shall cease and pass away shall our agreement pass away." That is what he said and we believed it. I think there is nothing that has been done by the people should abrogate them. We have kept every term of that agreement. The grass is growing, the waters run, the sun shines, the light is with us and the agreement is with us yet for the God that is above us all witnessed that agreement. He said to me that whoever did anything against me was doing it against him and against the agreement and he said if anyone attempted to do anything against

xxvi

me, to notify him for whatever was done against me was against him and therefore against the agreement. He said that he would send good men amongst us to teach us about his God and to treat them good for they were his representatives and to listen to them and if anyone attempted to molest us to, tell them (the missionaries) and they would tell him. He told me that he would protect me in all ways; that he would take care of my people and look after them; that he would succor them if they needed succor and be their support at all times and I told him it was all right and he wrote the agreement that way.

Now, coming down to 1832 and referring to the agreements between the Creek people and the Government of the United States; What has occurred since 1832 until today? It seems that some people forget what has occurred. After all, we are all one blood; we have the one God and we live in the same land. I had always lived back yonder in what is now the State of Alabama. We had our homes back there; my people had their homes back there. We had our troubles back there and we had no one to defend us. At that time when I had these troubles, it was to take my country away from me. I had no other troubles. The troubles were always about taking my country from me. I could live in peace with all else, but they wanted my country and I was in trouble defending it. It was no use. They were bound to take my country away from me. It may have been that my country had to, be taken away from me, but it was not justice. I have always been asking for justice. I have never asked for anything else but justice. I never had justice. First, it was this and then it was something else that was taken away from me and my people, so we couldn't stay there any more. It was not because a man had to stand on the outside of what was right that brought the troubles. What was to be done was all set out yonder in the light and all men knew what the law and the agreement was. It was a treaty—a solemn treaty—but what difference did that make? I want to say this to you today, because

xxvii

CHITTO HARJO'S TESTIMONY

I don't want these ancient agreements between the Indian and the white man violated and I went as far as Washington and had them sustained and made treaties about it. We made terms of peace, for it had been war, but we made new terms of peace and made new treaties. Then it was the overtures of the Government to my people to leave their land, the home of their fathers, the land that they loved. He said, "It will be better for you to do as I want, for these old treaties cannot be kept any longer." He said, "You look away off to the West, away over backward and there you will see a great river called the Mississippi River and away over beyond that is another river called the Arkansas River." And he said, "You go way out there and you will find a land that is fair to look upon and is fertile, and you go there with your people and I will give that country to you and your people forever." He said, "Go way out there beyond these two rivers; away out the direction of the setting sun and select your land—what you want of it—and I will locate you and your people there and I will give you that land forever and I will protect you and your children in it forever." That was the agreement and the treaty and I and my people came out here and settled on this land and I carried out these agreements and treaties in all points and violated none. I came over and located here.

What took place in 1861? I had made my home here with my people and I was living well out here with my people. We were all prospering. We had a great deal of property here, all over this country. We had come here and taken possession of it under our treaty. We had laws that were living laws and I was living here under then laws. You are my fathers and I tell you that in 1861, I was living here in peace and plenty with my people and we were happy; and then my white fathers rose in arms against each other to, fight each other. They did fight each other. At that day Abraham Lincoln was President of the United States and our Great Father. He was in Washing-

xxviii

CHITTO HARJO'S TESTIMONY

ton and I was away off down here. My white brothers divided into factions and went to war. When the white people raised in arms and tried to destroy one another, it was not for the purpose of destroying my people at all. It was not for the purpose of destroying treaties with the Indians. They did not think of that and the Indian was not the cause of that great war at all. The cause of that war was because there was a people that were black in skin and color who had always been in slavery. In my old home in Alabama and all through the south part of the Nation and out in this country, these black people were held in slavery and up in the North there were no slaves. The people of that part of the United States determined to set the black man free and the people in the South determined that they should not and they went to war about it. In that war the Indians had not any part. It was not their war at all. The purpose of the war was to set these black people at liberty and I had nothing to, do with it. He told me to come out here and have my laws back, and I came out here with my people and had my own laws and was living under them. On account of some of your own sons—the ancient brothers of mine—they came over here and caused me to enroll along with my people on your side. I left my home and my country and everything I had in the world and went rolling on toward the Federal Army. I left my laws and my government; I left my people and my country and my home; I left everything and went with the Federal Army for my father in Washington. I left them in order to stand by my treaties. I left everything and I arrived in Kansas—I mean it was at Leavenworth where I arrived. It was a town away up in Kansas on the Missouri River. I arrived at Fort Leavenworth to do what I could for my father's country and stand by my treaties. There at Fort Leavenworth was the orator [commander] of the Federal Army and I went and fell before the orator of the Federal Army. It was terrible hard times with me then. In that day I was under the Sons of my father in Washington.

CHITTO HARJO'S TESTIMONY

I was with the Federal soldiers. I am speaking now of this orator in the Federal Army. I went and fell before him and I and my people joined the Federal Army because we wanted to, keep our treaties with the father in Washington. Things should not have been that way but that is the way they were. The father at Washington was not able to keep his treaty with me and I had to leave my country, as I have stated, and go into the Federal Army. I went in as a Union soldier. When I took the oath, I raised my hand and called God to witness that I was ready to die in the cause that was right and to help my father defend his treaties. All this time the fire was going on and the war and the battles were going on, and today I have conquered all and regained these treaties that I have with the Government. I believe that everything wholly and fully came back to me on account of the position I took in that war. I think that. I thought then and I think today that is the way to do—to stand up and be a man that keeps his word all the time and under all circumstances. That is what I did and I know that in doing so I regained again all my old treaties for the father at Washington conquered in that war and he promised me that if I was faithful to, my treaties, I should have them all back again. I was faithful to my treaties and I got them all back again and today I am living under them and with them. I never agreed to the exchanging of lands and I never agreed to the allotting of my lands. I knew it would never do for my people and I never could say a b c so far as that is concerned. I never knew anything about English. I can't speak the tongue. I can't read it. I can't write it. I and my people, great masses of them, are unenlightened and uneducated. I am notifying you of these things because your Government officials have told me and my people that they would take care of my relations with the Government and I think they ought to be taking care of them as they promised. He said that if anyone trespassed on my rights or questioned them to let him know and he would take care of them and

xxx

CHITTO HARJO'S TESTIMONY

protect them. I always thought that this would be done. I believe yet it will be done. I don't know what the trouble is now. I don't know anything about it. I think my lands are all cut up. I have never asked that be done but I understand it has been done. I don't know why it was done. My treaty said that it never would be done unless I wanted it done. That anything I did not want to be done contrary to that treaty would not be done. I never made these requests. I went through death for this cause and I now hold the release this Government gave me. I served the father faithfully and as a reward, I regained my country back again and I and my children will remain on it and live upon it as we did in the old time. I believe it. I know it is right. I know it is justice.

I hear the Government is cutting up my land and is giving it away to black people. I want to know if this is so. It can't be so for it is not in the treaty. These black people, who are they? They are negroes who came in here as slaves. They have no right to this land. It never was given to them. It was given to me and my people and we paid for it with our land back in Alabama. The black people have no right to it. Then can it be that the Government is giving it—my land—to the negro? I hear it is and they are selling it. This can't be so. It wouldn't be justice. I am informed and believe it to be true that some citizens of the United States have title to land that was given to my fathers and my people by the Government. If it was given to me, what right has the United States to take it from me without first asking my consent? That I would like to know. There are many things that I don't know and can't understand but I want to understand them if I can. I believe the officers of the United States ought to take care of the rights of me and my people first and then afterwards look out for their own interests. I have reason to believe and I do believe that they are more concerned in their own welfare than the welfare [or] rights of the Indian—lots of them are. I believe some of them are honest men,

CHITTO HARJO'S TESTIMONY

but not many. A plan [man] ought fiat [first] to dispossess himself of all thought or wish to do me or my country wrong. He should never think of doing wrong to this country or to the rights of my people. After he has done that, then maybe he can do something for himself in that regard; but first he must protect the Indians and their rights in this country. He is the servant of the Government and he is sent here to, do that and he should not be permitted to do anything else.

All that I am begging of you, Honorable Senators, is that these ancient agreements and treaties wherein you promised to take care of me and my people, be fulfilled and that you will remove all the difficulties that have been raised in reference to my people and their country and I ask you to see that these promises are faithfully kept. I understand you are the representatives of the Government sent here to look into these things and I hope you will relieve us. That is all I desire to say.[1]

Chitto Harjo

Introduction

Some people thought he was a little strange, others were convinced that he was just a quiet soul. Dignified and proud, he stood tall with near-perfect posture. His long black hair hung loosely to his shoulders. He had a high nose and cheekbones and his clear dark eyes seemed to see beyond where he looked.[1] Mvskokes call this *hecetv*, to understand what you see. According to the Medicine Way, he was a White Stick, *Ehvtkecvlke*. Like his mother he was of the *hvlpvtv* or alligator clan, and therefore a patient hunter. As a White Stick, he was calm, thoughtful, and observant. In his early forties, Chitto Harjo possessed a powerful physique and strong intellect. He made a lasting first impression.[2]

Chitto Harjo had several names—Wilson Jones, Bill Jones, Bill Harjo, Bill Snake. People in his time called Chitto Harjo many things: troublemaker, rebellion leader, uncivilized Indian, martyr, murderer, and savage. In the eyes of many Mvskokes, Semvnoles, and traditionalists of other nations he was a hero, a defender of the old ways, a Native patriot, and a leader of the Medicine Way. Many people, including Mvskoke people, criticized Harjo and thought him crazy for fighting against progress and for outdated traditions and a Medicine Way of life, which they believed was dying out in Indian Territory.[3]

Chitto Harjo was a full-blood Mvskoke, and he was an unyielding soul. He believed in the metaphysical world of the Mvskokes that

INTRODUCTION

shaped people's lives, and he believed that it was essential to Mvskoke life. The Medicine Way was a positive continuum, older than the Mvskoke Confederacy itself. Harjo was one in a long line of Mvskoke traditionalist leaders who struggled to save the old Medicine Way, from Menawa, who fought against Andrew Jackson in 1813, to Opothleyahola (sometimes called Old Gouge) during the white man's war, and Isparhecher and Oktarharsars during the Green Peach War and the Sands Uprising. The fight to save the Medicine Way was also demonstrated by the leaders of other Indian nations. They felt the same threat of a white society that might one day control them, severing their connection to the past and altering the worldviews embedded in the generations of their peoples.

Chitto Harjo was a family man. He did not like to draw attention or criticism, but he believed in speaking up for what was right and fair. A man of ethics, Chitto Harjo was a natural orator, and he became the *henehv* or second leader at Hickory Stomp Ground. In this special role, Chitto Harjo gave the long talk at the beginning of each stomp dance to welcome visitors, making sure they felt included, and establishing the order of things for the rest of the dance according to the Medicine Way of *Epohfvnkv*.[4] The tall full-blood from Deep Fork Arbeka had a resonating voice of authority, so when he spoke, people listened.

In the mind of Chitto Harjo, the evil spirit of *Botha* had entered Christopher Columbus when he arrived on the shores of America. *Botha* lived inside of a great serpent that swam alongside of the eastern shore, and the evil spirit entered Columbus who was filled with greed and lust for gold, silver, land, and power. *Botha* transformed itself in becoming a part of Andrew Jackson, William McIntosh, and anyone, *este-hvtke* or *este-cate,* who supported land allotment and would do just about anything to get what they wanted. Such desire had become evil, but the Mvskokes believed this negative

INTRODUCTION

flow of energy was not forever and that it could be transformed back into "good."[5]

The increasing influx of white settlers into Mvskoke country and the rest of what had been called Indian Territory dismayed Chitto Harjo and his followers. They had never seen such a growing number of land hungry people. Harjo had heard stories from his elders about the white man's encroachment on his people's former homeland back in the Southeast. The Boomer movement had made a serious impact not just on Harjo and the Snakes, but on all the Indian nations in the territory. They were at the mercy of the federal government to protect their homelands, but soldiers in blue were not enough. In trying to preserve the Medicine Way of the Mvskokes, even by taking up arms, Chitto Harjo was in the wrong. He was not seen as a Native patriot but as the leader of a rebellion. From Harjo's viewpoint and those of the traditionalists, the outsiders or whites had disrupted the order of things. In this same light, they had caused a rebellion against the Medicine Way of the Mvskokes and other tribes in Indian Territory. But it all depended on whose point of view. Due to the large number of whites writing history, Chitto Harjo has been portrayed as the leader of the Crazy Snake Rebellion, a revolt against the newly arrived white population in the Indian Territory. In the same sense, Crazy Snake was wrong and blamed for standing in the way of progress and in the way of Indians becoming "civilized." Chitto Harjo, also known as Wilson Jones, was assigned Mvskoke Roll No. 7934, and his Census Card was No. 2718.[6] Chitto Harjo did not complete his selection of land as of July 2, 1902, and he was assigned an allotment on March 3, 1903. The certificate was signed by Tams Bixby, acting commission chairman. Bixby confirmed the allotment assignment on September 4, 1903, with a second certificate. Harjo was assigned an allotment of forty acres located at the northwest corner of the northwest quarter of section 16, township 11 north

INTRODUCTION

range 15 east of the Indian Meridian.[7] Although he was assigned an allotment, Chitto Harjo never lived there. What is important is that Crazy Snake lived his life as he wanted to and not at the hands of government officials, like Henry Dawes. Senator Dawes was from Massachusetts and he respected and tried to understand Native people. Yet, his bill in Congress became the Dawes Allotment Act in 1887. Although on opposite sides, Chitto Harjo and Henry Dawes understood each other, and both wanted to protect Mvskoke people and all other *este-cates* of the Indian Territory. But Dawes likely did not realize that the spiritual well-being was essential to the Mvskokes and for that matter, for everyone.

One of the important reasons for Chitto Harjo making his stand was based on at least two treaties that the Mvskokes had made with the United States. These two agreements were the Treaty of 1832, also called the Treaty of Cusseta, and the Treaty of 1866.

Throughout the world, only the governments of five countries have negotiated treaties with Indigenous people. Besides the United States, which has made 374 treaties and 94 agreements with the Indian Nations, Canada has made 70 treaties with the First Nations of Indigenous groups. The third country is New Zealand with 1 treaty affecting the Maori people, the Treaty of Waitangi in 1840.[8] France and Great Britain have made about 100 treaties and agreements with African Indigenous peoples.[9] The common ground for Indigenous treaties is they guarantee legal rights to Native people. Simultaneously, Native patriots like Chitto Harjo have had to remind the government to honor the treaties.

This book is also about the pain of *etekvlkē* (factionalism) that has a long history of dividing the Mvskoke people. Mvskokes fighting Mvskokes has been a theme in Mvskoke post-contact history spanning almost three hundred years. The Upper Mvskokes believed the Medicine Way of *Epohfvnkv* should be maintained as it always

INTRODUCTION

had been. Meanwhile, more and more Mvskokes of the Lower *tvlofvs* came into contact with Scottish, Irish, and British traders, which soon begin to alter the value systems of the Lower Mvskokes. They desired cultural goods that made life easier, and in time they became critical of the traditional Upper Mvskokes, who in turn criticized the Lower Mvskokes. Andrew Jackson understood that all the Mvskoke towns were not united as one nation, and he used this to convince many Mvskokes to help him. This dilemma carried on even after removal to Indian Territory where the two sides settled in different parts of the new Mvskoke Nation. Then the Sands Uprising led by Oktaharsars and his traditionalists in 1871 opposed the progressive Mvskokes led by Samuel Checote. The Green Peach War of 1881–83 continued the hostility with Isparhecher leading the traditionalists and Pleasant Porter leading Checote's Lighthorse. Even after the Crazy Snake movement from 1901 to 1909 and the Four Mothers Society forming, the cursed dilemma continued for the rest of the twentieth century.

Some people might suggest that this book is really about Indian nationalism, but these pages are about what it was like as a patriot to fight for the old Medicine Way. While other Mvskokes opposite of Chitto Harjo believed in nationalism and formed a national council and a national government like that of the United States, I argue that they did not feel the true patriotism that Crazy Snake felt. Native patriotism is much more than political nationalism; it is a loyalty to Mvskoke traditional identity that we call *Poyvekcv*. It is the same Native patriotism that Chitto Harjo felt and everyone feels dancing around the ceremonial fire. If you have been to a stomp dance and danced, then you know what I mean and you feel the spirit of *Poyvekcv*. At the end of the first quarter of the twenty-first century roughly 500 million Indigenous peoples live in ninety countries, but they make up only 5 percent of the world's population of 8 billion.[10]

5

INTRODUCTION

Most of these communities have their own stories of colonizer trying to erase or absorb them. Why have Indigenous peoples continued to resist?

The story of Crazy Snake has parallels among Indigenous peoples around the world trying to preserve their sovereignty against colonial imperialism. In the Southwest, Popé led his people with Apache allies to defeat the Spanish in the Pueblo Revolt in 1680. The Ottawa war leader, Pontiac, led the Pontiac Rebellion of Eastern Woodland tribes against the British in 1763. During the War of 1812, Tecumseh of the Shawnees recruited many warriors of Indian nations against the Americans. All these efforts enabled the Medicine Way of their peoples to survive.

The defense of traditionalism has been interpreted as rebellion instead of patriotism, and not just in the United States. For several months in 1669, Shakushain led the Ainu against the Japanese in Hokkaido.[11] From 1869 to 1871, José Santos Quilapán led the Mapuche in Chile against Spanish invaders.[12] In 1957 Indigenous activist leader Whina Cooper was recognized as "Mother of the Nation" of the Maori people, and twenty years later she led a protest march from Te Haua to Wellington demanding New Zealand recognize Maori land rights according to the Treaty of Waitangi.[13] In Paraguay Carlos Mareco led his Sawhoyamaxa community for twenty years to regain their ancestral lands in 2012.[14] And there are other parallel histories of Native patriotism to defend Indigenous cultures.

What contemporary newspapers described as "the Crazy Snake Rebellion" is presented here as the Crazy Snake movement illustrating Native patriotism. Native patriotism is about much more than one culture displacing another. As Cherokee scholar Robert Thomas shows, understanding four things—language, sacred history, religion, and land—enables us to understand Indigenous worldviews and traditional cultures.[15] Indigenous peoples have always wanted to be

INTRODUCTION

properly and respectfully understood, and a lack of understanding and respect has been at the center of conflicts between Indians and non-Indians. As Vine Deloria Jr., the late Lakota activist and scholar, put it, "The fundamental factor that keeps Indians and non-Indians from communicating is that they are speaking about two entirely different perceptions of the world."[16] Americans fail to grasp the need to sustain Native sovereignty among the Mvskokes and other Indigenous peoples. Or maybe they choose to ignore Native people fighting for their sovereignty, but the manifestation of this inherent sovereignty is that there are nearly six hundred federally recognized tribes in the United States at this date, even after generations of government attempts to extinguish them. It is said that history is written by the victors, but what about the other side of the coin? In recent years, Indigenous scholars, such as Taiaiake Alfred, Roxane Dunbar Ortiz, Kevin Bruyneel, Michael Witgen, and Ned Blackhawk, have answered this call with works supporting Indigenous sovereignty from Native viewpoints.[17] These are insightful works and have contributed greatly to understanding Native sovereignty in relation to U.S. sovereignty.

Chitto Harjo and many other Indigenous leaders were patriots defending traditions and homelands, although they have been othered as obstacles standing in the way of progress.[18] Their efforts have been called rebellions, revolts, and Indian wars. In the history of U.S.-Indian relations more than 1,500 Indian wars, attacks, and skirmishes have been authorized by the federal government against Native peoples.[19] Were traditionalists wrong to resist? Chitto Harjo and other Mvskokes like him, Opothleyahola, Oktarharsars, and Isparhecher, tried to preserve the Medicine Way of their people and went to war to defend the Mvskoke traditional worldview. In the twenty-first century the Keetoowah Cherokees are still dancing at the Redbird Smith Stomp Ground and at other Four Mothers Stomp Grounds,

INTRODUCTION

and ironically even at Chitto Harjo's Hickory Stomp Ground with Hickory No. 1 Church and Hickory No. 2 Church a couple of miles away.

If one does not defend one's traditional beliefs, then that particular perspective will be displaced by a different worldview. A worldview is how a person (that can include his or her community) perceives the world based on their values, environmental influences, and political and religious beliefs. And this perspective shapes decision-making, logic, and ethos.

The Crazy Snake movement took place in the context of decreasing traditionalism and an increase in Christianity being chosen over the Medicine Way, compounded by increasing numbers of outsiders, white and black, coming to the Mvskoke reservation and the rest of the Indian Territory. Through these rapid cultural changes *Poyvfekcv em eyoksicetv seko,* the "Spirit Everlasting," was and remains at the core of Mvskoke natural sovereignty into the twenty-first century. Culture continues because previous generations convince subsequent generations that it is relevant to them.[20] When increasing external influences threaten one's original identity it interrupts that process, producing a cultural inertia that inhibits patriotic resistance.[21] Thus Native cultural retention remains a vital part of the continuum of traditionalism. In the Indigenous mind, the continuum keeps Native identity alive.[22] In the process of colonization, Indigenous peoples are either absorbed, assimilated, or annihilated to the point of genocide and erasure from history. This is what Chitto Harjo saw, having witnessed the infusion of different peoples into the Mvskoke Nation with its resettling in the Indian Territory. Throughout the history of U.S.-Indian relations, at least thirty-three tribes have become extinct, and they risk being erased from memory and history. Other Indigenous peoples in the world, like the Batak in Southeast Asia, are on the cusp of extinction.[23] In the central area of the Santa Cruz River

INTRODUCTION

valley, the Indigenous tribes are gone.[24] In Africa alone, fifty-four tribes have disappeared. This is what Chitto Harjo feared and fought against as a patriot: to save his people and the worldview that distinguished their Mvskoke identity dating back to the mound builders in the Southeast.

Chitto Harjo applied Mvskoke logic, rhetoric, and stories in linking the greed of individuals like Andrew Jackson back to Columbus, and using oral tradition to remind the people of their heritage and who they were. Most important, Chitto Harjo used the maternal metaphor for Mother Earth and the Mvskokes' reverence for the earth as one of the four elemental powers (with fire, water, and wind) that should not be sacrilegiously disrespected. This kindred mother-to-people relationship is steeped in the cultural identities of Indigenous peoples. In the view of the Crazy Snake movement everyone should act according to "justice" and consider the right thing to do in their decision-making. Instead, most individuals chose to do what would be advantageous for themselves and their political interests. The history of U.S.-Indian relations has been a history of corruption, exploitation, colonization, and the disregard of the presence of Native people and what they thought.[25] This injustice implies westernization is not always "right" and more consideration needs to be given to Native perceptions, Indigenous writings, and the worldviews of American Indians and the Native ethos of other Indigenous peoples around the world.

The bottom line for trying to hang on to traditionalism is identity. But there is a fate worse than being othered into an identity that someone else has chosen, and that is to be misrepresented in history. In May 2021 the Muscogee Nation officially corrected their name from the Muscogee Creek Nation of Oklahoma to the Muscogee Nation of Oklahoma.[26] For over three hundred years, they had accepted the early foreign traders' descriptions of people living by the

INTRODUCTION

"creeks." Native nations have reclaimed the word "tribe" to use it with fresh energy and pride, some groups adding the word to their official names such as the Fort Sill Apache Tribe, Iowa Tribe of Oklahoma, and Otoe-Missouri Tribe. To reject the spirit that gives the Mvskokes strength, resilience, and pride to exercise their natural sovereignty as they always have is subordination, a willing acceptance of how other people have presented Indigenous stories and have written Indigenous history without so much as asking Indigenous people what they thought.

Perhaps a worse fate is to not be written about at all, to be erased from public memory. While there are at least 125 American Indian groups without a written history, at least for now they have stories in the oral tradition to share.[27] Finally, the absolute worst of all is when the people themselves forget who they once were. This is what Chitto Harjo saw happening during his lifetime, and this is what he feared the most. By assimilating the Mvskokes were deliberately foregoing their traditions. They were willingly taking up the white man's means of terminating their own identity, while easing the guilt of the white man for eradicating the Mvskokes with guns, Bibles, and diseases.

But carrying on in this *Poyvfekcv em eyoksicetv seko* is certainly more than survival and resilience. It is accepting change while maintaining the core identity intact. This was the new Mvskokeism— welcoming change from inside of the nation while not jeopardizing traditional identity. As a Native patriot, Chitto Harjo exemplified reconciliation or hybridity by wearing white man's clothes and understanding the worldview of whites yet embracing traditionalism and moving forward amidst external change. It is not an easy journey. This is walking in the seventh direction to pursue *fek herkv* "inner peace."

Momekvs! (It can be done!)

THE IMPORTANCE OF THE EAST
SIAH HICKS

The East was always a direction of respect to the early Indians—nothing was ever done, either in ceremonial or medicine, unless the East was faced. They believed that they were giving their respects to the East, as the old country in the East was a mother country and home to them and they never fully forgot their life there. They had first planted their customs and beliefs in the older Eastern country home where they were strictly observed and kept up and it was with this feeling of respect and the hope that their customs were or would be blessed and greater results could be expected. Hence, the number four would always be observed in all the rituals of their medicines and other observances—a thing was not completely done unless it had been done four times in succession in four sets at a time.

Then, the rising of the sun in the East denoted representative of the beginning of a life. It is believed, as the stories are told, that the old customs of the old country are being followed when the medicine of the tribe is taken when facing the East. The old country, in

THE IMPORTANCE OF THE EAST

the talks of the older Indians, have been often referred to and to them has been, "Hus-see O-sa Le-Cha" (Under the Rising of the Sun). Their homes had been in their Eastern country where they had enjoyed their own hunting grounds, their life as they wished it lived and the other things that came dear to them.

The health of the early Indians was gained from their time spent in the open and all they did was always for their bodily good. They thought that it was essentially to be long-winded as well as robust and tried to engage in environments that would be loved and enjoyed without being tiresome.[1]

1

The Medicine Way

Little boys and girls among the Mvskokes are taught to respect people, especially their elders. This lesson certainly applies to children respecting their close relatives since aunts and uncles play key roles in helping to raise a child. They teach their nieces and nephews to understand right from wrong, starting them on the good path to be honest, obedient, and helpful in the family. The importance of respect extends to animals, plants, spirits, and everything in life to form positive relationships. Disrespect invites bad luck. Even if you do not like a certain person, at least show respect for the individual, and the person should do the same for you.

Hvmmaketv (that's what they used to say)

When Mvskokes consulted their leaders in times of trouble or uncertainty, their leaders advised them to continue as they had always done, and *Hesaketvmesē* (the Maker of Breath) and the other supreme powers would protect them. The people devoted themselves to the ceremonies to curry spiritual strength and protection from the four elemental powers—fire, water, wind, and earth. *Posketv* (the Green Corn Ceremony) was (and remains) the primary means for giving thanks to the *Hesaketvmesē* and *Epohfvnkv*.[1] The ceremony is a series of dances preceded by taking medicine that looks like a brackish tea. Women and men wash their hands and face with it to purify

THE MEDICINE WAY

their bodies. But men also drink the medicine to purge or cleanse their bodies as a way of paying homage to the Maker of Breath. This rite of expressing gratitude is centuries old.

There is a story that the Semvnoles and Mvskokes share called "The Legend of Abuska." In the early years well before the Semvnoles separated from the Mvskokes, they were one people and life was hard. A young boy, *cēpvnē*, went into the forest looking for food, and he found his way to the lodge of a witch. The witch offered the starving boy a bowl of golden drink, and not knowing the ugly old woman was evil, the boy drank it. Cēpvnē visited the old witch many times when he was hungry and each time she gave him the golden drink. Being curious, Cēpvnē asked the old witch about the secret of this drink and how it made him grow handsome and strong. The witch could not share her secret: if the boy found it out, she would die a horrible death. One day, Cēpvnē approached the lodge of the old witch and listened to her magical song, and while she was making the golden drink she caught him watching her. She told him to run away and not look back, but to return in the spring. As Cēpvnē ran away, he saw the lodge of the old witch catch fire and heard her screams as she burned to death. The witch shrieked at him to follow her instructions.[2]

Cēpvnē's "heart was torn and he was sad for she was his only friend. Disobeying the witch's instructions, Cēpvnē watched and when nothing was left save ashes, he returned to his people. Many moons passed and the time came for him to go again to the deep forest. Eagerly he set out to the place where the witch had died." The boy was afraid, but his curiosity kept him going. "As Cēpvnē approached the place he beheld a tall green plant growing amidst the ashes. Among the broad leaves, which were turned to the sun, were the plump milky fruits of the plant. The boy rejoiced for he knew them as the source of the golden drink. No longer now would his

THE MEDICINE WAY

people have to depend solely upon the forest and streams for food. Each spring the plant grew plentifully and as the grains filled with milk they were dried and parched and ground into meal from which the *abuska* was made."[3] This is why the Green Corn ceremony provides faith to the Mvskokes during good times and bad times.

Other groups like the Cherokees and Choctaws practiced the Green Corn Dance as well. For them it was special, like a new year beginning in early July when important decisions were made. Among the Choctaws, for example, "At this [Green Corn] dance, all the boys of the tribe who were about four or five years old were brought before the Chief and he gave each boy a name, and a small piece of tobacco. The boy was called by that name after that."[4] During the ceremonial days, it was also the right time to put things in their natural order.[5]

Taking medicine was and is "the old ancestral way" of being Mvskoke.[6] Particularly during the Green Corn ceremony, taking medicine was the first integral part of preparation. An elder explained, "They started early the first day drinking their medicine which was to clean body, mind and soul, and leave them at peace with all of their fellowmen."[7] It is an ancient custom to consume what many called the black drink made from red root. Those who are unfamiliar with this custom could call it "a kind of religion," that has been carried on for centuries.[8] Red root is called *mēkko-hoyvnēcv*.[9] It involves a process of ingesting herbal liquid made from red root. In the Mvskoke language the ceremonial drink is actually called the white drink to symbolize its discoloring by purging it from the stomach. Early Europeans mistakenly called it the black drink due to the dark-brown color of the ceremonial tea and the Mvskokes adopted this misnomer in English.[10]

Red root was not always available nearby, and when it was not three to four of the strongest young men received instructions for where to find it and when to return. The medicine maker told them not "to take any tools or comforts with them, they were to sleep on the bare ground and dig the roots with their hands."[11] Some medicine makers were good and some were powerful. Like the Cherokees, no two medicine makers doctored the same way, and their remedies varied according to the patient's clan identity. Their knowledge was powerful. One Mvskoke elder said, "These medicine men have songs for the different medicines which are made for the different diseases. . . . They can make themselves invisible, or turn themselves into animals. The knowledge of these things are handed down from one medicine man to another and nobody else knows how they are made nor what they contain."[12]

Coming East

A Mvskoke story tells about a migration from the Red River to the East across the Mississippi River.[13] A very long time ago during one particular night, the Mvskoke people huddled together to keep warm and realized that in order to be less cold they had to keep moving forward. The people could not see because of the darkness but kept moving until they reached an opening. The people felt a strange mist and were afraid, so they sang together to make themselves feel connected for safety. In the next moment, they felt something like a spirit touching them, and it lightly blew the mist away. The Mvskokes had never seen the sun, and they were thrilled with happiness because they could see it for the first time ever and it provided warmth.[14]

The spirit that showed them the sun, *hotvlē*, became known as the "wind," an elemental power to the Mvskokes and Semvnoles. The people realized it was the same kind of power when they blew on their hands to keep warm. They also breathed in and exhaled *hotvlē*, and this mysterious power meant life for all the living. The Mvskokes ac-

THE MEDICINE WAY

knowledged the wind as one of the principal elements for life and other beings that they observed for the first time. The savior wind blew away more of the mist and the Mvskokes saw strange beings that became known as animals. And they saw that *hotvlē*, the power, was in the animals. In the forming of the people's worldview, animals and people were like relatives, but different. The people grouped the animals, including the powerful *hotvlē*, into clans or totems and acknowledged the savior wind as the most important.[15] And so the Mvskokes named the various clans with most of the twenty-two totems being animals, while a few were not. They included bird *Fuswvlke*, bog potato *Vhvlvkvlke*, cane *Kohvsvlke*, fish *Rvro-vlke*, hickory nut *Ocē-vlke*, maize *Vce-vlke*, salt *Okcvnwvlke*, and wind *Hotvlkvlke*, the most important clan. Small four-legged clans included mole *Tvkusvlke*, otter *Osvnvlke*, beaver *Eccaswvlke*, raccoon *Wotkvlke*, skunk *Konepvlke*, toad *Sopaktvlke*, and turtle *Lucvlke*, related to wind. Larger four-legged clans included deer *Ecovlke*, bear *Nokosvlke*, fox *Culvalke*, panther or tiger *Cahtvlke*, wild cat *Kowakkucvlke*, and wolf *Yvhvlke*, which is related to the bear clan.[16] Since the Semvnoles were an offshoot of the Mvskokes, they shared most all of the same clans, including alligator. Chitto Harjo's mother was of the alligator clan, and therefore so was he. The clans were strengthened by being in clusters and the alligator was categorized with the *Tämi* and turkey clans. All three lay eggs and some people have said the alligator was the uncle clan to the *Tämi* (large flying thing) and turkey clans.[17]

In learning about their new homeland, the people marveled at seeing so many different animals; they studied them for their strengths and abilities to such an extent that they began to identify with them. Some people became of the *Yvhvlke* clan, or wolf people; *Lucvlke* clan or turtle people; or *Hotvlkvlke*, or wind people, and so forth. It is said by the oldest elders that the mist returned, transformed into a storm, and it began to rain. The Mvskokes realized the rain tasted good, and they needed *uewv,* meaning water for life. As it rained, creeks flowed with uewv and turned into rivers. Thunder clapped and lightning flashed from the sky to the ground, frightening the Mvskokes during the rainstorm. Then, lightning struck a tree, creating *totkv* (fire). The people learned that *totkv* kept them warm as long as it was properly fed, and that it was essential to life like *hotvlē* and *uewv.* As the Mvskokes huddled around *totkv* to keep warm, they talked about the importance of the elements, and realized *ēkvnv,* the earth, was like a mother to all things. All four, *ēkvnv, uewv, totkv,* and *hotvlē* were celebrated by the Mvskoke people as the foundational powers within the vast realm of *Epohfvnkv.* Wind and fire were male powers and water and the earth were female powers, but *Epohfvnkv* was genderless.[18] In order for them to understand, the people humanized the wind and called it *Hesaketvmesē,* the "Maker of Breath," the same meaning as "Master of Wind."

The Mvskokes identified the East as the most important direction because the sun rose each morning, and the in-between of the dark at night and light of dawn was a powerful moment to pray or sing to celebrate the birth cycle of each new day. The opposite direction of East was West, which was associated with the end of life as daylight ended as a part of the great cycle. In their journeys to learn about their natural world, the Mvskokes accumulated much knowledge and recorded their experiences in stories. In all four main directions, there were sacred fires of other peoples. In the East, a white fire burned, and to the North, a red fire burned brightly. In the West, a black fire burned, and a yellow fired burned in the South.[19] The Mvskokes learned that the fire of the North provided warmth to their people and lighted the world. The northern fire made plants grow, and the people learned to plant corn. They celebrated the harvest of the green corn by holding dances. Collectively they became known as the Green Corn Ceremony that sometimes were called busk ceremonies. The people learned if they failed to respect nature and failed to do the busk ceremonies, they would disappear from the earth and fall into the oceans. They had been warned by the wisest ones, those who were known as *owalvs,* who were gifted to see the future. Although blessed with such power, they had to live strict lives, or the ability of prophecy would disappear.[20]

Some people say the tradition of *Posketv* goes back ten thousand years and perhaps longer, to the Mvskoke mound complex near present-day Macon, Georgia. Similar to the great mound complex of Cahokia on the Mississippi River, the Mvskoke mounds demonstrated the cultural depth of the inhabitants and descendants practicing the Medicine Way. What has enabled the continuation of the Medicine Way of the Mvskokes and Semvnoles is *Poyvfekcv* (the Spirit), or the spiritual force embedded in the people who believed in the old ways and practiced them. Mvskoke people and the Semvnoles, who were an offshoot of the Mvskokes, were dedicated to the Medicine Way.[21] This way of life formed an Indigenous worldview based on a combined physical and metaphysical reality where all relations were balanced within *Epohfvnkv.*

Tvlofvs

Mvskoke society was organized in towns called *tvlofvs.* Among the old *tvlofvs,* Tuckabatchee and Kialegee were the oldest. Both were mother Red Stick towns and gave rise to daughter *tvlofvs.* Tuckabatchee, the leading war town of the Upper Mvskokes, created Thlopthlocco town. The original White Stick mother towns included Cussetah, Coweta, and Arbeka.[22]

The confederacy of Mvskoke peoples included Evcees, Alabamas, and other groups whose *tvlofvs* rested along the black belt of rich soil stretched across the present-day states of Georgia, Alabama, and

Mississippi. Plentiful rains enabled the sixty to ninety riverine *tvlofvs* to grow corn and beans in the same fields as bean vines climbed the corn stalks. The people planted fields of squash, melons, and gourds. An abundance of white-tail deer, turkey, rabbit, and quail provided meat, plus varieties of fish swam in the streams.[23] The word *tvlofv* translates into English as "town," but it means much more than that: a community that defined one's connections with others through shared language, sacred history, religion, and land. These connections provided comfort, security, and a feeling of kinship.[24] To be a member of a *tvlofv* meant to have its physical and spiritual protection, and to have a place around the *totkv etkv* (ceremonial fire). Every member of the community knew every other member's clan and his or her family.[25] These relationships were like an extended family, and they also included non-humans. The Mvskokes saw themselves as a part of the natural world that contained a plethora of knowledge, and some of it was sacred.

Native people were bound to use the land with respect for the earth and for each other. "In the old days each family would have a hunting ground," it was said. "It would reach back from his [the] house to the river or mountain or some such boundary, regardless of who owned the land. It would be by agreement. And we wouldn't hunt on the other's hunting ground," according to a Mvskoke elder. "We would call it a 'hunting claim.' The oldest man would be the Head and everybody would listen to what he had to say; they weren't like they are now, he was the oldest so he knew [the] most."[26] The hunting domain for each family was known in the community and people asked permission to pursue wild game belonging to someone else. In a way, hunting claims were similar to land allotments, but they were not the same.

A hunting claim was men's space. Farming was women's space since the earth is female.[27] Women owned the gardens and the yield of vegetables and fruits grew in the female domain. But this did not mean the women owned the space of the garden since it was viewed as communal ownership held by the *tvlofv*.[28] The gardens used only enough space to support one family, without large fields of crops to be sold at a market. Corn, beans, squash, pumpkins, and melons were planted, while in the woods, berries and wild onions were gathered to go with the foods grown in the gardens. Scrambled eggs mixed with chopped wild onions made a cost-free and tasty dinner that required only a hen, a little grease, and some luck finding onions. Based on a moral economy that privileged community, no one in the *tvlofv* went hungry and every member was protected by the *tvlofv*'s men and medicine makers. This meant all *tvlofv* members had responsibilities and roles.

Mvskoke men fished and hunted prairie chickens, deer, raccoons, beavers, otters, wild turkeys, rabbits, squirrels, buffalo, and even skunks. Individual Mvskokes owned lots of cattle, hogs, and horses and typically had gardens of corn, rice, and oats. In contrast, mixed-bloods typically had large fields of cotton and wheat to sell commercially for exporting by riverboat to Fort Smith, where crops and slaves were sold and traded.[29]

For Mvskokes, planting, growing, and harvesting corn was central to life, and it was important to learn the cycles of the seasons. Provided by Mother Earth, the other universal elements blessed the corn with the rains of water, breezes of the wind to bring the rain, and the light of the sun that symbolized fire and life itself. Observing the activities of the seasons enabled the Mvskokes to develop their knowledge about the cycle of life. The harvesting of corn when it turned from green to yellow in the early summer enabled the people to celebrate by holding the Green Corn Ceremony.[30]

The cereal grain called corn was domesticated by Indigenous peoples in southern Mexico at least ten thousand years ago. Corn made its way into the Southwest along with trade, eventually reaching the Southeast where the Mvskokes, Semvnoles, Cherokees, Choctaws, and Chickasaws began to cultivate it with other crops. Much of the Western Hemisphere relied on this precious crop.[31] In the Mvskoke mind, rain and earth makes corn, makes sofkey, a traditional drink that was an acquired taste: the sourer the aroma, the better the sofkey. One Mvskoke woman described how to make it, shell "off of the cob, and when you get ready to use it you put it in cold water. . . . Beat it to take the husks off. . . . That will bring it to grits." Then, she said, "When making [it], put a pot of water on the stove. . . . When it is just about to boil, put the sofkey grits in. . . . When half done, drip some ashes into the sofkey. . . . Put it in a jar and set it aside until [the] next day [when] it's better and drink the liquid." Finally, she said, "Most people don't like it when it gets sour. I think it's better when it's two or three days old. The men sit around and smoke and drink sofkey."[32]

The communal idea was to make sure everyone had enough. To take more than what one needed upset the balance of things within *Epohfvnkv*. The idea of owning land seemed not only illogical but incomprehensible to Indian traditionalists who followed the Medicine Way of life. In their worldview, after emerging from the earth, it was not possible to own a part of your mother as you might own a horse, a basket, or an article of clothing. The earth provided for her children as a mother and in return her children would respect her and take care of her, respecting obligations and responsibilities to family, clan, and *tvlofv*.

While the Mvskokes and other tribes understood the earth culturally and philosophically as Mother Earth, the white man interpreted "land" as a commodity to be sold, leased, or owned. These two very different views of the land/earth have caused most of the conflicts between Indians and whites.

THE MEDICINE WAY

In the Southeast the vast Mvskoke Confederacy of about fifteen thousand people lived in sixty to ninety scattered riverine *tvlofvs:* the Upper towns along the Coosa, Tallapoosa, Chattahoochee Rivers, and the Lower towns along the Flint River.[33] A few towns contained small groups like the Alabama and Evcee, and Arbeka was actually a district of three or four small *tvlofvs.*

The dance ceremonies, which came to be called stomp dances, and other ceremonials bonded a community or town together. Old timers often referred to the stomp dance grounds as "square grounds."[34] Ceremonial laws were developed by a medicine maker and the town leader, and a *henehv* (orator) announced the laws to the people by delivering a ritual speech called "the long talk." All of this focused on the ceremonial fire in the center of the town and practicing the Green Corn Ceremony by stomp dances became the Medicine Way for each Mvskoke generation, and this was extended to other peoples to welcome them since they were included in *Epohfvnkv.*[35]

This lifeway proceeds in constant rhythm with the natural world. Long ago the natural environment was so immense that the people, in awe of the lush green flora and abundant fauna, attributed to the sacred fire the power of the sun and rain.[36] Overwhelmed by the natural world, the Mvskokes observed and learned from the surrounding plant and animal relatives. This became the medical and philosophical basis of their medicine knowledge. The plants and animals provided food and shelter, compelling the people to respect and depend on their non-human relations.

In the Mvskoke Medicine Way all human beings and animals come from *ēkvnv,* the earth. Because there were many kinds of animals and plants, the Mvskokes developed codes or laws of ranking their clans in a hierarchy. Hence those in authority came from certain clans, for example, the bird clan, that were placed in charge to

THE MEDICINE WAY

make sure people followed traditions. For instance, the highest clan was the wind people, and the *mēkkvke* (town leaders) came from the wind clan. The clan animals that could fly like a bird carried on the breath of winds from the "Maker of Breath" were regarded as higher than clan animals who could not fly. Hence in a *tvlofv* of the Mvskokes, the higher clans provided the leadership for war, peace, or medicine. People of medicine knowledge typically came from certain clans, like the bear clan, and their words carried much weight in decision-making during councils. These laws were carried out by the clans among the Mvskokes.

The Mvskoke people divided the towns into red towns and white towns, with the red towns being war clans and the white clans representing peace.[37] The *tvlofvs* were competitive, and even among the red towns or white towns friction developed such that the people might refer to another friendly town as *anhissi* (my friend), or *ankipaya* (my enemy or opponent). The Spirit Power or sovereign autonomy of competitive towns was demonstrated by the Mvskokes playing rough stick ball games also known as the "Little Brother of War."[38] The stakes of the competitive stick ball game were incredibly high. In the post-removal years Cusseta town defeated Coweta town three games in a row in 1876, forcing, by custom, the latter to accept subordination by becoming a friendly town to Cusseta. During these years, Hillabi earned a reputation for its superior stick ball players.[39]

The interactions of these external elements made up life, according to the Mvskoke and Semvnole. The "way" in which the external elements have been arranged by *Hesaketvmesē*, "Maker of Breath," is *heleswv*, "medicine," the Medicine Way. A part of the "way" was communicating with *Hesaketvmesē* by calling or praying or singing to the seven directions. Other Indian nations like the Cherokees, Choctaws, Evcees, Shawnees, and Chickasaws were included in the Mvskoke

24

universe of sociocultural relations. It was their historical or physical reality in a traditional sense, but it was only part of it. There was a spiritual dimension to life just as real as physical life, and it exists today.[40]

The people depended on the benevolence of the Maker of Breath and the four other elemental powers, which often bestowed upon them gifts of knowledge, blessings, prophecy, and assistance. The power of life from the Maker of Breath was told in the oral tradition of stories, legends, and myths that forms the combined physical and metaphysical reality for the Mvskokes and Semvnoles who believe in the old ways.[41]

The Medicine Way has continued through the ages. In the late nineteenth century, a young white settler, who grew up among the Mvskokes and Semvnoles around Okmulgee, Paden, Okemah, and Wewoka, remarked, "The Creeks [Mvskokes] and Seminoles had ceremonies for every major event in their lives; a ceremony for births, another for marriages, one for deaths, and special ceremonies before they set out upon any undertaking. They held a Stomp Dance before they met to play their [stick] ball games, for instance. And they had dances and ceremonies when their corn began to be edible in the summertime. They seemed to think that their ceremonies made it all right for them to go ahead with anything, brought them luck and appeased the spirits. . . . The Indians believed in dreams, and thought they were signs and omens from spirits and they were very susceptible to the phenomena of Nature; they were very much afraid of thunder and lightning, and they saw omens in flying birds and running animals."[42]

The metaphysical realm, always present and nearby but not usually visible, ruled over the physical. The Mvskokes understood the universe to function according to the four elemental powers. Since the Mvskokes emerged from the earth, the people continued to pay respect to the four powers that were the pillars of *Epohfvnkv*. This is the Medicine Way of the Mvskokes as it has always been.

Churches and Schools

Churches and schools challenged the Medicine Way. As the number of Christian Mvskokes increased, Chitto Harjo and the traditionalists of all the tribes had good reason to be concerned. The fact that Christianity was exclusive and *Poyvfekcv* of the Medicine Way was inclusive could not be overlooked. The white man's Christianity denied the validity of the traditional beliefs of the Mvskokes. In the Christian mind, there was just one way, but some Mvskokes practiced both the Medicine Way and Christianity, to the dismay and often criticism from conservative Christians. The long history of Christianity is filled with persecution and the struggle to exist among older religions. This same competition and the displacement of other beliefs was a part of the Christian crusade introduced by the missionaries going back to the old Mvskoke Confederacy. With the intrusion of Christianity, Mvskoke traditions, including the Green Corn Dance ceremony, were labeled as being pagan and heathenish. The patriotic Mvskokes believed the missionaries and Christians had upset the order of things according to *Epohfvnkv*, whereas Christians saw themselves as the only righteous people.

Due to the inclusivity of *Epohfvnkv*, Mvskokes added Christianity to their worldview, but in their own way. They saw many parallels between *Poyvfekcv* and Christianity. Specifically, the East is a supreme direction of the seven cardinal directions—North, East, South, West, Up, Down, and Inside of our hearts. East is where the power of light comes from; the sun rises in this direction, enabling us all to see and bringing warmth. This is the gift of life provided by every daybreak. When telling stories in the Bible, missionaries in-

THE MEDICINE WAY

formed the Mvskokes that the star of Bethlehem under which Jesus was born was in the East. That Jesus would come to earth again from the East lined up with the significance of the East to the Mvskokes, and the Semvnoles believed this, too. One Mvskoke said, "It is believed that . . . he will come from the east with the sunrise."[43] Justice of the Peace Larkin Ryal, a white man who married a Mvskoke woman, recalled a baptism at a Mvskoke church: "It was absolutely according to the Bible. They went down into the water and came up out of the water just as it says in the Bible. They all knelt down and prayed, it was a pretty sight."[44] Going to water was one of the Mvskoke traditions: water possessed power to replenish life by quenching thirst and was essential for life and rebirth. Mvskoke traditionalists understood the tradition of baptizing people, as they could easily identify with emerging from water with new life.[45] "Going to water" was also a ritual for medicine makers and prophets, who could see the future in the reflection of clear, calm water.[46] Because the Semvnoles share the same traditions as the Mvskokes they also believe in "going to water"; the Cherokees have the same belief in the prophetic power of water and its ability to heal.

Some Mvskokes converted to Christianity completely and stopped practicing the Medicine Way of the Green Corn Dance ceremony. Other Mvskokes converted to Christianity, went to church, and prayed, but they also continued to embrace the Medicine Way and enjoyed going to stomp dances. In this way, they could do both, and they saw no conflict of interest. But the purists of believers like Chitto Harjo viewed Christianity to be a threat to *Poyvekcv*.

Many of the early Mvskoke churches were a hybrid of a one-room building with a traditional arbor attached to its front. The stomp grounds had three brush arbors representing North, West, and South, with the East side open to welcome the dawn of life for a new day. Always the Mvskoke and Semvnole churches faced east, as the stomp

27

grounds do, with the greatest respect for the special cardinal direction of rebirth. The idea of the arbor made a lot of sense for humid summer days and evenings. At some churches, a deacon blew an antler horn or rang an old iron bell, like those used on plantations, that was near the church to announce the beginning of church services. During bad weather, the bell was rung when a tornado was sighted. The deacons of the church played a similar role with responsibilities to "those who pick the leaders" to lead the next song at stomp dances. These two roles of authority insured that everyone followed the order of things—to focus on the sermon or on the song of the stomp dance.

Another parallel developed and it was called Fourth Sunday. It is hard to say when the tradition of Fourth Sunday started, but it was sometime during the early proliferation of Mvskoke churches after the Civil War. The practice followed the pattern of stomp grounds clustered together in groups of three or four grounds, going back to the estimated sixty to ninety *tvlofv* in the Southeast. An original stomp ground as the cultural center of a *tvlofv* was called a mother stomp ground. As more people joined, due to the inclusivity of *Epohfvnkv*, the ground would split, forming a new ground. This happened repeatedly as more people attended. The new grounds developing from a mother ground became sister stomp grounds with other new *tvlofvs*, and they were usually in close proximity for convenient travel between them.

The sister stomp grounds developed from the same idea as a mother or original church creating new churches with the spreading appeal of Christianity. Typically clustered in fours, the churches would receive visitors from the other three churches on the Fourth Sunday of a month. But not all the members would visit the church holding Fourth Sunday services. Instead they continued with their regular worship services.

The Fourth Sunday tradition was and remains an all-day church service of worship. After the early morning teaching of Sunday School, a deacon would ring a bell or blow an antler horn to announce the beginning of a sermon delivered by the church minister, who would present his message in the Mvskoke language and then preach the same sermon in English. A noon meal was offered at the various camp houses surrounding the church, making sure the visitors were fed, very similar to stomp dances where camps at the stomp ground would feed visitors first, then the members of the camp. After the meal, a deacon again rang the church bell or blew an antler horn, and the host minister would then recognize a minister from a sister church, who gave a sermon in the Native language or English. Sermons by guest ministers continued until the end of a long afternoon, often interspersed with singing church hymns and certainly ending the Fourth Sunday service with an invitational hymn for those in the audience to come forward to convert to Christianity, rededicate their lives to God, or request a prayer for a relative or friend in need of emotional assistance or spiritual guidance.[47] Only a few churches could afford a piano, perhaps a used one, but in the late nineteenth and early twentieth centuries, most congregations did not have one, much less a member who could play it. It was, however, customary to have a song leader. The first pew or a bench was reserved for sinners wanting to repent and those wanting to become newborn Christians. These individuals would step forward during the invitation hymn, which would be repeated or a different one sung until the invitation opportunity was ended by the host minister. From the outside it appeared that many Mvskokes and Semvnoles had converted to Christianity, and they did so as church-going Indians. Yet although they accepted the major Christian tenets, they persisted in being *este-cate* "Indian."

THE MEDICINE WAY

The inroads made by Christianity posed a threat to the Medicine Way of the Green Corn Ceremony and added to the concerns of Crazy Snake. Chitto Harjo was not only fighting against allotment, physically, culturally, psychologically, ideologically, and philosophically. He was also fighting against churches and schools because they were replacing the worldview of his people. Christianity and the white man's education worked in tandem with land allotment as Harjo saw it.

He was not wrong. In late 1882 Interior Secretary Henry Teller took a bold step in directing Hiram Price, the commissioner of Indian Affairs, to terminate Indian traditions. Teller told Price, "I regard as a great hindrance to the civilization of the Indians, viz, the continuance of the old heathenish dances, such as the sundance, scalp-dance, & c." Teller added, "Another great hindrance to the civilization of the Indians is the influence of the medicine men, who are always found with the anti-progressive party."[48] Price established a set of Indian offenses and sent them to Indian agents on reservations. The list of outlawed offenses included the sun dance, scalp dance, and war dance, plural marriages, drinking liquor, and the practices of medicine men. On March 30, 1883, Commissioner Price instructed the Indian agents to establish "at each Indian agency, except the agency for the five civilized tribes in the Indian Territory, a tribunal, consisting of three Indians to be known as 'the Court of Indian Offenses.'"[49] Indian police officers were introduced to help the Indian agent enforce the rules. Although the Five Nations were exempted, the new rules affected the western half of the Indian Territory and sent a clarion message declaring that the federal government was abolishing all Indian traditional practices. Four years later, John D. C. Atkins, then commissioner of Indian Affairs, issued an order prohibiting Native children from speaking their tribal language in any schools on reservations, although at the time the Mvskokes were using books published in their Native language in their schools.[50]

During the removal years, the first Mvskoke parties to arrive in Indian Territory became attracted to churches. Missionaries who had started churches and schools among the Mvskoke *tvlofvs* in the Southeast were frustrated by the possibility that their hard work would be for naught, and so they continued their efforts while the Mvskokes began to rebuild and put down fires. In the early 1840s, immediately upon the Natives' arrival in the Indian Territory, the American Board of Commissioners for Foreign Missions sent missionaries to work among the Mvskokes, Semvnoles, and Chickasaws.[51] They carried their Bibles and pamphlets with them and read the gospel.

The early schoolbooks used by missionary and Mvskoke teachers were written in English. But as early as 1834, a book in the Mvskoke language appeared in print: *Mvskoki imvnaitsv / Muskogee (Creek) Assistant* written by Reverend John Fleming, an early missionary to the Mvskoke. The following year John Fleming published *A Short Sermon: Also Hymns* and *Istutsi in naktsokv* or *The Child's Book.*[52] Two other enterprising individuals, R. M. Loughridge and David Winslett, published a well-used hymnal in 1851. Nine years later, H. F. Buckner and G. Herrod produced a grammar book, a song book, and a translation of the Gospel of John in the Mvskoke language. During the next two decades, Loughridge and Winslett's *Nakcokv esyvhiketv* or *Muskogee Hymns* was in such demand that a fourth edition appeared in 1880.[53]

One of the problems for people wanting to learn to read and write the Mvskoke language was the fact that several alphabets were employed to write Mvskoke. To solve this, in 1853 the Mvskoke government adopted a standard that enabled a smoother translation of the Mvskoke spoken word into a written language.[54] The first Bible in the Mvskoke language was published in 1887. Publications in Mvskoke and the devotion of missionaries undoubtedly helped to influence the founding of schools, although most of the white teachers taught only from books written in English. Mvskoke students who attended the Koweta Mission School during the 1850s studied Salma Hale's *History of the United States* and learned about the idea of building a nation-state. At Asbury Manual Labor School, located at North Fork Town, the students read R. M. Smith's *Modern Geography,* published in 1848, and Jedidiah Morse's *Geography Made Easy,* published earlier, in 1814. Both works stressed nationalism.[55]

While some Mvskokes became Christians during these years, most of the people followed the Medicine Way. Not all Mvskokes welcomed Christianity, especially following removal. Many of the settlers and politicians who forced the Mvskokes to remove claimed to be Christians. In 1843 a conservative national council passed a law that barred any Mvskoke or African American from preaching Christianity. In order for a white missionary to preach the Good Word to Mvskoke communities, special permission had to be obtained from the council, and it was reluctant to grant it. To enforce the law, the Mvskoke government sent Lighthorse patrols to stop the missionaries from preaching and Mvskokes from praying like Christians.[56] During the rebuilding years, Mvskoke laws became stricter, disallowing Christian preaching or holding meetings. Violations meant fifty to one hundred lashes on the bare back, with a second offense warranting an ear to be cut off. Even wearing white man's clothing was not permitted. Mvskokes who did not attend busk ceremonies or take medicine received fines between $2 and $3.50.[57] These prohibitions, however, did not halt the imposition of white religion and literacy.

Mostly the Indian churches were either Baptist or Methodist. They included Thewathle Methodist Church, Weoguffke Methodist, Hutchachuppa Baptist, Thlop Thocco Baptist, Sand Springs Baptist, and Alabama Baptist, considered to be the mother church of all

Baptist churches.[58] In 1858 the Methodists laid the cornerstone for a log mission school called Asbury, reported to be the largest mission school in Indian Territory.[59] The Mvskoke leadership also approved the construction of a manual labor school by the Presbyterian Board of Foreign Missions. The Mvskokes agreed to pay one-fifth of the cost of building the school, with the Presbyterian Board paying the rest. On March 1, 1850, a three-story brick building proudly opened its doors to eighty students. In the following years, cedar, hickory, and oak trees shaded the grounds where students played when not in class, and rose bushes lined the path to the front door. The school grounds included an orchard of apple, peach, and quince trees. During recess, the students picked wildflowers, including anemones, black-eyed Susans, butterfly weeds, innocences, red buds, spring beauties, and violets.[60] Several months later, in 1851, Loughridge Boarding School opened for operation.

Christianity proliferated during the Civil War years. The aftermath of the war left many people—Indians, whites, African Americans, and mixed-bloods—feeling uncertain about their futures. They hoped, looking for a sign and wanting to believe in a higher power. Then, in September 1876, everyone in the Mvskoke Nation and in the Indian Territory witnessed a supernatural event. As R. L. Nichols, a white settler, recalled, "There was a total eclipse of the sun that happened about 3 P.M. It got dark as night and everybody was really scared as they were not expecting such a thing to happen. The chickens all went to roost as though it was night. No one took [news]papers in those days to see what was going on what was going to happen and if they did take newspapers there was no mail delivery."[61]

For the Mvskokes, the darkening of the sun enacted the sacred. According to the Medicine Way, light and dark meeting signified the cycle of the end of the day transforming into the approaching darkness of night. Was this a sign, an omen? This phenomenon occurred

THE MEDICINE WAY

when the powers of light and dark as universal constants acted inconsistently, with night taking over day for seven and a half minutes. Such an extraordinary event caused *ehosa* for young Mvskokes and Semvnoles until elders shared their memories of previous experiences when the sun turned black. In the Mvskoke way of counting lunar moons, a full lunar eclipse occurred every eighteen years. The eclipse represented the wedding of the moon and sun and signaled a new spiritual generation of young people. Many generations ago, all of this began one moonless night at a stomp dance when a Mvskoke trickster, the Rabbit, diverted the people's attention and put the ceremonial fire into a bag to steal it. Hurriedly the sly rabbit hopped away but stumbled, causing the moon to fall out of the bag; the fire fell next, then the sun.[62] From that point on, the people learned to protect and respect the fire, moon, and sun; in return they would take care of the Mvskokes.

During the 1870s and 1880s, the Mvskokes operated the Coweta School, Hillabee School, Okmulgee School, Owekofker School, Tullahassee School, and the Arbeka School not so far from Arbeka *tvlofv*.[63] During the last quarter of the nineteenth century, the Mvskoke Nation operated seven boarding schools, plus three for descendants of freedmen. The Mvskoke government paid teachers a standard salary of twenty-five dollars per month with a requirement of at least ten students, and teachers received an additional two dollars for each pupil above the ten students. The students typically began their studies with the *Muskokee or Creek First Reader / Nakcokv Es Kerretv Enhvteceskv*. By the first decade of the twentieth century, the Mvskoke Nation reported that an estimated 95 percent of the people could read and write the Mvskoke language.[64]

By the late 1880s, many Mvskokes combined stomp dancing with church-going and saw no conflict between the two. The *Indian Chieftain* of Vinita reported that on Fourth of July weekend in 1888 in

Tulsa, a Saturday night barbeque beef dinner and stomp dance was followed by a Sunday church service with Parson Haworth preaching on "God's abundance," and dinner on "a table near one hundred feet in length" was laid. The evening services followed with everyone enjoying the sermons and fellowship, and the people found the singing "very entertaining."[65] Naturally this cultural hybridity did not appeal to the traditionalists.

The Ghost Dance

At first the Northern Cheyennes doubted the rumors they heard about an Indian prophet called Wovoka and his teachings about something called the Ghost Dance. From the Paiute reservation in Nevada, Wovoka shared his visit to the sky and being instructed to deliver a divine message to everyone who would listen to him. In early 1890 the Ghost Dance movement began to spread hope across reservations in the West. A couple of Northern Cheyennes, Black Coyote and Sashee, were sent by their people to investigate. They traveled on the railroad to the Walker River reservation to learn directly from Wovoka. Upon their return to Indian Territory, their enthusiastic descriptions inspired kinsmen to believe Wovoka's Ghost Dance promise of a reborn Mother Earth, the return of loved ones who had passed on, and the doing away of all evil, convincing the Northern Cheyennes and the Arapahos to adopt the new religion.[66]

The Southern Cheyennes learned about the Ghost Dance from Cheyenne boarding school students who received letters from relatives and friends in Montana. Expectation spread with the news to the Caddo, Wichita, and Kiowa. In September 1890 the Cheyenne and Arapaho held the largest dance ever on the North Fork of the Canadian about two miles from the Darlington Indian agency. After a Southern Arapaho named Sitting Bull traveled to Montana to meet

THE MEDICINE WAY

Wovoka, he claimed to have met the messiah. Wovoka chose him as an apostle to convince others of the spiritual power of the Ghost Dance. Wearing a wide brim black hat adorned with an eagle feather, Sitting Bull instructed his Southern Cheyenne people how to do the Ghost Dance. After two days of dancing, he paused the dancers. He walked slowly toward a young Arapaho woman, and passed his eagle feather several times in front of her eyes, putting her to sleep. During the singing, Sitting Bull did the same to more than a hundred dancers who fell unconscious. After their sleeps, the awakened dancers told how they enjoyed visiting the spirits of loved ones who had passed on.[67]

The spread of the Ghost Dance to Indian Territory succeeded due to the disorder of things and the imbalance felt among the traditionalists of all tribes. Some traditionalists criticized the Ghost Dance for having some parts that appeared to be Christian. The traditionalists refused to be influenced by the white man's religion.

Yet with the Ghost Dance another new religion began emerging in western Indian Territory: the Native American Church. Using peyote as a primary sacrament, the Native American Church arrived from the Southwest and spread to the Comanches, under the leadership of Quanah Parker, on the southern plains in the late 1800s. In addition to Christianity and politics causing so much upheaval, Chitto Harjo watched *ehosa* spread over the land. The beliefs of *estecates* of various Native groups like the Native American Church and Ghost Dance clashed with old Native worldviews, leaving doubt in the wake.

A BLACK PREACHER PUNISHED BY THE CREEK LIGHTHORSE IN 1845

JESSE ISLAND

One of them came and tied another rope around my wrists; the other end was thrown over the fork of a tree, and they drew me up until my feet did not quite touch the ground, and tied my feet together. Then they went a little way off and sat down. Afterwards one of them came and asked me where I got this new religion. I said in the Old Nation. "Yes," replied the Indian. "You have set half of this nation to praying and this is what we are going to whip you for." Five men were going to give me five strokes each. When I saw the sticks my heart faint a little and I said, "My friends, do take a gun and shoot me and don't whip me so." Then the Indians said, "We don't want to kill you; we will give you fifty lashes for the first time, the next time we will give you one hundred, and the third time you are known to hold religious meetings we will kill you." Then another Indian said, "You tell our people that Christ was hung up and we do the same for you."[1]

2

Moving Fire

Being connected to your people is important for everyone in all cultures, and this is imperative for Mvskokes. An essential part of this connection is for a person and his or her family to belong to a *tvlofv* known as a town community, but it is much more. Among the Mvskokes, a person and his or her family, plus a person's clan have a place around the fire. Knowing one's place and respecting other people and their positions is relevant for belonging to the *tvlofv*. By pulling together, the *tvlofv* functions as an effective community. This togetherness helps to create a harmonious balance as it was meant to be.

Hvmmaketv (that's what they used to say)

The confederation of Mvskoke *tvlofvs* has always had differences of opinion because the numerous town leaders did not always agree on the same issue. This *etekvlkē* (division of factionalism) dates back to the beginning of Mvskoke contact with European traders.[1] The Upper Mvskokes believed in *Poyvekcv* (Spirit), the energy force that remained embedded forever in the people who were "believers." They described themselves as *este-cates* (Indians, red people). The Lower Mvskokes relished the material goods received from Irish, Scottish, and British traders who traded these goods for pelts. Led by William McIntosh, the Lower Mvskokes favored the white traders and began dressing like *este-hvtkes* (white people).[2] McIntosh had led many

Lower Mvskokes to join Andrew Jackson and some Choctaws and Chickasaws to fight other Mvskokes in the Red Stick War of 1813–14.[3] At least twenty-one towns were involved, with the majority of the Red Sticks coming from the Upper Mvskokes.[4] This feud set up a long-running tradition of *este-cate* versus *este-hvtke* factionalism among the Mvskokes. This split has sometimes been described as being between "full-bloods," who were the main loyalists to traditions, and "mixed-bloods," who took up the ways of the white man and strayed from the Medicine Way, though these descriptions were not always literal: there were exceptions, for example, patriotic mixed-bloods upholding the Medicine Way and full-bloods who fully embraced non-Indian ways.

Assimilation or Removal

The conflicts of 1813–14 were far from the last as white settlers increasingly encroached on the lands of the Indians of the Five Nations, who lived on what was later to become the heartland of the cotton South. The federal government debated two conflicting policies when it came to Indians: assimilation and removal. Assimilation urged by missionaries would enable Indians to become Christians and to learn literacy and Anglo culture, which would supposedly allow Indians to live within a white world. On the other hand, removal would free up land for white settlement in the East and avoid future conflicts by guaranteeing permanent Indian ownership of land and permanent federal government protection west of the Mississippi.

The idea of moving the Mvskokes provoked considerable debates among Indians, whites, slaves, and non-slaves. The Mvskokes' signing of the Treaty of Indian Springs (sometimes called the McIntosh treaty) in 1825, which gave up Mvskoke lands east of the Flint River in exchange for the same amount of land in Indian Territory, was controversial and divided the Mvskokes into supporters of the McIntosh treaty, the progressive mixed-bloods, and the conservative traditionalist full-bloods. Naturally Mvskoke leader William McIntosh favored removal, since the U.S. government agreed to pay him $40,000 (about $1.2 million today). The acceptance of a bribe of this size reflected opportunism and greed entirely outside of Mvskoke values. Although opposed by many Mvskokes, this agreement finalized their removal from Georgia.

Assimilation was tested by the Cherokees, whose leader Sequoyah had developed an alphabet for the Cherokee language and who adopted a constitution asserting sovereignty over their lands, bringing them into conflict with the state of Georgia. When a deer hunter accidentally discovered gold on Cherokee lands, triggering a rush of over four thousand people (known as '29ers) looking to get rich, the Cherokees sued the state to keep white settlers out. The resulting Supreme Court decision affirmed that states could not pass laws interfering with Indian treaties.[5] This ruling increased popular support for Indian removal after 1829. President Andrew Jackson along with others in the federal government argued that the eastern tribes would be safer from settlers arriving in Georgia if they agreed to move to the West. Jackson told the Creek Nation

> Friends & Brothers, listen: Where you now are, you and my white children are too near to each other to live in harmony and peace. Your game is destroyed, and many of your people will not work and till the earth. Beyond the great River Mississippi, where a part of your nation has gone, your Father has provided a country large enough for all of you, and he advises you to remove to it. There your white brothers will not trouble you; they will have no claim to the land, and you can live upon it you and all your children, as long as the grass grows or the water runs, in peace and plenty. It will be yours forever. . . .

My children, listen: My white children in Alabama have extended their law over your country. If you remain in it, you must be subject to that law. If you remove across the Mississippi, you will be subject to your own laws, and the care of your father, the President. You will be treated with kindness, and the lands will be yours for ever.[6]

Jackson instructed his secretary of war, Lewis Cass, to investigate Indian affairs in the South. Cass knew very little about Indians, but he got things done. His task was to determine if the Mvskokes and the rest of the Five Nations were capable of farming the land and living alongside the settlers in Georgia and Alabama. Not taking into consideration that Mvskokes and other nations were horticulturalists and grew corn as their main food staple, Cass reported that the Indians were hunters and gatherers and concluded that they would be in the way of the settlers who could civilize the land by planting crops and building homesteads.[7]

In early 1830 when Congress took up legislation for Indian removal to the West many congressmen recognized the proposed legislation as white greed. Hugh White, the Tennessee senator who served on the Committee on Indian Affairs, spoke against it on February 22. Senators Theodore Frelinghuysen of New Jersey, Asher Robbins of Rhode Island, and Peleg Sprague of Maine stood firmly in opposition, as did the tall canebrake congressman (five feet, eight inches), Davy Crockett of Tennessee. Opposing Indian removal, the legendary frontiersman voiced his opinion in a letter to a friend. On Christmas day when he was in Washington, Crockett, though barely literate, put pen to paper: "I am truly afread that a majority of the free citizens of these united States will Submit to it and Say amen Jackson done it."[8] Outside of Congress, opposition included the American Board of Commissioners for Foreign Missions, who argued that removal would cause suffering and death among the Indians, and that it would be inhumane to move such large numbers of people, especially the elderly, sick, women, and children.[9]

For seven days in April, the Senate debated Indian removal. For three of them, Senator Theodore Frelinghuysen held the floor, speaking for more than six hours each time to repudiate removal. Representing the view of the Cherokees, the Mvskokes, and other tribes, Frelinghuysen criticized the Georgia settlers for not remaining on their own lands. He did not believe that the settlers should take Indian "forests and rivers, these groves of your fathers, firesides and hunting grounds" "by the right of power, and the force of numbers."[10]

The representatives voted 102 to 97 to pass the bill, the Senate, 28 senators to 19. By both vote counts, Congress was divided over the forced removal of Indians. But on May 28, 1830, President Jackson signed S. 102 into law. The amendments included a $500,000 appropriation to purchase new lands, plus funding for the removals of the Indian groups to the West.

> Be it enacted by the Senate and House of Representatives of the United States of America, in Congress assembled, That it shall and may be lawful for the President of the United States to cause so much of any territory belonging to the United States, west of the river Mississippi, not included in any state or organized territory, and to which the Indian title has been extinguished, as he may judge necessary, to be divided into a suitable number of districts, for the reception of such tribes or nations of Indians as may choose to exchange the lands where they now reside, and remove there.[11]

The eastern tribes were to exchange their homelands for new lands west of the Mississippi. In early spring 1832 a group of Mvskoke delegates arrived in Washington to begin the negotiations that resulted in the Treaty of Cusseta. The first article summed everything up: "The Creek tribe of Indians ceded to the United States all their land, East of the Mississippi," or about five million acres in Alabama. The Mvskokes' land in the East would be exchanged for new homelands in the designated Indian Territory. Article 10 stipulated that the sum of $16,000 "shall be allowed as a compensation to the delegation sent to this place [Washington], and for the payment of their expenses, and of the claims against them."

The seven Mvskoke delegates were Opothleyahola, Tvcebatcheehadgo, Effematla, Tvcebatche Micco, Tomack Micco, William McGillivray, and Benjamin Marshall, a Coweta headman. According to the agreement, the Mvskokes could remain in Alabama if they wished. Article 2 of the Cusseta Treaty called for the ninety Mvskoke *mēkkvke* (leaders) to be allotted a full section of land and a half section of land per head of family. "At the end of five years, all of the Creeks entitled to these selections, and desirous of remaining, shall receive patents therefore in fee simple, from the United States." But the Mvskokes realized that they would be surrounded by whites greedy for their homelands, and that state authorities would be on the side of the settlers in land or title disputes. The intrusion of settlers and land speculators ruined the crops, and droughts in 1830 and 1831 added hunger to misery. When they received their allotted lands in Alabama many were so short of food that they were forced to sell them. A location agent in charge of removal informed Lewis Cass that the Mvskokes were too trusting and could easily be swindled out of their land allotments: a common practice was for an opportunist to persuade a Mvskoke who had a starving family to pretend to be another Mvskoke in order to receive a treaty land allotment, then sell it.

The most significant part of the Cusseta Treaty was Article 14, in which the U.S. acknowledged the sovereignty of the Mvskokes to govern themselves as a nation if they moved west. "The Creek country west of the Mississippi shall be solemnly guaranteed to the Creek Indians, nor shall any State or Territory ever have a right to pass laws for the government of such Indians, but they shall be allowed to govern themselves, so far as may be compatible with the general jurisdiction which Congress may think proper to exercise over them." This important point and the rest of the treaty seemed acceptable, and the Mvskoke leaders signed the treaty.[12]

Trail of Suffering

Convincing all the people to leave their homelands and forsake their relationship with Mother Earth was not easy. News spread to all the Mvskoke *tvlofvs* and the other southeastern tribes that they could no longer live in their homelands and would need to move west, beyond the Mississippi River. As they were making removal plans late on Tuesday night, November 12, 1833, stars began to fall and appeared to shoot across the sky. Hour after hour, the stars fell in enormous numbers until dawn. The *New York Evening Post* reported that the event was "magnificent beyond conception. The general direction of these meteors was westerly, and their tracks as they descended towards the earth were nearly parallel, so that it appeared as if the cope of heaven was raining down a shower of fire, which was driven in an oblique course by the wind."[13] The oldest elders said that the stars in the sky at night are the ceremonial fires of ancestors. And as the stars went west, the Mvskokes understood the prophetic message to be to take their fires with them and put down their ceremonial fires in the new westerly homeland.

People from New Haven, Boston, Georgia, Ohio, South Carolina, Maryland, and Missouri saw tens of thousands of falling stars for several hours. In time, it would be discovered that the Leonid meteors cycled every thirty-three years, but the event in 1833 was the greatest storm in history to this date. Many people believed it was the end of the earth. Missionaries, preachers, and churchmen of all kinds recited Revelation 6:13, "And the stars of heaven fell unto the earth, even as a fig tree casteth her untimely figs, when she is shaken of a mighty wind." In the end of the world, as described in the Bible, the sun will become black, earthquakes will move mountains, and the moon will become like blood.[14] During the following weeks, people studied the sky at night. One day after Christmas, a full lunar eclipse plunged the full moon into total darkness, lasting one hour and thirty-eight minutes. Afterwards, the moon appeared to be stained with deep orange and red.

Like the Mvskokes, the Plains Indians watched the ominous rain of stars and recorded the strange phenomenon in their winter counts.[15] The medicine makers and *owalvs* (prophets) watched the falling stars in awe, but they also wondered if this was an omen.

The starving Mvskokes had become desperate to drive out the white settlers in order to save themselves and their homelands. They resented settler encroachment and other insults: during the hostilities a phrenologist explored Mvskoke grave sites, digging up many of them to collect the skulls of dead Mvskokes.[16] During the winter of 1834–35, ill feelings between Mvskokes and settlers from Georgia erupted into outright hostilities. It all started in the Chattahoochee valley when white intruders from Georgia provoked the Red Stick warriors of the Lower Mvskoke *tvlofvs* of Jitchitta, Yuchi, and Chiaha. In May warriors from the three towns burned down several homes, other buildings, and a tavern on the Federal Road. Then the Lower Mvskokes attacked a stagecoach near Tuskegee and set it on fire. When the passengers tried to escape, the Mvskokes beat them to death with their red war clubs.[17] The series of raids that followed became known as the Mvskoke War of 1836. Each attack was more violent than the last, but Mvskokes were far from united: the Lower

Mvskoke warriors were the driving force, while the traditionalist Upper Mvskokes remained at peace.[18] The war dragged on into the early months of 1836, when the Mvskoke leader Eneah Micco realized that his force of about one thousand was outnumbered by about eleven thousand soldiers and militia. Having no choice, he surrendered.[19] The hostilities continued and blended with the Second Semvnole War from 1835 to 1842, and many Mvskokes fled to Florida to join the Semvnoles as allies.[20]

Attacks between Indians and whites continued until more Indians migrated to the West. The journey of about 850 miles took about two and a half to three and a half months, depending on availability of supplies, steamboats, and livestock to pull wagons. As early as summer 1834, 630 Mvskokes agreed to leave under the leadership of Eufaula Harjo. After a meager harvest, their removal began under Captain John Page of the U.S. Army. Most of the removal party were poor, except for Sampson Grayson, who owned thirty-four slaves, and the widow Sally Stidham, who owned twenty-three slaves. While it would seem logical to avoid travel during the cold months, the Mvskokes did not want to migrate during spring and early summer due to the swelling of the rivers, which often washed away the bridges over the Cahaba, Black Warrior, and Luxapalila. Page urged the Mvskokes to navigate impassable roads and to endure prairie blizzards in open spaces that the people had never experienced before. Eufaula Harjo's party finally reached the Verdigris River in late 1834.[21]

While most of the Mvskokes suffered and starved during the group's removal, a few wealthy Mvskokes, led by John Stidham from Sawokli, migrated on their own in 1834. Influenza killed several Mvskokes who contracted the disease from white settlements they had passed along the way. On the Arkansas River, a severe snowstorm tormented the group 150 miles from their destination of Fort Gibson.

MOVING FIRE

The journey dangerously affected the Mvskokes during 1834 and 1835. Some individuals became lost in *ehosa,* others became frustrated from anger, provoking a rash of suicides with warriors fleeing into the woods and hanging themselves with grapevines.[22]

The removal of the Mvskokes to the West has been called *Estemerketv Nene* (the Road of Suffering).[23] The 14,609 Mvskokes in Alabama, of which the War Department listed 2,495 as being hostile, were divided into five removal parties. Opothleyahola, the respected leader whose name meant "highly acknowledged ceremonial crier to 'Yahola' one of the two male pure spirits above us," gathered eight thousand of his kinsmen from Kialigee, Thlopthlocco, Thlewarle, Hillibi, Fish Pond, and Autauga. Roughly two thousand Mvskokes from the Coosa and Tallapoosa districts prepared themselves to start on the Road of Suffering to the West.[24] Opothleyahola was a traditionalist and although he did not speak English he excelled as an orator of the Mvskoke language.[25] He was born about 1780 in the Upper mother *tvlofv* of Tuckabatchee. Opothleyahola was born a Red Stick with a warrior persona, ready to take action, but he learned to be wise. In the Mvskoke War of 1813–14, he had fought alongside the Red Sticks against Andrew Jackson. An articulate speaker, Opothleyahola shared his view against the Lower Mvskokes who were becoming less traditional with each generation. Simon Jackson, a Mvskoke elder, remembered a story about an incident when Opothleyahola practiced the Medicine Way. Jackson recalled, "It is said that he was once in prison back in the old country for eight days. He neither ate nor drank for those eight days but even then there was no change in his physical appearance to show any weakness. He chewed the root which is classed as the most useful herbal medicine among the Muskogee-Creeks. This herb is called Mēkko Ho-ne-cha (Wild King)."[26]

Along the Path of Suffering, some of the *tvlofvs* carried their fire with them, and the Mvskokes called this tradition "moving fire."

Mose Wiley of Fish Pond town in Oklahoma described the ritual in detail. When the Mvskokes of a *tvlofv* found out that they had to join a removal party, they prepared to take their fire with them. They selected two men to do this. According to Wiley, "Each of them took a burning piece of wood from the fire and each was to keep this piece of fire from going out on the journey. When they made a camp these men made a new fire from the burning wood they carried. When they broke camp they took two other pieces of burning wood and brought it on with them."[27] The ritual for building a new fire for a new *tvlofv* was called "put down fire."[28]

The mother fires of Artussee and Tuckabatchee of the Upper Creeks joined the movement. In preparation for the march going west, Opothleyahola declared that Mvskokes would "take our last black [medicine] drink." The Mvskoke leader said he would "put out his old fire and never make or kindle it again, until he reaches west of the Mississippi." The Mvskoke leader wanted a new start and a new ceremonial fire to give rebirth to the Mvskokes. Opothleyahola and his removal parties arrived in Indian Territory on February 2, 1836, and chose as their home the valley where the North Fork of the Canadian branched off from the Canadian River.[29] Hostilities in the homeland continued through June 1836. As Opothleyahola reflected on the turmoil, he was convinced that whiskey and land speculators, known as sand shakers, were much of the cause, for they stood to profit most from all of the chaos.[30]

In early September 1837 the five sacred brass or copper plates were ceremonially removed from under the Tuckabatchee Council House to be carried along with twenty-three thousand Mvskokes on the Road of Suffering.[31] Sacred objects held in the highest regard, the plates were made from metal from the earth, like the Mvskoke people, and had been gifted by strangers called conquistadors.[32] They were kept at Tuckabatchee, one of the earliest and most significant mother *tvlofvs* of the Mvskokes, signifying its respected status among all the people. All removal parties of the Mvskokes experienced hardship; they were cold, hungry, and sick. Many died, and sometimes death was welcomed as a means to escape the pain and agony. But they had to go on, to keep moving to survive, much as in the migration legend when the people were cold, in the dark, huddling together to keep warm as they kept moving forward to finally emerge from the earth into the world and everything that would be known as *Epohfvnkv*.[33]

To help them to endure the suffering, the Mvskokes prayed to the Maker of Breath, and to sustain themselves they sang this song over and over:

> *Espoketis omes kerreskos,*
> This may be the last time, we do not know.
> *Espoketis omes kerreskos,*
> This may be the last time; we do not know.
> *Mekusapvlke vpeyvnna,*
> The Christians have gone on,
> *Espoketis omes kerreskos.*
> This may be the last time; we do not know.
> *Pumvpvltake vpeyvnna,*
> Our others have gone on,
> *Espoketis omes kerreskos.*
> This may be the last time; we do not know.
> *Cvwantake vpeyvnna,*
> My sisters have gone on,
> *Espoketis omes kerreskos.*
> This may be the last time; we do not know.
> *Espoketis omes kerreskos,*
> This may be the last time; we do not know.
> *Espoketis omes kerreskos,*
> This may be the last time, we do not know.[34]

One Mvskoke elder explained that Christian Mvskokes and slaves on the Trail of Suffering shared songs to get them through the anguish of the march to the new homeland in the Indian Territory.[35] Undoubtedly the Mvskokes looked to all sources of strength to urge their people to continue moving along, so they blended Christian and traditional beliefs to help themselves. As many as eighty-one of them died along the Path of Suffering. At first they experienced bowel problems and fever from salt rations and drinking bad water, resulting in death from dysentery, diarrhea, and cholera.[36] On September 3, 1836, a large group of Mvskoke "hostiles" finally arrived at Fort Gibson.

During 1837 as many as four to five thousand Mvskokes were gathered together by soldiers at Montgomery, Alabama. Many of them had served as volunteers for the United States in the Second Semvnole War. From Montgomery, the majority of the Mvskokes were steamed downriver to camps at Mobile, guarded by soldiers. From Mobile, the military planned to load the Mvskokes on steamboats to begin their journey to Indian Territory.[37] The U.S. Army had negotiated for transportation with the Alabama Emigrating Company, which engaged three steamboats, *The Yazoo, John Nelson, The Monmouth*. After a night of heavy rain and low visibility on the Mississippi, *The Monmouth,* filled to capacity with 611 Mvskokes, ran into a sailboat being towed by another steamboat, hit an island, and broke in half. An estimated 311 Mvskokes drowned in the murky waters of the Mississippi.

In 1837 the rest of the people of Arbeka removed; they were one of the last of the Mvskoke *tvlofvs* to move to the West.[38] Those who did not die had no choice but to keep moving along the way. When they arrived at Fort Gibson, the Mvskokes began to locate new square grounds for their new towns in their new homelands. The western tribes had their own view about the Mvskokes and other tribes from the Southeast moving their fires to Indian Territory. A Mvskoke man later recalled that the Osage, Kansas, Comanche, and Kickapoo peoples opposed the newcomers. The western tribes moved their camps, "going to grassy places during the winter months and returning with the return of warm weather," and they attacked the newcomers in order to protect their domains.[39]

In all an estimated 3,500 of 23,000 Mvskokes died along the Road of Suffering from cholera, influenza, pneumonia, and starvation.[40] The survivors kept pushing on to complete the long journey. Upon arrival they rebuilt their fires throughout the new Mvskoke Nation. New ceremonial fires had to be put down in the following manner. It was said, "The ground has been cleaned, nothing unclean has been left on the ground. Some clean dirt, about a wash-pan full, is piled where the fire is to be made and smoothed down on top. Two lines are made, one going exactly north and south, the other going east and west on the top of the dirt. Some herbs are put in the spaces between the lines. Four, two and a half foot logs are placed with the end touching in the center. Then four roasting [corn] ears are placed between them."[41]

By 1859, 13,537 Upper Mvskokes lived in forty-four to sixty-three *tvlofvs* along the Canadian River; the rest were Lower Mvskokes living in thirty *tvlofvs* along the Cimarron River and in the Three Rivers area.[42] Although removal had tested the Medicine Way of the Mvskokes, they rebuilt their towns based on the old system in the Southeast.[43] The Mvskokes and Semvnoles shared a common culture and core of values as the means for constituting their societies. Steeped in centuries of tradition, they transported this culture and set of values with them along the infamous Road of Suffering to Indian Territory during the 1830s and 1840s. The physical environment had a great influence on shaping culture and influencing human behavior, and the Mvskokes and Semvnoles experienced a new homeland of green flora and humid summers with a similar climate to the homeland they had left. Hence the physical reality remained virtually the same, enabling the continuity of the metaphysical reality that they had known. The Mvskokes and Semvnoles were only a part of the painful forced migrations that included other tribes—the Cherokees, Chickasaws, Choctaw, and twenty-plus other groups from the eastern woodlands.

Realizing they were caught in between the old Medicine Way and the white man's capitalism, many of the Lower Mvskokes preferred an economy based on keeping their slaves.[44] This decision added to the hardship of the slaves traveling with the Mvskokes on the Path of Suffering. In the post-removal years, 267 Mvskokes owned 1,651 slaves. Benjamin Marshall, a signer of the Cusseta Treaty and a wealthy Mvskoke, owned more than 100 slaves, and 19 accompanied him during removal. Most slavery operated on a small scale compared to the large white plantations. Mvskokes assigned their slaves tasks to do, and when these jobs were done, the slaves went to their own homes to work in their own fields. The slaves could be adopted as Mvskokes with rights, including property ownership, but they could not be assigned a clan since this identity was according to blood connection on the mother's side.

As many as five thousand African American slaves belonging to the tribes walked the Path of Suffering, as well as a handful of missionaries. A slave girl moved with the self-migrating Mvskokes of Thlopthlocco *tvlofv,* and she described how they walked in groups separately during the day but camped together at night.[45] One Choctaw elder told of how his parents and his brother walked the trail in 1854, three years before his birth. He said, "My mother, Lydia Simmons Choate, was a white woman," and she suffered the hardship of removal.[46] Another Choctaw elder said her people "thought it was a disgrace to come here by being driven like cattle, as they were."[47] In experiencing the shared agony, blacks and whites had become *este-*

cate (Indian). By the completion of the Semvnole removal, roughly twenty-five *tvlofvs* completed the trek to the West. The Semvnoles established their new communities of *tvlofvs* between the North Fork of the Canadian River and the Canadian River.[48]

Treated inhumanely, the Mvskokes, Semvnoles, Cherokees, Choctaws, and Chickasaws incredibly survived forced migration and genocide.[49] Those in charge of the removal parties did not really care if the Mvskokes and other Indians lived or died on the trail, forcing them to march during the cold months of winter. Their only concern was to make sure the Mvskokes, Semvnoles, and other groups left their homelands. The pain of watching loved ones die along the Trail of Suffering was traumatic for the Mvskokes, but greater was the shame and humiliation of being forced from their homelands and leaving a part of themselves attached to Mother Earth. With heavy hearts, the Mvskokes continued their journeys of agony, singing, "This may be the last time, we do not know," to keep moving forward and sustain each other. Symbolically it was like the first time, when the earth opened up and the Mvskokes struggled together out of darkness, singing to comfort each other until they saw the light in the East. This is how the stomp dance tradition was born with the people dancing through the dark of night to greet the sunrise in the East.

A WHITE BOY'S FIRST STOMP DANCE
WALTER GARY, INTERVIEWED IN 1937

The sun had just gone down, and it was early night. There was no moon, but the stars were thick and bright. And I could feel excitement tensing the muscles of my abdomen and making my heart beat faster. . . . I wish I could make you see all this just as I saw it that June night back in the old Creek Nation forty-four years ago. There we were; three white men going to an Indian dance, and we knew there wouldn't be any more white men at the dance. There were only six white men living in a radius of twenty-five miles, and we knew where the other three were. There would be hundreds of Indians at the dance; this was the "New Yorker" [Nuyaka] dancing ground just ahead. . . . One of my companions, a young man about twenty-something, grunted and stopped walking. His name was Frank Payne. Jeff Gentry, my other companion, grasped my arm and we both stopped too. Ahead of us the sky was red. "That's the dance fire," Jeff said. . . . I gazed with open mouth, awed and thrilled; I was sixteen then, and impressionable. The brush thinned out, giving way to grass, and we could see the huge camp. The fire in the

A WHITE BOY'S FIRST STOMP DANCE

middle leaped high in the air, casting a sort of wavering, unreal light over milling Indians, tents, wagons, and brush arbors. We went forward again, keeping close together. "Gosh, I'm kind of scared among all these Indians," Jeff whispered.

Finally there were nearly two hundred of them out there, all dancing and chanting in unison. The chant had changed too, I noticed; it was sort of [a] song now, smoother and with more words than at first [chanting]. Then the women got into the dance. I became conscious of a rattling sound; it went, "Chink, chink! Chink, chink, chink!" "Hear that!" Jeff whispered. "That's caused by pebbles rattling in terrapin shells. The women wear 'em strapped to their ankles." After a while they must have decided that they wanted some more dancing, because they started in all over again. Some of them were Indians that hadn't danced before. Jeff and Frank and I joined in, too, this time. The Indians would dance and then rest, and this went on until about three o'clock in the morning. Then they began to drift off to bed. Some of them slept in the tents, and some under the brush arbors. A lot of them just lay down on the grass under the sky, and slept that way; you couldn't have run me off with a club. I woke up the next morning to the sounds of a stirring camp; the Indians were talking, laughing, and moving about. Little cooking fires winked in the fading darkness, and the sun was just coming up in the east. At the table nearest us were three old men with staffs about four feet long in their hands. One of them came up to me and grasped

A WHITE BOY'S FIRST STOMP DANCE

me by the arm; he pushed me gently toward the table, pointing with his staff. I didn't need any urging; I felt starved. I got a tin cup full of coffee—strong and black, with no sugar or cream—and made a sandwich out of a biscuit and a piece of pork. There was beef on the table too; a kind of small corncake made from blue Indian corn; called "blue bread," a dish called "sof-kee" made of corn boiled and slightly fermented. And, of course, the new corn, boiled on the cobb. I hated to leave. "Come on kid," Jeff called tolerantly. "This isn't the last green corn dance you'll ever see; there is one every year."[1]

3

The White Man's War

We must believe in doing the right things, according to the Medicine Way of *Epohfvnkv*. By doing the proper things in preparation, we prevent problems. It is also wise to take precaution and protect yourself and your family, and the order of things will provide balance. This has been said many times by elderly aunts, uncles, grandmothers and grandfathers, and parents who believed in the Medicine Way.

> *Hvmmaketv* (that's what they used to say)

Chaos and the need for order troubled the post-removal years. Although the Mvskokes continued to form a loose confederacy of towns acting in their own *Poyvekcv yekcetv,* an important change began to occur. The *tvlofvs* based on communities of the twenty-two-clan system began to move toward a centralized government. In the old country in Alabama and Georgia, the Ocmulgee mound complex represented the annual meeting site for all *tvlofv* leaders. In the West, Eufaula No. 1 along the Canadian River began to emerge as the central *tvlofv* among the Mvskokes. The divisions between the Upper Mvskokes and the Lower Mvskokes persisted in the new Mvskoke system of towns.

THE WHITE MAN'S WAR

Centralized Government

In 1840 the Mvskokes moved increasingly away from their former loose confederacy consisting of *tvlofvs* and toward a centralized government with a national council. The Mvskokes established a court system, and a police force, the Lighthorse tribal police, was created to arrest and punish criminals. Mvskoke justice operated according to lash laws. If a person was found guilty of stealing a horse, mule, jack, jenny, or cow, the Lighthorse administered fifty lashes with a hickory switch with the tips burned over a fire to harden them. A second offense for the same crime called for one hundred lashes and the loss of an ear. A third violation for the same crime mandated a death sentence. The crime of rape called for the same harsh degrees of punishments. It was against the law for a Mvskoke man to marry an African American woman, and hiding a runaway slave warranted a fifty-dollar fine or one hundred lashes. Blacks in the Mvskoke Nation who were over twelve years old had to pay a three-dollar annual tax, in addition to a tax on a wagon and livestock.[1] A white man, Larkin Ryal, who was married to a Mvskoke woman, served as justice of the peace for the Mvskokes. He described some of the details of Mvskoke law: "A book the size of your hand contained the Law. . . . They used hickory switches, some were pretty smooth and others were rough. They would tie him [criminal] up by a tree so that the switch wouldn't go all around and cut him in the front. Just his back was whipped."[2]

In 1842 there were only twenty-two white men and no white women living on the Mvskoke reservation. Each white man had an Indian wife and six of them were licensed traders. This situation changed with more whites arriving—missionaries, teachers, doctors, or men working for the railroad, including strayed cowboys. Before 1870 North Fork emerged as the largest populated settlement among the Mvskoke *tvlofvs,* with several hundred people and several stores along the Texas Road. Unfortunately such prosperity invited violence with more people arriving. In 1872 the first railway, the Missouri, Kansas, and Texas Railroad, known as the Katy railroad, crossed the Mvskoke Nation connecting the towns of Mazie, Wagoner, Muskogee, Checotah, and Eufaula. But it did not happen without a heavy price. Mvskokes killed the first two surveying teams for the railroad.[3]

Any missionary preaching in the Mvskoke Nation had to obtain permission from the National Council, according to a law made by the council in 1843.[4] It was an effort to reduce the number of young Mvskokes who were converting to Christianity and abandoning the old traditions.[5] From the late 1700s to the early decades of the nineteenth century, the Second Great Awakening, a nationwide movement seeking to make the tenets of Christianity part of everyone's life, was felt among the Mvskokes and all Indigenous peoples in the country.

The Mvskokes adopted a constitution in 1859 and another one in 1860. The first one acknowledged the natural sovereignty of the *tvlofvs*. Within a year the National Council produced a second constitution, which reflected the distance of the political leadership from the people living in the *tvlofvs*.[6] The revised constitution changed the governmental infrastructure, in calling for a principal chief and a second chief to be elected by tribal members from four newly created districts. Each district had a judge appointed by the principal chief. Above the district judges was a court of five supreme judges who ruled over cases based on Mvskoke national laws in the constitution.[7]

Loyalist Mvskokes, Confederate Mvskokes

At first, the white man's war starting east of the Mississippi did not concern the Mvskokes and other tribes in Indian Territory. Opothleyahola had arrived at the decision to stay out of it. In early

1861 he explained his plan to everyone who would listen. When asked what was the best thing to do, Opothleyahola replied that everyone should find a place where they could stay out of the way of white men of the North fighting the white men of the South. Old Gouge was wise and intelligent, and had become successful at planting and harvesting cotton, so people listened to him. But as the fighting moved ever closer to Indian Territory, it threatened everyone like an unwelcome rainstorm. If the Mvskokes moved farther west, they would be out of harm's way, but of course they would have to make peace with the Plains tribes. In the coming weeks, Old Gouge's followers set up a camp on the banks of the Red Fork, also known as the Cimarron River.[8] For now, Opothleyahola believed they had a chance to stay neutral.

Many people began to believe that Old Gouge was right, but Opothleyahola began to doubt himself and rethought things; he reconsidered whether in the event the U.S. lost the war it would continue to honor its 1838 treaty provisions of providing annuities to the Mvskokes.[9] Would the Five Nations be able to keep their lands? In these days of uncertainty, the Mvskoke way called for doing the right things for the best things to happen. If things were out of balance, one of the four powers would make the disorder known to the people by a flood, tornado, or some other catastrophe. In 1860 people talked about the drought, the worst anyone could remember. With no rain in sight, things were out of balance as the sun mercilessly scorched the cornfields.[10] The Mvskoke *tvlofvs* held their Green Corn dances, hoping the power of water would bless them.

During the early summer of 1861, a stranger stood on the horizon: Albert Pike, a smooth-talking type from Arkansas but without a southern accent. The large bear of a man, six feet tall and three hundred pounds, arrived to council with the Mvskokes. With his shoulder-length hair and long beard, his words sounded odd since he was actually born and raised in Boston. He claimed the Confederacy needed their help to win the war, and he tried to persuade the Mvskokes and as many Indian nations as possible to fight for the Confederate States of America.[11] Pike's offer was enticing; with a Confederate victory Indian Territory would become a part of the Confederate States of America, he claimed, and tribal leaders would be invited to send a delegate to sit in the House of Representatives of the Confederate government. Acting on his own without the full confidence of Confederate president Jefferson Davis, Commissioner Pike added that Indian Territory could become a state in a future Confederate States of America.[12]

Opothleyahola spoke vehemently against signing the treaty,[13] but forty-five leaders, influenced by Pike's assurances that the Confederacy's promises were "so long as grass grows and waters run," signed a treaty with the Confederacy on July 10, 1861, at North Fork Town on the Canadian.[14] The war between the whites divided the Mvskokes and their old nemesis of factionalism reemerged. Some thought it best to remain loyal to the U.S. while others felt the pressure to go with the southern states. Some Mvskokes reminded others it was Alabama and Georgia settlers who had driven their people from their homelands.

Two days later, the Choctaws also signed a similar treaty with the Confederacy. The Semvnoles did the same on the first of August.[15] Yet Old Gouge continued to preach that staying neutral was the best for the welfare of the Mvskokes and, in fact, for all the Indian nations of the territory. By the end of Albert Pike's smooth talk, roughly twenty tribes, including separate bands of tribes, decided to accept the promises of the Confederacy.[16]

On August 15, 1861, the Mvskoke *mēkko* Hutkko and Opothleyahola wrote a letter to President Abraham Lincoln.[17] They posed the question, if the Mvskokes remained loyal to the U.S., would the president promise to protect them? "Your children want to hear your word, & feel that you do not forget them. I was in Washington when you treated with us, and now white people are trying to take our people away to fight against us and you. . . . I well remember the treaty."[18] About a month passed without an answer, then Lincoln responded through a special commissioner, E. J. Carruth. If they remained neutral and could make it to Fort Row in Kansas, the soldiers there would protect them.[19] Carruth sent letters to the Choctaws, Chickasaws, Semvnoles, Witchitas, Iowas, Caddoes, and Comanches, requesting them to meet in Kansas. Fort Row had been built that summer as a buffer against Confederate attacks in the area. Located about two dozen miles inside of the southeast corner of Kansas on the south bank of the Verdigris, the fort was built to house about eighty local militia men.[20] Much happened before any Native group could reach Fort Row.

Several Native regiments were formed from those who signed treaties with the Confederacy. The First Regiment of the Choctaw and Chickasaw Mounted Rifles, the First and Second Creek Rifles, plus a unit of Semvnoles came under the command of Confederate Colonel Douglas Hancock Cooper.[21] The Ninth Texas Cavalry was under Lieutenant Colonel William Quayle, and Douglas Cooper was the overall commander.[22] Cooper saw that the Mvskokes were undecided, and that their possible loyalty to the Union posed a threat to the Confederacy's control of Indian Territory.

Cooper had anticipated the actions of the neutral Indians and quickly tried to vanquish any plans of Opothleyahola and his followers to escape. Many of the neutral Indians suddenly realized the danger their lives were in. Women and children traveled in wagons, on horseback, and walked while trying to keep up with the growing caravan of people, wagons, and livestock. The neutral Indians, instead of being found, surprised Cooper's men north of the Red Fork

THE WHITE MAN'S WAR

in the late afternoon and attacked. In dismay Cooper's men had to retreat as reinforcements arrived. The two sides fought for the rest of a cold winter afternoon in what became the Battle of Round Mountain or the Battle of Red Fork. Opothleyahola's fighting force consisted of Mvskokes, Semvnoles, Comanches, Delawares, Kickapoos, Wichitas, and Shawnees, along with slaves who had nowhere to go but to join their masters. Fighting into the early darkness of the short winter day, Old Gouge ordered the prairie grass to be set on fire to hold off any further advance from Cooper's soldiers.[23] The wind was an ally in spreading the fire toward the soldiers. But it was not a victory for either side to celebrate. The temperature dropped and the weather changed for the worse, alternating between pelting sleet and falling snow.[24]

Cooper was not convinced that Opothleyahola and his followers wanted to remain neutral. Not taking any chances at Round Mountain, Cooper ordered an attack against the Indians and the slaves. But Old Gouge drove their attackers back, and he avoided making the terrible mistake of pursuing and running into Cooper's counterattack with the main force of his men. Opothleyahola had no choice but to retreat, but he had outwitted Cooper who now realized the large Indian group had one main objective—making it to Kansas where Union soldiers could protect them.

Flight to Fort Leavenworth

The bitter winter only added to Douglas Cooper's frustration, but Opothleyahola and the loyalist Indians and slaves had it worse on their journey. Each new day brought more snow, and staying together became a laborious task in those conditions. Freezing snow also meant starvation: game was scarce. A Mvskoke elder recalled, "I have heard my mother tell of that flight. To comprehend it you must bear in

THE WHITE MAN'S WAR

mind that Oputhliyahola was taking all of his followers with him, women, children and even the aged and sick."[25] The only hope for Opothleyahola and his suffering group was to remain out of the reach of Cooper's men. But they could not stay very long in one place. The group started to splinter as some of the neutral Indians and slaves left to try to reach Kansas on their own.

Opothleyahola needed help and he prayed earnestly to the Maker of Breath and Mother Earth. It helped. His scouts found some banks with shallow caves at Bird Creek—a good sign, Old Gouge believed, for the group to make a last stand here. They were low on food and ammunition. At Bird Creek, more Indians joined Old Gouge. One guess is that three-fourths of the Mvskokes had decided to join Opothleyahola, but this seems to be an exaggerated estimate.[26]

On Monday morning of December 9, 1861, Cooper's weary men closed in on the neutral Indians, who became known as Union loyalists. In the early afternoon, Cooper ordered his soldiers to attack. After four hours, Cooper's men could not pry the Indians and slaves from the caves. Opothleyahola's side managed to lose only about ten of their men while killing twenty-five of Cooper's soldiers and wounding another thirty-five.[27]

After surviving the Battle of Bird Creek, the exhausted Indians continued their pilgrimage, slogging north.[28] Cooper's men were running low on ammunition, and Opothleyahola's warriors had almost none. Both sides wanted to avoid a third battle, but too much hung in the balance: for the loyal Indians, protection in Kansas, and for Cooper, preventing more Indians from joining the Union side. Cooper needed reinforcement and sent word to Colonel James M. McIntosh at Van Buren, Arkansas.[29] Then he waited. Three days before Christmas, McIntosh and his heavily supplied force of 1,380 marched from Fort Gibson in the cold to meet up with Cooper.

McIntosh's scouts discovered Old Gouge's temporary camp in Osage country at Chustenahlah. McIntosh sent this information ahead to Cooper. Cooper's returning messenger reached McIntosh on Christmas Day, ordering him to attack the loyalists as soon as he could.

At noon the next day, McIntosh attacked the encampment of the Union loyalists, located northwest of Tulsa *tvlofv* on Shoal Creek.[30] With Opothleyahola and his followers at the top of a hill, the wind and snow affected the Confederate soldiers much more.[31] Outfoxed, McIntosh had to march his freezing men uphill, into blasts of cold wind coming from the north. But knowing Old Gouge's warriors were low on ammunition, McIntosh marched his soldiers on foot to draw more fire from the loyalists. The Mvskokes, Semvnoles, and other Indians and slaves could not hold off the soldiers.[32] The winter's short days dropped the temperature, but the early darkness provided little protection for Opothleyahola's weary party. The cold became the greater enemy with each passing hour. In the remaining hours of fighting, the loyal Unionist Indians and slaves lost their horses and wagons and were forced to flee with nothing except for the clothes on their backs, and some of the slaves were "captured and took [*sic*] back to their masters."[33]

At least 250 of Opothlevahola's group died along the way to Fort Row, over a hundred miles away. Along the snow-covered miles, the Union loyalists straggled along the best they could against the cold northern wind. The military had never intended Fort Row to be more than a supply stop for patrols to water and rest their horses and pick up supplies, if the post could spare them. Fort Scott was the main post, but it was farther away. More and more loyalist Mvskoke survivors continued to arrive, overwhelming the resources at the fort. Many were dying, and more people continued to arrive until the number of refugees rose to 7,600. The fortunate received a blanket, the only protection between their bodies and the cold frozen ground.

THE WHITE MAN'S WAR

Dr. William Kile trying to provide care had to amputate over 100 frostbitten arms, legs, fingers, and hands.[34]

One of Opothleyahola's descendants, Don Cook, lamented, "The suffering among the Indians . . . was almost indescribable. They had abandoned their farms, homes and stock, and few of them had tents or shelter of any kind. Most of them were scantily clothed and many were without shoes. Food was scarce and many died of exposure in Kansas."[35] A former slave remembered, "They suffered a great loss at the hands of the Confederates, and they finished their trip into Kansas in a terrible storm in the dead of winter, sick, dying, and destitute. They were very angry at the Confederates and all of them enlisted in the Northern Army."[36] "Many of the survivors died during the night of the last battle, if it could be called that," said the ex-slave. Many came down with pneumonia, like Opothleyahola himself. Old Gouge and several others managed to make their way to a Sac and Fox agency at Quenemo, but there the noted Mvskoke leader fought his last battle.[37] Up in years even for an elder, Opothleyahola died at eighty-five years old; he was buried next to his daughter. It was almost impossible to bury him because of the frozen ground, but now Opothleyahola's long journey ended in *feke ofv*, the seventh direction, and his body was transported to where he rests near present-day Belmont, Kansas.[38] The war had ripped the Mvskoke Nation apart and caused similar harm to the rest of the Indian Territory. Many of the Loyal Mvskokes who reached Kansas joined the Union forces to fight against their brethren or anyone who sided with the Confederacy.[39]

Having survived what he called the "terrible hard times" to make it to Fort Row, Chitto Harjo remained a loyalist and fought on the Union side.[40] Years later, he recalled, using the term "my father" for the president of the United States: "I arrived at Fort Leavenworth to do what I could for my father's country and stand by my treaties.

THE WHITE MAN'S WAR

There at Fort Leavenworth was the orator [commander] of the Federal Army and I went and fell before the orator of the Federal Army." He remarked, "In that day I was under the Sons of my father in Washington. I was with the Federal soldiers. . . . I went and fell before him and I and my people joined the Federal Army because we wanted to keep our treaties with the father at Washington. Things should not have been that way but that is the way they were. . . . I went in as a Union soldier. When I took the oath, I raised my hand and called God to witness that I was ready to die in the cause that was right and to help my father defend his treaties."[41] An undetermined number of Native men fought for the Union, largely coming from the Mvskoke, Semvnole, Cherokee, and Osage nations.

By 1864 the tide of the war had turned in favor of the Union. News of General Robert E. Lee's surrender on April 9 at Appomattox Court House in Virginia did not reach Indian Territory until early May.[42] Chief Peter Pitchlynn and his Choctaw unit surrendered on June 9, 1865.[43] Two weeks later, General Stand Watie and his battalion of Confederate Mvskokes, Semvnoles, Cherokees, and Osages surrendered and signed a peace treaty, though Watie had held out and was the last Confederate general to surrender. Following the lead of Stand Watie and the Choctaws, Governor Winchester Colbert represented all the Chickasaws when he surrendered on July 14.[44]

The Treaties of 1866

While they have been called treaties, the four surrender agreements signed by the Five Nations in 1866 were punitive measures, punishing even the loyalist Indians who had fought for the Union side. The 1866 treaty with the Creek Nation forced the Mvskokes, "in view of the alliance with the Confederacy of the United States," to accept the military occupation of their lands by U.S. soldiers, to sell the western half of their lands (3,250,560 acres) to the United States at thirty cents per acre "whereon to settle other Indians," and to allow railroad companies to build through Mvskoke land, and it set aside land for missionary enterprises and schools. Further, the treaty stipulated that slavery was to be abolished and that all freedmen must be admitted to full tribal citizenship with the same rights as tribal members. Finally, the treaty required the Mvskokes to accept federal legislation provided it did not "in any manner interfere with or annul their present tribal organization, rights, laws, privileges, and customs." It further stipulated that a representative legislative general council was to be established, presided over by the superintendent of Indian Affairs, and that a court system be established "with such jurisdiction and organized in such manner as Congress may by law provide."[45]

The other four nations faced the same treatment. The government made the Semvnoles sell all their land—2,169,080 acres at fifteen cents per acre for a sum of $325,362. Then the Semvnoles had to purchase a much smaller area, about 20 percent of their former land: 405,120 acres at fifty cents per acre. The government mistreated the Cherokees the same way and made the Choctaws and Chickasaws sell their leased district of an estimated seven million acres for $300,000.[46] The 1866 treaties created smaller reservation lands for the Mvskokes and the other four tribes. The federal government asserted more control over the Five Tribes and made them subject to current and future federal laws. All of this undermined the sovereignty of the Five Nations and compelled them to establish new governments like that of the U.S. government.

The Mvskokes had little choice but to begin to rebuild and reorganize their national government at Okmulgee. Facing pressure from the federal government, the Mvskokes completed a new constitution in October 1867 representing forty-seven *tvlofvs,* including three new freedmen towns.[47] One Mvskoke elder recalled that the new constitution followed "somewhat the outlines of the Constitution of the United States. There was to be one principal chief and one second chief, elected for four years; two houses, the House of Kings, made up of one representative from each town, and the House of Warriors, one representative from each town and one additional for each 200 persons belonging to the town. The Mvskoke Nation was divided into six districts, a judge, prosecuting attorney and company of Lighthorsemen for each district. A company of Lighthorsemen consisted of a captain and four [to six] privates."[48] The six districts were Coweta, Deep Fork, Eufaula, Mvskoke, Okmulgee, and Wewoka.[49]

The adoption of the constitution by the Mvskokes signified the compliance of the Lower Mvskokes, who represented the progressive faction. The Upper Mvskokes reluctantly accepted the constitution, which they viewed as a threat to Mvskoke sovereignty. On top of the political changes came the increasing influence of missionaries and Christianity, which was at odds with traditionalist culture. The new "Great Seal of the Muscogee Nation I.T.," adopted following the Civil War, depicted a sheaf of wheat in the center with a yeoman's plow in front of it—though the prized crop of the people had always been corn. The new seal seemed to signal acceptance of the transformation of the Mvskokes into Christianized farmers who harvested wheat, as in the description of Joseph's dream, recounted in Genesis 37:7: "For, behold we were binding sheaves in the field, and, lo, my sheaf arose, and also stood upright."[50] Some years later, Mvskoke churches would sing the gospel "Bringing in the Sheaves."

The war had devastated the Mvskoke Nation and the rest of Indian Territory. The Mvskokes continued their customs as they had always and welcomed others to their dances. One African American said, "I used to go to Stomp Dances and have a good time. Every year, usually in July, the Stomp Dances were held for three or four days at a time and every one for miles around would come. . . . Indians and the negroes like myself, all mixed, mingled and danced together."[51]

Neighbors helped each other through hardships. One young white boy remembered his father helping a lot of people. He said, "My father was a doctor and would ride horseback, sometimes being gone from home for a week at a time. The [Choctaw] Indians would call him the white Medicine Man. The Indians had their own Medicine Man and they made all their own medicine from herbs that they would gather from the woods."[52] People did not have much money. A white farmer who lived with his wife near Hickory Ground recalled, "Everybody farmed and bought on credit. But people worked at any other work they could get, and there were plenty of jobs to be had for the settlers and transients, too. There were cleaning, picking cotton, cutting wood, gathering strawberries and blackberries to sell in town, building houses and fences." The farmer added, "The turkey and deer had been killed out then but there were opossum and skunks that were hunted for the hides."[53]

Cattlemen frequented the Mvskoke Nation and Indian Territory, and trying to keep their cattle out of the corn patch or gardens proved to be a challenge. A young farm girl named Emma described how "her mother used to have to get out and run the long horned cattle away from their home, to keep them from horning and rubbing the corn down." Emma said her mother "sometimes would take a sheet and hold it wide and run at them. It would scare them almost to death. They would snort and run with their tails in the air, bawl, paw and shake their heads. The scare with the sheet would keep them away at least for a while."[54]

The cattle loved plains bristlegrass, sand dropseed, little bluestem, and cane bluestem that grew waist high. On the frontier where not enough rain fell, however, prairie fires were a danger. In 1894 a settler from Texas witnessed "a fire several miles in length with flames leaping twenty feet in the air . . . an awe inspiring spectacle and I saw just that a few weeks after we arrived." The broad prairie fire consumed "the country clean, burning up everything in its path." A neighbor boy lost a wagon loaded with fence posts to the fire. The settler exclaimed, "I saw lots of fires after that but none that thrilled me like that one. I have seen fires at night so big one could read a newspaper by the light several miles away."[55] Fires presented such a hazard that Fish Pond *tvlofv* passed a law that prohibited fires during certain times of the year, "especially during the windy months, the law being strictly enforced and observed. If a fire was started and the wind blew the fire along and accidently burned some property of a neighbor or other people, the person starting the fire had to replace the property burned."[56] Mvskoke elders seeing such destruction likely wondered if the people had done something wrong to provoke the wrath of the elemental power.

By the 1890s the Mvskoke Nation and the rest of Indian Territory entered a form of *ehosa,* a state of such confusion that it was certain that things were out of order and out of control. Like the growing prairie fire in 1894 that consumed everything, only blackened ruin and the stench of destruction remained behind. Too many outside forces were at work causing imbalance to the changing Mvskoke world beyond the people's control. One has to wonder if the *owalvs* foresaw this happening.

The horizon for the Mvskokes at the end of the Civil War did not look promising; everyone struggled for the next ten years. The war had torn the Indian nations apart and destroyed many homes, farms, and buildings. Like a prairie tornado, it damaged everything and affected most everyone in its path. Some soldiers had no homes to return to, nor did all people who fled to escape the fighting. Devastation, destruction, and depression colored the landscape,

THE WHITE MAN'S WAR

hollowed-out towns and cities struggled to get by. The ruins provoked many opinions about how to rebuild the Mvskoke Nation, but politics stood in the way.

Cēpvnē

Among the Mvskokes and Semvnoles, the word for little boy is *cēpvnvke,* and when the child starts to grow, he is called *cēpvnē* (boy).[57] Chitto Harjo was like most young male children of the Mvskokes and Semvnoles: his mother and father called him Cēpvnē until he achieved a more distinctive name. The Mvskokes and Semvnoles lived according to a matrilineal system where everything was based on the mother's side, as it is done culturally today. Clan membership was an integral part of a Mvskoke's upbringing and kinship place around the ceremonial fire. Cēpvnē's mother was of the alligator clan, which meant that Cēpvnē's clan was alligator as well.

Chitto was born in the post-removal year of 1846. His parents, Aharlock Harjo and his wife Milley, were married in the new Mvskoke Nation sometime in the early 1840s. Aharlock and Milley had three children, Polly, Wilson, who would become known as Chitto, and Mollie. All three took the last name of Jones after the Indian agent, James Logan, persuaded the parents to select an English name.[58] Wilson's father was a farmer, and he taught his young son how to hunt, read herbs, plant crops, and take care of livestock.[59]

By nature, Cēpvnē was a White Stick. This means he was an introvert who did not impulsively react to crises. Rather he preferred to study situations and think about them before deciding what to do. His way followed the ancient tradition of White Sticks who were deemed peaceful at heart, calm in mind, and studious by nature. White Sticks represented the half of Mvskoke philosophy that promoted peace, tranquility, and knowledge.

White Sticks also produced the medicine ones, individuals who were conjurers, healers, or curers called *heles hayv* and *kērrv* (persons of special knowledge), or fortune tellers and prophets called *owalvs*. They were the ones who kept the knowledge of the past and sacred knowledge of medicine. As effective listeners, White Sticks were counselors and advisors. And as they grew older, their years of accumulated wisdom made them trusted elders for they had encountered many things in their lifetimes.

A White Stick was not instinctively a warrior, but this did not mean he or she could not be a warrior. Polly and Mollie and other little girls were observed in the same manner as little boys. Like boys, they would be a White Stick or a Red Stick, according to their nature. A Red Stick was a warrior by nature. One's instinct was to take action immediately, and the strength of a Red Stick was in the blood. Red Sticks were the first ones wanting to go to war to defend the Mvskoke and Semvnole *tvlofvs*.[60] They earned the title of "Hadjo," meaning one showing reckless courage and fearlessness to the point of appearing crazy. A Red Stick might be known as Arbeka Hadjo, "Fearless Person of Arbeka Town," or Eufaula Hadjo, "Fearless Person of Eufaula Town." It was hard for a Red Stick to be calm due to the emotional nature of a person born with a spiritual readiness to take action. Red Sticks were the first to get angry and often had to be calmed down, and generally they were not good negotiators for peace.[61]

Cēpvnē grew up embracing the Mvskoke worldview of the Medicine Way. As a boy, he entered training to become a young man and followed the teachings and advice of his father and uncles. Like all children, Cēpvnē participated in the Green Corn dances in celebration of the corn harvest and gave thanks to *Epohfvnkv*.[62]

THE GREEN PEACH WAR

AGNES KELLEY, SAMUEL CHECOTE'S DAUGHTER, 1937

I was eight or nine years old. We lived on the home-place northwest of Okmulgee, and were sitting on the porch. A whole lot of people came riding upon horses, I suppose they were Isparhecher's soldiers. One of them gave Daddy a letter and he gave it to one of his Light Horsemen to read to him. Then he wrote an answer and sent it back by these people. Then he came to town and stayed all night at the Council House where he had soldiers to protect him. Both sides had Light Horsemen. Daddy was a Democrat as he served on the Southern side. Isparhecher was a Republican who had been on the Northern side. They both had scouts out to see if the other side was near.

After they made peace they found out that they were close kinfolk. They didn't know it before the [Green Peach] war. Daddy was a Tiger, and Isparhecher was a Tiger too, so Daddy and Isparhecher were Tiger Clan kin.[1]

4

The Sands Uprising and the Green Peach War

An old saying the elders used is *Hesaketvmesē em vnvtaksetv,* which means to look up at the Maker of Breath. While traveling, especially when using dirt roads, it is wise to observe the weather because it changes so quickly. The same advice applies to trying to walk the good path in life, to keep your head up, certainly when the politics became thick and problematic. When things are chaotic and out of order, then it is essential to keep your head up to see what is happening and what might be approaching on the horizon.

Hvmmaketv (that's what they used to say)

Isparhecher had a habit of thinking a lot before he decided what to do. He was a full-blood traditionalist of the Lower Mvskokes and after removal he lived at Cusseta *tvlofv* along Deep Fork of the Canadian River.[1] People respected him as he possessed deep knowledge of the old Medicine Way shaped by the ancestors, and he knew what to do in dangerous situations. He kept his head up and often talked to the elemental powers, especially to *Hesaketvmesē* (Maker of Breath). By watching the clouds and studying the wind, a person could tell when a bad storm was approaching, even a *hotvle rakko* (tornado). Isparhecher knew to point his hunting knife or a sharp edge into the wind, praying to the Maker of Breath to divide the wind, so that it would go around him and the other people in its path so that they might be spared: *Hesaketvmesē pon Hesaketvmesē, Poth key hul we lay gets cv.* (Maker of Breath oh Maker of Breath, You that are powerfully high above us.)

The divisions and factionalism that predated the Civil War never stopped festering. As Don Cook, a Mvskoke mixed-blood from the Wewoka District, recalled about this period, "A disagreement arose among the Creek people; Oktarharsars Harjo with Isparhechar as commander on one side and Samuel Checote with Pleasant Porter as commander on the other side." The long-standing disagreement between the progressive mixed-blood Lower Mvskokes led by Porter and Checote and the traditionalist full-blood Upper Mvskokes led by Oktarharsars Harjo and Isparhecher came to a head in summer 1881 in a series of violent encounters known as the Green Peach War.

Pleasant Porter was born in Indian Territory in 1840, the son of a mixed-blood Mvskoke woman and a white father. He was educated in both English and Mvskoke, and studied at Tullahassee Presbyterian Mission School. Raised on a plantation, during the war he had served in the Confederate Company A of the First Creek Regiment under Colonel Daniel Newman McIntosh and had fought against Opothleyahola at Round Mountain and Bird Creek in 1861.[2] After the Civil War Porter became the superintendent of schools, and starting in 1872 he was the nation's representative in Washington. He served on the National Council for twelve years, and ran for principal chief three times, winning twice.[3]

Samuel Checote was born in the Chattahoochee valley in Alabama in 1819, and at the age of ten, before the Indian removal bill was passed, he migrated with his parents to Indian Territory. As a young man, Samuel Checote converted to Christianity. Filled with the Holy Spirit, he preached the Bible to Mvskokes and to anyone who would listen. But this did not sit well with the conservative

THE SANDS UPRISING AND THE GREEN PEACH WAR

traditionalists who controlled the government at the time. The National Council passed a law in 1843 to punish anyone preaching Christianity with fifty lashes on the back.[4] Taking heed, twenty-four-year-old Checote fled the nation until Chief Chilly McIntosh dismissed the law. In 1852 Checote joined the Indian Mission Conference of the Methodist Episcopal Church and spread the Gospel until the outbreak of the Civil War.[5]

During the early constitutional years, a new faction formed among the traditionalists of the Upper Mvskokes under the leadership of Oktarharsars Harjo, also known as Sands.[6] Sands was a full-blood and he had survived removal to Indian Territory. His followers were called the Sands, and under his leadership they refused to attend the council meetings of the Mvskoke Nation.[7] The Sands proudly called themselves *este-cates,* and they referred to Checote and his party as Mvskokes who acted like *este-hvtkes.* Two issues drove the Mvskokes further apart. The first was the election of 1867, the first election after the new postwar constitution: because the voting system had been changed from the raising of hands to a secret ballot, allegations surfaced that Checote had cheated.[8] The second was the federal government's payment from the tribal funds, which was to be distributed among all tribal members. Because the U.S. recognized Samuel Checote instead of Oktarharsars as the legitimate winner of the 1867 election, all payments went to his government, which then distributed the federal funds only to the Lower Mvskokes.[9] To make matters worse, in 1868 the Checote government tried to negotiate an amendment to the Treaty of 1866, calling for additional sums to be paid to the Mvskokes for their loyalty to the Union during the war. The National Council ratified the amendment to the treaty immediately, but the U.S. Senate did not.[10] During the winter of 1868–69, Checote's delegates went to Washington to lobby for the Senate's ratification of the treaty. The Sands party, suspecting that the newly negotiated

THE SANDS UPRISING AND THE GREEN PEACH WAR

sums would go to the Checote faction, sent its own delegates to Washington to try to stop the process. But their disruption led Indian Agent J. W. Dunn to denounce the Sands party, including their efforts to restore the old ways of justice. Meanwhile the treaty never made it out of committee, even with the supportive recommendation from Commissioner of Indian Affairs Ely Parker, a Seneca, who confirmed it represented the desire of the Mvskoke people.[11]

In an attempt to bring about a peaceful resolution, the Board of Indian Commissioners agreed to hear Sands and his followers. Sands claimed that Checote partisans had cheated him in the 1867 election, but as he was not able to provide any evidence, the Board of Indian Commissioners could do nothing to remedy the situation. In 1869 L. N. Robinson, superintendent of Indian Affairs, stated that in the view of the federal government the Mvskoke constitution justified Checote being the elected chief. On this basis, the U.S. recognized Checote's administration as the official government of the Mvskoke people. Checote's government was "devoted to the interests of the nation favoring religion, education, progress, and works of internal improvement." The superintendent added, "If need be, the Creek authorities should be furnished a force sufficient to put down insubordination or insurrection; and unless strong measures are used at once, I greatly fear the Creek people will soon be involved in civil war."[12] The war has been called the Sands Rebellion, but it depends on one's point of view. From the Checote view it was a rebellion against Chief Checote's government, but in the eyes of Sands it was Native patriotism trying to keep the traditionalists in power.

Robinson's fears were not misplaced and tensions erupted in the Sands Uprising in 1871. That fall of 1871 Sands ran once again for principal chief, unsuccessfully, as the Mvskoke people reelected Samuel Checote. When Checote attempted to call a meeting of the National Council, three hundred Sands followers swept into Okmulgee

THE SANDS UPRISING AND THE GREEN PEACH WAR

on horseback to disrupt the council. Anticipating trouble, Checote had put Pleasant Porter in command of the Lighthorse. Porter was standing in front of Sangers Store on South Morton Avenue in Okmulgee when the Sands Mvskokes, heavily armed with rifles and pistols, rode by. One of the riders shouted a warning to Porter, "You need not count us, we are too many for you." Porter counted them anyway. Then he turned to tell Sanger, who was also a Lighthorse under Porter's command, to close his store immediately and take his family and clerks out of town. Porter gave the same command to the other shopkeepers in town.[13]

As both sides began rechecking their guns, emotions turned to anger. Cotchochee, the leader of the Sands warriors, realizing a lot of bloodshed was imminent, made a rash decision: he rode to the Severs store and through an interpreter he asked Captain Severs to stop Porter from gathering his men. When Severs delivered the message to Chief Checote, Checote replied, "Today is Monday; tomorrow, Tuesday, our constitution says for our Council to meet; if Costsochy's [Cotchochee's] men have not evacuated, there will be time for you to use your troops," meaning Porter's Lighthorse.[14] The risk of carnage persuaded Sands supporters to lay down their arms. In the following months, Sands unexpectedly fell ill and he soon died. Without Oktarharsars's leadership, the traditionalists of the Upper Mvskokes abruptly ended their uprising.[15] But this led other traditionalists, like Isparhecher and Chitto Harjo, to step forward to preserve the Medicine Way. They would take their places in the Mvskoke split between traditionalists and progressives.

Boomers

In the midst of such divisions, white settler incursions into Indian Territory and a federal government policy hostile to tribal sovereignty threatened Mvskoke life. In 1871, the House of Representatives passed the Indian Appropriation Act, a routine funding bill with an important add-on supported by representatives from the western states. The bill outlined a major change in federal policy relating to relationships with Indian tribes: henceforth the federal government would no longer recognize Indian tribes as independent nations with whom the U.S. government would sign treaties. "No Indian nation or tribe within the territory of the United States shall be acknowledged or recognized as an independent nation, tribe, or power with whom the United States may contract by treaty."

In the 1880s the Mvskokes and other tribes in Indian Territory faced a continual wave of outside pressure largely coming from the Boomer movement. Some of the lands forcibly sold to the U.S. in the 1866 treaties, ostensibly for the resettlement of other Indians, created an island not designated by the federal government for any tribes. This island within Indian Territory, known as the Unappropriated Lands, enticed settlers from Kansas who saw the "surplus" land as an opportunity.[16] It was illegal for whites to settle in Indian Territory (except for missionaries with permission and Indian agents), and government officials spent countless days sending the military to arrest Boomers and escort them off the Indian reservations. Starting in the late 1870s Boomer settlers relentlessly petitioned Congress and any government official who would listen to release the Unappropriated Lands in Indian Territory to white settlers. This nearly three-thousand-square-mile area looked almost like a square carved in the middle of Indian Territory from the Treaties of 1866.

Boomers envisioned Indian Territory as an opportunity for colonization. In their view any open land needed to be settled, farmed, and civilized. The Boomers were encouraged by the Homestead Act of 1862, which made public lands available for settlement and fee-simple ownership after five years of improvements to the land.[17] They recruited new members and planned continuous expeditions into

THE SANDS UPRISING AND THE GREEN PEACH WAR

Indian Territory to start colonies, and they used lobbying tactics, rhetoric, propaganda, even the Bible to make their case. Missionaries pointed out that in the book of Genesis, "The Lord God took the man and put him into the garden of Eden to dress it and to keep it."[18]

Land hunger prompted Senator Richard Coke of Texas to introduce the first Indian land allotment bill in Congress. With politics in his blood, Richard Coke was raised in a prominent family in Williamsburg, Virginia. After finishing his law degree, Coke, like many young men at the time, caught Texas fever. With his law books in hand, he arrived in Waco in 1850. He was elected governor of Texas as a Democrat in 1874, and after a two-year term was elected to Congress in 1876. Texas had entered the Union in 1845 as the largest state, with 269,000 square miles and as many as 125,000 newcomers. Coke realized that land was needed to raise cattle and cash crops, especially cotton.

When the 45th Congress convened in March 1877, the senator from Texas introduced a bill allotting tribal lands to individual members of the Indian nations. In Coke's opinion the vast tracts of prairie north of the Red River that were set aside for Indians were far more than the tribes needed. The fact that the core identities were community oriented did not matter to Senator Coke. The senator had his eye on the "surplus" lands left over after allotment, which he believed should go to white settlers.[19] Both houses of Congress found the bill intriguing, but neither took action. Similar bills over the next few congressional sessions also died, but the idea of allotting tribal lands remained in the halls of Congress, and the senator from Texas would not give up.[20]

Alarmed at the actions of Senator Coke, the Mvskokes, Semvnoles, Cherokees, Choctaws, and Chickasaws sent a memorial to Congress entitled "Protest of the Representatives of the Indian

Territory" and signed by leaders of three tribes: D. W. Bushyhead, Cherokee principal chief; P. N. Blackstone and George Sander of the Cherokee delegation; Pleasant Porter, Ward Coachman, and D. M. Hodge of the Mvskoke Creeks; and Peter Pitchlynn of the Choctaws. "We have understood that such [allotment] bills were not intended to apply to the Indian Territory, as there is no provision for white settlement in that country, and the treaties define that this allotment in severalty can only be done on the request of the Indian nations."[21]

Allotment had several goals, the most prominent ones being to "free up" "surplus" Indian land for white settlers and to force Indians to modernize by breaking up traditional culture. In the House of Representatives, the Indian allotment bill triggered extensive debate. A report from the House Committee on Indian Affairs rejected the idea of civilizing the Indians through individual land ownership and preparing Native people for assimilation into the mainstream with American citizenship. Colorado Senator Henry M. Teller, an outspoken opponent of allotment, pointed out that "the real aim of this is to get at the Indian lands and open them up to settlement. The provisions for the apparent benefit of the Indians are but the pretext to get at his lands and occupy them. With that accomplished, we have securely paved the way for the extermination of the Indian races upon this part of the continent. . . . If this were to be done in the name of greed, it would be bad enough; but to do it in the name of Humanity, and under the cloak of an ardent desire to promote the Indian's welfare by making him like ourselves, whether he will or not, is infinitely worse."[22]

Teller grew up as a Methodist farmer in New York, moved to Colorado Territory, and started practicing law in 1861. Proud and righteous, the tough-as-they-come senator summed up his view on allotment, stating, "If I stand alone in the Senate, I want to put upon the record my prophecy in this matter, that when thirty or forty years shall have passed and these Indians shall have parted with their title, they will curse the hand that was raised professedly in their defense to secure this kind of legislation, and if the people who are clamoring for it understood Indian character; and Indian laws, and Indian morals, and Indian religion, they would not be here clamoring for this at all."[23] Realizing they needed to do something, the leaders of the Five Nations sent their best orators who could fluently speak English to convince members of Congress to vote down the bill.[24]

In January 1884, when the Board of Indian Commissioners of the Bureau of Indian Affairs took up the issue, Senator Henry Dawes addressed them. Pointing out that "the Indian problem has always been with us," Dawes touted the bill as "a way to solve a problem which hitherto has been found to be insoluble by the ordinary methods of modern civilization, and soon I trust we will wipe out the disgrace of our past treatment, and lift him up into citizenship and manhood, and co-operation with us to the glory of the country."[25] Henry Lauren Dawes was born on October 30, 1816, in Massachusetts. He went to Yale, studied law, became a Republican, and wanted to enter politics. Something of an intellectual, Dawes became curious about Indians, read about them, studied their cultures, and made more than one trip to the Indian Territory. As a senator he became chairman of the Senate Committee on Indian Affairs. Dawes was one of the rare politicians in Congress who understood the Medicine Way of the Mvskokes, Semvnoles, Cherokees, Choctaws, and Chickasaws. Many people called him one of the best friends of the Indians.[26]

Dawes was a part of a group of reformers who met yearly at the Lake Mohonk resort in upstate New York. There so-called friends of the Indian held discussions and presented papers on how to influence Congress, the Department of the Interior, and the president to pass laws to benefit Native people. Dawes educated himself, traveling several times to the West to learn about Native ways and Indian traditions, and about Harjo and others like him, such as Redbird Smith. Although Dawes respected the Medicine Way he viewed the coming of the white man's civilization to Indian Territory as inevitable, and as he observed mixed-blood Indians changing he concluded that the Medicine Way was doomed to be lost to modernity.

Although Dawes felt the momentum in the halls of Congress surging overwhelmingly towards allotment, he continued to argue against it. But in December 1885, as chairman of the Senate Committee on Indian Affairs, Dawes radically changed his strategy. He agreed to support the allotment idea to lessen the potential damage to all tribes. In fact, his changed position in favor of allotment displaced Senator Coke as its primary advocate.

The annual Lake Mohonk "Lake in the Sky" meetings in the Catskills Mountains of New York took up Indian land allotment in continual conversations, especially in early 1887. The goal was to gather the best minds "interested in Indian affairs so that all should act together and be in harmony, and so that prominent persons connected with Indian affairs should act as one body and create a public sentiment in favor of the Indians."[27]

Initially most clergy and missionaries stood against land allotment because they believed it interrupted their work. Since 1819 the Civilization Fund Act had authorized the president to "employ capable persons of good moral character" to introduce to any tribe adjoining a frontier settlement the "arts of civilization." Yet other leaders of church organizations supported the allotment bills. Lyman Abbott, the well-known editor of the *Christian Union* in New York, advocated allotment in the name of the social gospel, believing that Indians required social and individual salvation for entrance to the kingdom of God. Although Abbott had never seen a reservation and

THE SANDS UPRISING AND THE GREEN PEACH WAR

had met only about ten Indians, he argued that as long as the Indians remained on reservations the "Indian problem" of savagery and poverty would persist and Christianity, civilization, and salvation could not happen.[28]

Dawes criticized Abbott and government officials for risking the breaking of Indian treaties made with every tribe by supporting allotment without the consent of the Indians. Dawes argued that the true "friends of the Indian" were Indian reformers—the author Helen Hunt Jackson and the Women's National Indian Association, which had petitioned Congress to uphold its treaty responsibilities to the Native peoples.[29] Jackson had become noted for the publication of her book, *A Century of Dishonor,* blaming the federal government for the impoverished conditions on Indian reservations.[30]

The allotment idea caught the attention of churchgoers, humanitarians, and all kinds of do-gooders who feared Indians were being exploited for their remaining lands. But the last bill drafted seemed to have the best chance of being passed. The group that met regularly at Lake Mohonk sincerely believed the "Indian problem" had to be solved to alleviate deplorable living conditions and misery on the nearly two hundred reservations.[31]

At the end of the first week in February 1887, the Senate and the House passed the General Allotment Act, also known as the Dawes Act, by voice vote.[32] It authorized the president of the United States to cause reservation lands to be surveyed and allotted in severalty to any Indian located on the reservation, but Section 8 explicitly excluded "the territory occupied by the Cherokees, Creeks, Choctaws, Chickasaws, Seminoles, and Osages, Miamies and Peorias, and Sacs and Foxes, in the Indian Territory, [and] any of the reservations of the Seneca Nation of New York Indians in the State of New York."[33] It would seem that the Mvskokes and the rest of the Five Civilized Tribes were protected since their lands were excluded, but the greed

THE SANDS UPRISING AND THE GREEN PEACH WAR

for Indian lands proved too great. Just ten years after the Dawes Act passed, whites established forty-nine towns in the Mvskoke Nation along the Katy and Frisco railroad lines; Muskogee blossomed as the most prosperous one.[34] As a result of the Dawes Act, Native Americans ceded control of about one hundred million acres of land by 1934, or about two-thirds of their holdings when the act passed in 1887.

The Green Peach War

Federal policy sought to transform Native people into individual landowners, similar to white yeoman farmers. This idea represented something of a threshold for the American Indian: to step over into a different world of civilization where a new life awaited, earned through the sweat of his brow by harvesting his own crops, building a homestead for his family, and worshiping in a church. But among the Mvskokes, the church was the square ground outdoors that represented the seven directions. Isparhecher is an example of that way of life. He was born in 1828, and his father was Yarteen Tustenugee and his mother was Kechiahteh.[35] Isparhecher was a full-blood and he spoke only Mvskoke. In his prime, he stood six feet tall and weighed two hundred pounds, a solid, strong man with dark brown penetrating eyes. Isparhecher wanted to preserve the Medicine Way for the Mvskoke people, and welcomed all other Indians.[36] In 1867 Isparhecher was elected to the House of Warriors. After about a year, he resigned to become the judge of the Okmulgee District, a position he held for a little over two years. As a judge, Isparhecher wanted to preserve the old Medicine Way of his people. Following his campaign promise to "drive from the country the thieves and outlaws who had for years infested it," he sought to use the Lighthorse to do just that.[37]

THE SANDS UPRISING AND THE GREEN PEACH WAR

The spring rains did not come as usual in 1881. Only a couple of years after the territory and the rest of the U.S. started to recover from the country's first Great Depression, crops failed and deep cracks formed in the barren ground as the summer heat forged a serious drought. Amidst the Mvskokes's mounting problems several white families—intruders—had illegally fenced off large areas in the Mvskoke Nation, and the Indian agent and U.S. military were slow in helping the Mvskoke leadership to get rid of them.[38] Outlaws and trespassers infested the Mvskoke Nation, compelling Judge Isparhecher to order his Lighthorse to drive out criminals. One of the Lighthorse arrested a man who illegally had a pistol in his possession. The Lighthorse turned the prisoner over to the Lighthorse of another district, but when the criminal's friends rescued him from jail, they threatened Isparhecher, prompting other Mvskokes to come to his aid.

Frustrated with the incursions into their lands and with great respect for the Mvskoke leader, many loyal Mvskokes from the *tvlofvs* of Tuskegee, Artussee, Kialegee, and Tuckabatchee supported Isparhecher in forming an opposition government at Nuyaka. The traditionalist leader commanded about 350 warriors from the local area, including about 30 Semvnole warriors.[39] Hearing the news, Chief Checote ordered his Lighthorse to arrest Isparhecher for sedition. Not wanting the indignity of being arrested, Isparhecher and his friends, including his Lighthorse warriors, asked the U.S. Indian agent, Jonathan Q. Tufts, for formal recognition and protection.[40] Isparhecher led the traditionalists of the Upper Mvskokes and Checote led the mixed-bloods of the Lower Mvskokes. Their longtime differences clashing in fights during the spring months of 1881 became known as the Green Peach War, when peaches are still green on the tree.

The two sides of Lighthorse tangled near Springtown in the Deep Fork District in July 1882, killing ten of the Checote Lighthorse but

THE SANDS UPRISING AND THE GREEN PEACH WAR

none of Isparhecher's. Isparhecher received a message from the Checote government assuring him that if he returned to Okmulgee he would not be harmed. Knowing his Lighthorse was outnumbered and with the federal government favoring Checote, Isparhecher returned, but he soon learned that a militia was organizing to hunt him down.

As Reconstruction was ending, new elections for the leadership of the Mvskokes did not produce a solution to the conflict. In fact, it created further political turmoil by pitting them against each other yet again. One elder remembered Isparhecher running against Sam Checote. The elder recalled, "The Checote party defeated the Isparhecher faction who would not accept defeat and started a rebellion. Isparhecher enlisted all the Indians that he could and then sought to enlist the colored people." The elder reminisced, "I was too young to fight but I was old enough to listen to what was said."[41] One of Isparhecher's recruits was Chitto Harjo who was thirty-six years old at the time and convinced the ways of the progressives were not best for true Mvskokes.[42]

Once again an election controversy sparked a war. John Harrison, a Mvskoke freedman, recalled that the Green Peach War reignited with charges of fraud in the Mvskoke election of 1882. Harrison remembered the results of the election "was that Ischarsphieche was defeated for Creek Chief and he enlisted forces against the Checotah faction as he did not want to permit the Checotah faction to take charge of the Creek Nation." The conflict had gone beyond arguments, and the fighting could not be stopped. Harrison specified, "There were hundreds of men lined upon both sides and I believe their first squirmish [sic] was near the present town of Taft, . . . , and another near the present town of Yahola." The fighting lingered at intervals until the late fall of 1882. Harrison said it came to an end

THE SANDS UPRISING AND THE GREEN PEACH WAR

"when Ischaraphieche agreed through his spokesman Lee Perryman to quit the rebellion."[43]

The old *etekvlkē* curse persisted. The postwar years produced almost no rest for traditionalists, who felt the mixed-bloods had seized control of the government and everything else. The pro-allotment Checote administration had the support of federal officials who wanted to survey Mvskoke lands into quarter sections, then collect the names of all Mvskokes on a roll and assign them lands: 160 acres to a head of household, 80 acres to a single person or orphan, and 40 acres to a child less than eighteen years old. But making Indians individual landowners and farmers went against the fundamental tradition of communal use of tribal lands.

During the early summer months of 1882, Opothleyahola's nephew Tuckabatchee Harjo of Tuckabatchee *tvlofv* realized the importance of siding with Isparhecher, and he gathered two hundred Mvskokes, including many families, from the Tuckabatchee area. He was joined by Sleeping Rabbit, a Cherokee who aligned with the traditionalists of both Cherokees and Mvskokes and commanded one hundred of his own people. Together they began to plan their reinforcement expedition to Mvskoke country. Confronting James Larney and the Checote-controlled Lighthorse three miles east of Okemah, at Battle Creek, Tuckabatchee Harjo left a half dozen of Larney's men dead within an hour. The Harjo party retreated to Boley, a freedman settlement, to regroup and then decided to travel north to join Isparhecher at Nuyaka.[44]

Elder Alex Blackston remembered that in late July 1882, Isparhecher and Sleeping Rabbit "met the Checote army in skirmishes on Pecan Creek and Sugar Creek. After these skirmishes a partial treaty was made with Esparhechar to quit fighting but that fall the trouble all flared up again; this time near the Creek Capital at Okmulgee."

In its wake Isparhecher and many of his men retreated to the Sac and Fox country, whereas Sleeping Rabbit and at least two others were captured and locked up in the Council House in Okmulgee, where Sleeping Rabbit was later shot to death as he tried to escape.[45]

The Sac and Fox leadership, wanting to avoid bloodshed on their reservation, urged Isparhecher and his followers to move on. They "retreated to the Cheyenne Country" where "the United States Soldiers took all of them captives and marched them to Fort Gibson and held them prisoners. Esparhechar saw that there was no use to go farther and he signed a treaty agreeing to quit fighting."[46] Isparhecher's followers were released and allowed to go home, but this did not end the hostilities.

The Green Peach War, also called Spa-he-ch's War, broke out again on Christmas Eve day 1882 when a small group of men out scouting for Checote came upon Isparhecher's camp at Nuyaka. Among the oaks, hickories, and elms, the two sides fired at each other. Seven of Checote's scouts were killed, but Isparhecher's roughly 250 followers would be badly outnumbered by Checote's nearly 800 men, who were yet to arrive. But before the gun smoke had even cleared Isparhecher's early victory inspired his men to believe they could defeat Checote's Lighthorse and any troops sent by the U.S. government.[47]

Chief Checote sent word to Pleasant Porter to return immediately from Washington to put down the insurrection.[48] Porter caught the next train to Indian Territory and took full command as soon as he arrived in Okmulgee.[49] Behind the scenes the federal government, considering Isparhecher to be a rogue leader who threatened their preferred leadership, worked to defeat him. In early January 1883 Checote requested troop support from the federal government.[50] He received a shipment of "300 repeating rifles and 300 Colt's revolvers" from St. Louis. In early February 1883, Porter began "drilling and

THE SANDS UPRISING AND THE GREEN PEACH WAR

organizing his troops at Okmulgee rapidly," although he believed he would "have a bloodless victory." Porter speculated Isparhecher and his force to be about eighteen miles due west of Okmulgee. The *Vinita Indian Chieftain* reported that a notorious Black outlaw, Dick Glass, and Gabriel Marshall, a known troublemaker, were Isparhecher's main advisers.[51]

Meanwhile the Indian agent, Jonathan Q. Tufts, invited Checote and Isparhecher to each send five representatives to discuss peace at the Union agency in Muskogee. Checote immediately named five representatives, but Isparhecher claimed that his important persons were scattered and it would take some time for them to be notified. As Tufts put it, "Isparhechee and his men will listen to nothing looking to a peaceful settlement." He told Isparhecher that he could request "a full investigation either by a commission appointed by the Department or by a commission composed of the Chiefs of the Cherokee, Chickasaw, and Choctaw Nations," but if he refused the "Creek Nation should be permitted to exercise its authority and crush the rebellion in its own way."[52]

Pleasant Porter did not wait. His Lighthorse pursued Isparhecher on the Sac and Fox reservation, where Isparhecher had once again requested protection. But the Sac and Fox Indian agent advised him to turn himself over to Porter. About the same time, Daniel "Goob" Childers, a mixed-blood Mvskoke, was reported to be on his way to the Sac and Fox agency "to deliver the word sent by the Commissioner of Indian Affairs for them [Isparhecher] to return to their homes and occupy their lands." Childers also reported that a few days earlier some of Checote's men had killed Sleeping Rabbit while he was escaping from jail in Okmulgee. Sleeping Rabbit was one of Isparhecher's trusted friends.[53]

During the first two weeks in March 1883, Isparhecher's followers camped at the Sac and Fox agency and prepared to face Pleasant

Porter's Lighthorse. Much ceremony occurred to prepare for battle, and protection medicine invoked requests for assistance with songs and prayers. Men reflected on their pasts, their families, and how they would face death. When Porter's men came, they rode through the agency taking captive every man they could find wearing a hat with a corn husk—a marker of being one of Isparhecher's warriors. Both sides, "well armed with Winchesters and revolvers, drew up in battle line on the prairie within sight of the Agency." Rendered powerless by the situation, Agent Jacob V. Carter conveyed the request of the Sac and Fox leaders to both parties, insisting that no fighting take place on their reservation. While Carter spoke, Isparhecher and his outnumbered followers hastily retreated in the direction of Shawnee and the reserved lands of the Kickapoos, Potawatomis, and Shawnees nearby. Porter and his men pursued them but soon gave up the chase and returned home toward Okmulgee. In the coming weeks, when the grass grew higher to graze their horses, they would return to pursue Isparhecher. Word had it that Isparhecher and his followers had reached the Kickapoo area. They were starving, but even with plenty of money, they were afraid to return to the Sac and Fox agency to get supplies for fear of Porter's men waiting for them.[54]

Isparhecher refused any advice to surrender. He trusted only the closest people to him and retreated westward to the Comanche reservation, where the Comanche leader Asa Habbe protected him. Other nations saw that Isparhecher was in need of protection and provided it for him, but bureaucrats and missionaries saw him as a threat to the coming of civilization and Christianity. Winter's months passed into spring. Isparhecher and his followers received word that they would be protected if they surrendered on April 1. U.S. troops would escort them in the Mvskoke Nation to Okmulgee.[55]

In early August 1883 the Checote and Isparhecher parties worked out a peace agreement of seven articles. The first and second articles

THE SANDS UPRISING AND THE GREEN PEACH WAR

stated both sides would continue to recognize treaties made with the U.S. and the Mvskoke Constitution of 1867. Article 3 stated, "We agree that a full and unconditional amnesty and pardon shall be granted for all alleged criminal offences, political or otherwise, committed prior to the present date, as provided by the Act of the National Council of Oct. 16, 1882, it being understood and agreed upon that should there be any dispute as to whether any offence charged against any person is such a one as has grown out of the late trouble in the Nation, then in such care the facts shall be submitted to the Indian Agent whose decision shall be final." Article 6 stated a fair coming election would be carried out and Article 7 asked for the U.S. troops to stay as needed to maintain peace at Okmulgee and to assist civil officers and the Indian agent.[56]

Chief Checote resigned unexpectedly on August 19, 1883. People could only guess why; possibly Checote felt his life threatened by Isparhecher. A Mvskoke elder said, "Esparhecha was a firm believer in the supernatural. He was a medicine man himself. He had as his councilors in the war, the medicine men, and many unbelievable things were performed by these men."[57]

The Elections of 1883 and 1895

Samuel Checote's resignation led to a new national election for principal chief. Three individuals vied for the office. Joseph M. Perryman was the candidate of the Mvskoke party. Isparhecher had the support of the Loyal party, and, unexpectedly, Samuel Checote entered the race for the Pin party. Although Checote collected a large number of votes, on September 3, 1883, the competition really was between Isparhecher and Perryman. The tribal constitution stated under Article 2, Section 1, that "the Principal Chief of the Muskogee Nation shall be elected for a term of four years, by a majority of the votes."[58] Perryman had the plurality of the votes, more than Checote or Isparhecher, but he did not have a majority of the votes.

Checote and Perryman agreed that Isparhecher would travel to Washington as a delegate to seek a solution from Henry Teller, now secretary of the Interior. Isparhecher left for Washington in late January 1884. From the nation's capital on February 26, Isparhecher wrote Perryman that Teller had not yet decided and suggested a re-election be called. The next day, Secretary Teller responded "that the words 'majority' and 'plurality' are synonymous ones as understood and used by the Muskogee people." Secretary Teller instructed the Indian agent Jonathan Q. Tufts to acknowledge Joseph Perryman as the legitimate winner of the election. He served his four-year term.[59] The influence of the federal government over the Mvskoke election demonstrated that Mvskoke sovereignty was being usurped, and it was becoming clearer that due to the Mvskoke government's lack of military and economic power, the U.S. paternalistically controlled the Mvskokes and the rest of the Five Nations.

Political differences within the Mvskokes, the Cherokees, and the other Five Nations worked in the best interests of white opportunists wanting to settle on Indian lands. The common ground of trying to hold back the outsiders temporarily united the patriotic members of the Five Nations. In this sense, they were fighting to preserve their identities as *este-cates,* "Indians."

The western halves of the lands of the Mvskokes, Semvnoles, and Cherokees continued to appeal to non-Indians. The external interest in Indian Territory had predictably increased at the end of the Civil War. Settlers, both white and African American, encroached on Indian lands, sometimes with the approval of Indian agents who should have been protecting Indian interests. Agent Moses Neal at the Sac and Fox reservation "permitted intruders, in violation of positive orders, to remain at his agency, and . . . he has personal knowledge

THE SANDS UPRISING AND THE GREEN PEACH WAR

of many on the Sac and Fox, Kickapoo and Iowa reservations that have no permit and ought to be put out," according to the *Indian Chieftain* for July 8, 1888.[60] In the same issue, the newspaper reported about 3,500 freedmen in the Cherokee nation were "entitled to Cherokee citizenship," according to the Treaty of 1866, but it had not yet been granted by the tribe.[61]

The four 1866 treaties continued to wreak havoc due to the provisions forcing U.S. control over the Mvskokes, Semvnoles, Cherokees, Choctaws, and Chickasaws. Chaos reigned with rustlers stealing cattle from Native ranchers and farmers, and outlaws running rampant. In addition to the developing Boomer movement in 1879 and afterwards, the expansion of railroads and coal mining produced an increasing flow of whites to Mvskoke country and to all of Indian Territory. Apprehensively the Mvskokes and other four nations tried to maintain law and order on their reservations, but the bureaucrats in Washington continued to undermine their political sovereignty. On March 1, 1889, the U.S. government established a federal district court for Indian Territory at Muskogee, with the Chickasaw Nation and southern part of the Choctaw Nation assigned to the court at Paris, Texas.[62] This act of paternalism in the eyes of Chitto Harjo and other traditional patriots was an example of the white man taking control over everything, especially the justice system.

Turmoil over land allotment further divided the Mvskoke people. In the disputed national election of 1895, the Mvskokes elected Isparhecher, who defeated Samuel Checote. The Checote side tried to keep Isparhecher and his supporters powerless. In one incident, William Bruner said, "The Isparhecher men thought they had a right to carry guns the same as the appointed Lighthorsemen, but the rules of the Creek Nation were that it was against the tribal law for any one to carry a gun unless allowed to do so by the captain of the Lighthorsemen." Bruner, a Mvskoke, explained, "The Creek judge

THE SANDS UPRISING AND THE GREEN PEACH WAR

or captain of the Lighthorsemen sent some of his men to arrest some of the Isparhecher men for disobeying the new constitution or law."[63] The infighting was superseded by trouble on the horizon, rolling in like a heavy blue thunder storm. The increasing flow of settler intruders caused *ehosa* "confusion" for the Mvskokes.

Even the most progressive Mvskokes were not in control, although some people still believed Pleasant Porter was in power. Mvskoke elder John McGilbray recalled, "Due to the great influence of General Pleasant Porter, the council refused to recall the delegates and negotiation continued, providing for the individual allotment of the Creek lands and the winding up of the Creek tribal affairs, which was a crushing blow to Isparhecher." Feeling very depressed, the full-blood leader remained for several months in seclusion. During his long silence, wild rumors spread as to what Chief Isparhecher's next move would be. In February, Isparhecher made the following public statement in an open letter written on his behalf.

> Okmulgee, I.T. February 15, 1898, I see in the public prints much surmising concerning myself. Some think I have retired to my country home to saw wood; others that I have accepted the inevitable without a further struggle; and still others say that I am planning either war or a general exodus of my people to Mexico. None of these surmises disturbs me in the least, for I do not regard them as more than the idle passing wind. Yet, inasmuch as my silence seems to annoy some people. I will now ask you to give the public my views of the situation as I now see it. The United States Government has by its late acts of Congress abrogated the treaties heretofore made with the Indians of the Indian Territory, disregarding their wishes and ignoring their treaty rights. I feel that this is an assumption of power unauthorized by the organic laws of the American Union, and simply a declaration of war, which would be resisted as such treatment was attempted against the similar rights of any nation other than the

weak, defenseless tribes of the Indian Territory. In other words, it is a challenge of power without affording the Indians any weapon of defense. The Indian is simply a target to stand up and be shot down. This is not fair. Let the Indian have an equal show and, if he then proves himself an unequal match, his defeat cannot be charged to unfairness.[64]

The Mvskoke leader stressed equality and justice. Undoubtedly he felt the pressure of the federal government usurping the ability of the Mvskoke government to govern its own people. Ending his letter, Isparhecher wrote, "Is it fair that the Creeks shall be denied the use of their money to use as they please? As they are not free born, and entitled to the exercise of the rights guaranteed to a free people?" Isparhecher emphasized, "Yet we, the Creeks are denied the use of the means necessary to protect our joint rights in the courts of the United States. The great president of a free people says we cannot have the money to test our constitutional rights in the courts. Thus it seems that we, the Creeks, have no right of self-control, and are to be dealt with as little children only."[65] As Mvskoke settlers, Eliza Palmer and her family believed that Isparhecher was right. She said: "Our family was on the Isparhecher side, who believed this country should be kept as it was; that is, undivided, and we still believe he was right. If it had been that way there would have been no rich or poor Creeks as each would have shared equally in the riches."[66]

But times had changed, even beyond the control of the Mvskokes. The outside political influences caused considerable confusion. Isparhecher faced extreme pressure, losing respect from his supporters, and he lost the trust of the traditionalists who were against the whole idea of owning parcels of Mother Earth.[67] A pressing federal government became less interested in its treaty obligations to the Mvskokes, Semvnoles, and other tribes as it simultaneously asserted increasing control over Indians.

THE SANDS UPRISING AND THE GREEN PEACH WAR

The allotment process for the Five Nations occurred during radical transitional years for the nations. The process provided Indians with allotments of the poorest soil that could not be farmed: rocky, filled with sandstone, located on hills. No one thought that the worthless allotments held anything of value. But coal rested beneath Choctaw lands and oil beneath that of the Osages, Semvnoles, and Mvskokes. The launching of the automobile industry and airplane travel spurred the creation of the petroleum industry, turning black crude into black gold.

Reconstruction was, among the Mvskokes, a lasting ordeal that involved the greatest degree of *etekvlkē* (factionalism) the Mvskoke people had ever experienced. Traditionalists like Isparhecher believed people were forgetting who they were—Mvskoke. One can only imagine the grand full-blood leader on his last day looking up at the Maker of Breath and praying. He believed in the old ways all the days of his life of ninety years, until he died in Okmulgee in 1903 on Christmas Eve. He had served his people in the affairs of the nation for sixty years.[68] Being connected to one's people and the past was becoming less important as newcomers brought Christianity and materialism, as the European traders had in the Southeast, tilting the balance of *Epohfvnkv* to the point where non-Mvskokes were gaining increasing control. Was this meant to be? The traditionalists continued to follow the Medicine Way in the Green Corn Ceremony, heeding the old stories that warned if the Mvskokes did not live accordingly, "they would disappear from the earth and fall into the waters of the ocean."[69]

Chief Sam Checote.
Oklahoma Historical Society Photography Collection. Photographer unknown. Courtesy of Oklahoma Historical Society. Accession 570.

Nighthawk Society.
Oklahoma Historical Society Photography Collection. Photographer unknown. Courtesy of Oklahoma Historical Society. Accession 682.

The Dawes Commission. Front row, left to right: M. H. Kidd, H. L. Dawes, A. S. McKinnon. Back row, left to right: A. L. Wright, Anna L. Dawes, assistant, and H. M. Jacoway, stenographer.
Oklahoma Historical Society Photography Collection. Photographer unknown. Courtesy of Oklahoma Historical Society. Accession 819.

Daniel Bob, Choctaw.
W. P. Campbell Collection. Photographer unknown.
Courtesy of Oklahoma Historical Society. Accession 3416.

Crazy Snake rebels under arrest.
W. P. Campbell Collection. Photograph by Robertson Studio.
Courtesy of Oklahoma Historical Society. Accession 3730.

Chitto Harjo (Crazy Snake). W. P. Campbell Collection. Photographer unknown. Courtesy of Oklahoma Historical Society. Accession 3905.

Crazy Snake's home.
W. P. Campbell Collection. Photographer unknown.
Courtesy of Oklahoma Historical Society. Accession 3938.

Hickory Ground, Crazy Snake's camp.
Grant Foreman Collection. Photographer unknown.
Courtesy of Oklahoma Historical Society. Accession 2407.

Crazy Snake Rebellion.
Oklahoma Historical Society Photography Collection. Photographer unknown.
Courtesy of Oklahoma Historical Society. Accession 3936.

Pleasant Porter.
Walter Ferguson Collection #70. Creek Tribe #6 Binder. Courtesy of Western History Collections, University of Oklahoma Libraries.

Chitto Harjo, Crazy Snake, leader of Creek Rebellion.
Phillips Collection #1534. Creek Tribe #6 Binder. Courtesy of Western History Collections, University of Oklahoma Libraries.

Opothleyahola.
Campbell Collection #2138.
Courtesy of Western History
Collections, University of
Oklahoma Libraries.

Stand Watie.
Phillips Collection #1459.
Courtesy of Western History
Collections, University of
Oklahoma Libraries.

Redbird Smith, a Cherokee medicine man.
General Personalities Collection #67. Cherokee Tribe #2
Binder. Courtesy of Western History Collections,
University of Oklahoma Libraries.

FUS FIXICO'S LETTER TO PLEASANT PORTER ABOUT ALLOTMENTS, 1905

So, the full-blood Injin was about to die and go [to] the Happy Hunting Grounds. So he has called you all together to hear his will. He want you to take his sofky [corn] patch and make a big farm out of it, and raise wheat and oats and prunes and things like that instead a flint corn and gourds. He want you to tear down his log hut and build a white farm house with green window blinds. He want you to take this three hundred pound filly with the pestle tail and raise Kentucky thoroughbreds. He want you to round up his mass-fed-rasor-back hogs and raise Berkshires and Poland Chinas. He want you to make bulldogs and lap poodles out a his sofky curs. He want you to [know that he] had no understanding with Oklahoma.[1]

5

The Snakes

Mvskoke elders believe a person should only take what he or she needs. Leave the rest for others, who should also take only what they need to live, whether it is wild game, fish, natural foods in the woods, or anything. The moral of the story is if a person takes what he or she "wants" rather than what the person actually "needs," the desire for more will turn into greed. A greedy person becomes evil when he or she will do anything to get what they "want." Greedy people will eventually destroy themselves because they cannot stop from "wanting," even when they have enough. In order to walk the good path in the seventh direction for inner peace, it is important to learn the difference between what you need and not to take more than that.

Hvmmaketv (that's what they used to say)

While the territories occupied by the Five Civilized Tribes were protected in the Dawes Act, the punitive land cessions that the Mvskokes and Semvnoles had been forced to make in their 1866 treaties with the United States, an area known as the "Unassigned Lands," were not. By the terms of these treaties, these lands were to be used for resettling other Indians, not whites. But Pleasant Porter, as the Mvskoke Nation's delegate in Washington, agreed to remove this restriction on the Unassigned Lands in exchange for a payment

THE SNAKES

of $2.25 million. Then, following years of pressure from Boomers, President Benjamin Harrison issued a proclamation opening the Unassigned Lands to settlers at high noon on April 22, 1889. Roughly fifty thousand people participated in the Land Run of 1889.[1]

Porter believed the best and only way forward for the Mvskokes was assimilation.[2] He told a delegation of visiting officials and newspapermen in late September 1889 that "in every treaty, every agreement, the United States had tried to advance the Indian. This was the underlying idea in all the treaties and it was the Indian's only hope. . . . Every change has been a betterment—an improvement." Porter, according to contemporary newspaper reports, "urged the adoption of statehood and advancement in every direction, and declared that the Indian must live outside his native superstition—must outlive it. The laws of nature are inexorable—we cannot stand still; we must advance or recede."[3] He would come to regret his words.

The speed of white settlement on Indian lands alarmed the Five Nations. The Mvskoke National Council sent a message to President William McKinley during October 1889 reminding him of the need to uphold the eighteen ratified treaties the United States had signed with their tribe.[4] But burdened with running the country during a recession, McKinley had other things on his mind. A year after the land rush, Congress enacted an Organic Act for Oklahoma Territory. The law created seven counties—six in the Oklahoma District, and a seventh which became known as the Oklahoma Panhandle or No Man's Land. The act called for appointing a governor, a secretary, and three judges with an elected two-house legislature. Harrison named George W. Steele of Indiana as the first governor of Oklahoma Territory. It was not an easy job in a rapidly growing region: the population of Oklahoma Territory shot up from 80,000 in 1890 to 400,000 in 1900.[5]

THE SNAKES

The Curtis Act

Although the Mvskokes and ten other Indian groups had escaped the Dawes Allotment Act, the success of the land rush encouraged demands for more Indian lands to be made available to settlers. As mentioned earlier, the Dawes Act exempted the Mvskokes, Semvnoles, Cherokees, Choctaws, Chickasaws, Miamis, Peorias, Osages, Sacs and Foxes in Oklahoma, Senecas of New York, and Red Lake Ojibwe in Minnesota. In the meantime, a young newly elected member of the U.S. House of Representatives was working to help the Indians of the Five Nations become American citizens. Charles Curtis was part Indian (Kaw or Kansa, Osage, and Potawatomi): born on the Kaw reservation, he was the son of a white man but spoke his people's language and was raised by his Indian grandparents in the Kaw Medicine Way and by his white grandparents to attend public schools with whites. Although his classmates ridiculed him as "Injun Charley," this made him only more determined to study law.[6] He believed that Indians should honor their Indian cultures as well as assimilating into the majority culture. He eventually became Senate majority leader and vice president (in Herbert Hoover's administration)—the first Native American and the first multiracial person to reach those offices. On December 7, 1897, young Congressman Curtis introduced House Resolution 8581, "For the protection of the people of Indian Territory." The Curtis bill was amended forty-two times in twenty-four pages of changes, and by the time it passed on March 3, 1898, it bore little resemblance to Curtis's original draft.[7]

Far from being the protection that Charles Curtis had intended for the Five Nations in Indian Territory, the new law represented sudden political death for the Mvskokes, Cherokees, Choctaws, Chickasaws, and Semvnoles. The Curtis Act dissolved the governments of the tribes effective in 1906 and extended the provisions of the Dawes Act to the Five Civilized Tribes. It forced them to enroll, accept al-

110

lotments, end communal ownership, and incorporate towns and town lots to be surveyed and sold. It also provided for male residents of Indian Territory to vote, and authorized the federal government to collect taxes from the "white citizens of the Indian nations in the territory."[8]

While some Mvskokes, like Porter, supported land allotment, others did not. Although he did not agree with Porter most of the time, Isparhecher was a realist. He called an intertribal council meeting of the Five Nations at Eufaula in July 1896, where he relented in the best interest of the people. He sincerely believed allotment was going to happen anyway, and he urged the delegates to try to understand and make the best of their situation.[9] In an open letter to the National Council, Chief Isparhecher asked the council members and the Mvskoke people to be resilient and accept land allotments. "In such division I would suggest that all the land be divided and taken up, each citizen receiving an equal share of the lands of the nation wherever he may select the same, without intrusion on the rights or improvements of another citizen." Isparhecher advised "leaving no surplus lands anywhere for the possible future operations of trusts, land syndicates and similar corporations" from "the surrounding states." The Mvskoke leader added, "The lands so allotted should include everything of value found beneath as well as on the surface."[10] Like Senator Dawes, Isparhecher realized that the momentum for allotment created unstoppable political pressure, and he saw it as perhaps the last chance to accept the divided up land, or they would risk being removed again by the government.

The Dawes Commission

Having been given the authority to start enrolling members of the Five Nations for land allotments, Dawes, in 1893, led a "commission to negotiate agreements with the Choctaw, Creek, Chickasaw,

THE SNAKES

Seminole, and Cherokee Indian tribes."[11] Many individuals served on the Dawes Commission, including Indians, for example, governor of the Semvnoles John W. Brown, who led his people for thirty years. At times, the commission met at Brown's home.[12] Indian reformers sometimes served as interpreters to the Dawes Commission in their work to enroll individuals for allotments. George Tiger, a full-blood Mvskoke and a tribal lawyer and judge, "believed in allotment" and

> took a staunch stand for the sectionizing of the land and was an interpreter during the time the Dawes Commission was at work enrolling Indians. He was an influential and good speaker for any cause he thought was right, any cause he thought would be of benefit to his people.
>
> There was only one man he could not win over to his side or change his mind on the subject—Chitto Harjo. The Dawes Commission sent him on the mission to see what he could do with Chitto Harjo's group but he reported that he could do nothing with them.[13]

Chitto Harjo, whose name means "Crazy Snake," was also known as Wilson Jones. He was a traditionalist who rejected the allotment of Mvskoke land and believed his people should live the Medicine Way. Years later Chitto Harjo's daughter, Salina Jones, recalled: "Chitto realized that his influence over time was dwindling as he was becoming increasingly aware that we would not be able to keep our tribal hunting grounds. Even with his influence as a great orator, he knew he was losing his followers to the White man's greed. . . . In spite of all this, Chitto still felt strongly that with his words and reasoning, he could change the ways of the Whites."[14] In the Mvskoke tradition, it was believed that a person who had become bad could be turned back into a good person, and Chitto Harjo was convinced

THE SNAKES

that the *este-hvtkes* could become like Mvskokes, similar to many tribes accepting the Medicine Way.

Henry Jacobs, a Mvskoke freedman, recalled that after the Curtis Act passed "the Creek fullbloods at once called a council and declared Chitto Harjo as their hereditary Chief who at once set out to re-establish the tribal courts and customs and who at once declared Hickory Ground as the capital of the Creek Nation instead of Okmulgee."[15] Harjo's resistance to allotment became well known throughout the Mvskoke Nation. It was said, "As everybody knows Chitto Harjo would not allot. . . . The ones who would not allot gave up their homes and some had good homes and let others file on because they did not want allotment[s]."[16] Joe Grayson recalled of the Snakes, "When the allotments were plotted, those settlers who had made their homes and improvements on the land which they claimed as their own were forced to abandon them and, they did not leave without removing the buildings and sometimes even burning them. They did not want anyone else to have use of the buildings as they have been through hard work to make all that had been made."[17]

Winey Lewis, a full-blood of Tuckabatchee, recalled that her parents enrolled for an allotment, but the parents of her future husband, Saley Lewis, a Kealigee from Nuyaka Town, refused to enroll. Winey Lewis described her parents as having already homesteaded some land, "so they went and ask for land they had so improved. Sometimes another Indian beat them to it and he would have to move off to another place." Lewis admitted, "We were lucky and got the home place where we were all born. Father was born one mile north of here but he filed on the place a quarter [mile] west, where he and mother lived. It was just like a race, the first ones there got what they wanted."[18]

For traditionalists, refusing land allotments was a form of protest and an action to support the Medicine Way of the Mvskokes.

THE SNAKES

The idea of allotting tribal land to the Mvskokes as individuals did not make sense. Harjo's daughter Salina described her father's frustration. "Even after the induction of the Dawes Act my father was very active in working to keep out [our] tribal lands as common land amongst us for hunting and gathering of herbs and plants. We enjoyed doing our work together with other Creek families and did not understand why our common land had to be divided with set boundaries and fences."[19]

Some settlers had a different view of the traditionalist stance on allotments. LeRoy Ward recalled:

> Chitto Harjo started complaining about the Indians accepting the acreage allotment. He wanted the whites to come in and develop the country and then move out leaving the country to the Indians. In 1884 he met the United States senators at Tulsa Town and said he would accept allotment if the land was not deeded. If the land was allotted to the Indians and not deeded, it could not be taxed nor sold. In that way it would be of no use to anyone but the Indians. He wanted ground left for the towns and villages, too. Chitto Harjo was smart and qualified to talk in almost any language. He was against the Dawes Commission and in 1899 he organized a council and was going to make the non-citizens move out of the country when he saw fit. He made tours to keep in contact with his five thousand members. His strongest followers were from Deep Fork country. There were some from most of the tribes but none from the Osages.[20]

A deputy U.S. marshal later recalled:

> Chitto Harjo was a leader type and due to his teachings that, "Way back in Alabama the government said, Go to this country and we will give it to you forever and now we are only asking them to live

THE SNAKES

up to that treaty they made before we came here," they wanted to continue to hold all the land they could and have their own tribal government. The allotment would put them under federal law. . . .

When the Dawes Commission began to enroll the Indians and Crazy Snake and his followers refused, the commission had the federal court issue a summons to him to appear before the court and show some cause for not enrolling. . . . Harjo lived 14 miles west of Checotah, had a good farm, plenty of horses, was considered a "well set-up" Indian. He was very personable sort of fellow, keen-eyed and shrewd."[21]

By no means was Harjo wealthy, but he made a modest living with his family on five to ten acres where they raised the usual crops of corn, beans, melons, squash and also had a small orchard.

In observing the power of the court system, Chitto Harjo realized that his concerns had to be addressed at the federal level. Harjo sought advice from Albert Gallatin "Cheesie" McIntosh, the first Mvskoke to practice law in the federal court system, on how to overturn the allotment process.[22] In late 1899 Harjo took his case to Washington, D.C., together with representatives from the Five Nations and Mvskoke leaders, including Lahtah Micco, Hotulke Fixico, and Hotulke Yahola. Although they did not succeed, while they were in Washington they were advised by Lorenzo A. Bailey, a Washington attorney, to "proceed with their old customs and ignore the new order of affairs." Bailey had told Harjo and the others that although the Indian commissioner favored allotment, the president did not. Furthermore, Bailey advised, the 1832 Treaty of Cusseta protected their legal rights and allowed them to set up their tribal government. The other three delegates caught smallpox in Washington, and so Harjo returned home alone. On his return he began to travel to stomp grounds to share what the delegation had learned in Washington.

THE SNAKES

While Lahtah Micco, Hotulke Fixico, and Hotulke Yahola recovered from smallpox, Pleasant Porter, hoping to nip the movement in the bud, contacted William Jones, commissioner of Indian Affairs, asking him to detain the three potential troublemakers as long as he could. By the time the three returned in January 1901, Chitto Harjo had set up a separate government based at Hickory Ground.[23] "Upon returning home the commission called a meeting of the representatives of the tribes to be held at Hickory Ground, a point about twenty miles southwest of Okmulgee, in the Creek Nation. That meeting was attended by ten Choctaws, two Chickasaws, two Seminoles and an indeterminate number of Creeks and Cherokees. . . . The Indian Commissioners reported the results of their mission to the City of Washington, laying particular stress upon the advice of the unnamed attorney; 'to ignore the new order.'" This occurred in 1901.[24]

Mrs. Willie Blair, a white settler, remembered:

All there was to the 1901 uprising was that Chitto Harjo and some others did not want to accept the rule of the white people; the allotment nor the laws nor the churches though some of them had accepted the churches. . . . They wanted to be free with their own land, homes and wild game without interference from white people. They were not committing any crime by meeting out there at their Hickory Ground town but were holding Council, trying to talk the different things over and see what they could do about it. As usual there was nothing they could do.[25]

Many of the Cherokees also expressed opposition to land allotment. A Cherokee full-blood politician, Benjamin Knight, recalled, "The Allotment Law was passed by the legislature also, but some of the leaders of the Cherokees protested this and it was left up to the common people to vote on the bill. A band called the 'Night Hawks' among the Cherokees did not vote in this election and this lack of

THE SNAKES

interest caused the bill to pass."[26] Like the Mvskokes, the Cherokees experienced their own factionalism of traditionalists—the Nighthawks and Keetoowahs, who were against Cherokees who called themselves progressive. Realizing the implications of the Dawes Act, the Keetoowah Society began actively opposing land allotment in the 1890s. Known for their secrecy, the Keetoowahs began to reemerge when Redbird Smith, a member of the Cherokee National Council, separated from the Keetoowah Society and formed the Nighthawk Keetoowah Society that grew to about 5,500 members.[27] On March 15, 1902, the U.S. district court in Muskogee ordered Redbird Smith and eleven Nighthawk Keetoowahs to enroll for land allotments. The Nighthawks appeared on the designated date but refused to enroll, and authorities put them in jail until they changed their minds. After one night behind bars, Smith and the others went to the Dawes Commission and accepted enrollment.[28] Many Semvnoles believed as Chitto Harjo did and reluctantly accepted land allotments. The Semvnoles had signed an agreement with the Dawes Commission on December 16, 1897, and the allotment process was completed in 1907.[29]

Traditionalists from the Five Nations

The members of the Dawes Commission had their hands full negotiating with the Mvskokes, Semvnoles, and Cherokees. In each negotiation, the commission met resistance from conservative factions that opposed the individual ownership of land. For some traditionalists the most important aspect of the imposition of land allotment was that it insisted on property ownership and inheritance along patrilineal lines whereas all Five Nations were matrilineal. In the traditions of the Medicine Way, women had equal power in how things were done, and they certainly had more power than white

THE SNAKES

women did. But when white men began to intermarry with Five Nations women, they went against the grain and disregarded this equal division of powers. It did not sit well with traditionalists.

Whereas the majority of Choctaws and Chickasaws accepted their land allotments, a faction of traditionalists resisted. With the influx of more settlers and miners who came to dig coal from beneath Choctaw land, the Choctaws and Chickasaws felt the pressure of the growing numbers of whites, many coming from various parts of Europe, from Ireland to eastern Europe. Workers were needed in the coal mines of the Choctaws, also in the Mvskoke reservation as Henryetta sprang up as a coal-mining town. Eastern European miners were willing to do dangerous work for low pay. Some Choctaws and Chickasaws felt they were becoming quickly outnumbered, as they had in their previous homelands in the South. Traditionalists agreed things were getting out of control, and that there were fewer and fewer Choctaws and Chickasaws every year, especially now that many elders were dying, compounding the numbers of those who had passed to the other side along the Trail of Suffering as they traveled to reach promised homelands in Indian Territory. They did not want to lose control of these new homelands, which had been promised to them in the removal treaties.

The traditional Choctaws and Chickasaws had heard of Chitto Harjo and the Keetoowahs and the Nighthawks. The Mvskoke traditionalists shared with the other tribes the belief that they were a part of the Earth Mother, and that their relationships with the earth dated back centuries within the Medicine Way. This lifeway represented the belief that people come from the earth, which they should respect as they do their mother. In this view of the Medicine Way, the earth is a whole and should not be divided up in individual allotments as proposed by the Dawes Act and the Dawes Commission.

THE SNAKES

When the Mvskokes and the ten other Indian nations were exempted from the Dawes Act, Chitto Harjo, like other Indians, probably assumed everything would be all right. News and information about allotting tribal lands for all the Indian nations were shared by those who could read the newspapers and understand English. For certain two forces were at work: change coming from outside of the Mvskoke Nation caused by the Dawes Act and change from within due to the people being less traditional and becoming more like *este-hvtke*.[30] That the Mvskoke people were becoming less *este-cate* (Indian) deeply concerned Chitto Harjo.

The Dawes Commission had begun to record Mvskokes' assigned allotments on what came to be known as the Dawes rolls. Survey crews staked out the allotted areas and drew maps according to section, township, and range lines. The final rolls contained more than 101,000 names compiled from 1898 to 1914, although over 400,000 people had tried to sign up for allotments.[31]

In 1899 Pleasant Porter, elected due to his campaign promise to work with the Dawes Commission, replaced Isparhecher. Porter believed that the commissioners worked in the best interests of the people, and those who agreed with him reelected him four years later.[32] In a lengthy speech before the National Council at the courthouse in Okmulgee, Porter extolled allotment and the future of the Mvskoke Nation. A majority of the Mvskoke Nation signed up for allotments. According to Chief Porter, "More than two-thirds of the Creek people have made selections of allotments of the use of the surface of the land, under the provisions of the Curtis Act and have received certificates from the Dawes Commission for such selections." Porter concluded that the Mvskoke people believed that allotment was in their best interest and that they "assented to and accepted the allotment and partition of their lands."[33]

THE SNAKES

Chitto Harjo, as the second leader at the Hickory Stomp Ground, insisted that all traditionalists of the Five Nations who believed in the Medicine Way, including freedmen, come together. Creating an intertribal coalition that included freedmen would bring many loyal bodies together, necessary due to the prevalence of rumors, gossip, and yellow press newspapers predicting an Indian war. Settlers, seeing the increasing number of traditionalists and freedmen arriving to join Harjo at Hickory Ground as military gatherings, panicked.[34]

The Snake followers came from everywhere, Salina, Chitto Harjo's daughter, recalled. "Many were Creeks but there were Cherokees, Choctaws, Chickasaws, Seminoles and freed slaves that came as far away as Louisiana to support the Creek Indian cause of saving our land, as one land, to become the Crazy Snake tribe. My father sent out representatives to look for old slaves or descendants of slaves who were glad to be of service to their old masters. These [former] slaves left their homes in Louisiana and elsewhere to return to Indian Territory." Ex-slaves and Indian traditionalists working together frightened whites, and local gossip spread bad feelings toward Indians and African Americans.[35]

Following Bailey's advice in Washington, Chitto Harjo insisted that the 1832 Treaty of Cusseta, in which the federal government had promised the Mvskokes that they could govern themselves, was still in effect.[36] "Being the children of Chitto," said Salina, "we grew to live in fear of the white man. We could not fully understand as children, why, if we treated our land with care and, if we left the White man alone, why were we continued to be harassed." She added, "There were Whites that would call us names and treat us with disrespect because we wouldn't follow the allotment procedures; to them we were savages, not Indians." In other words, in the view of whites to be Indian meant to complacently follow the guidelines of the government, but to insist on self-determination was to be a savage In-

THE SNAKES

dian. Chitto Harjo's daughter Salina recalled that the traditional Mvskokes "desired to return to their old ways of life, absence of fences, having common property and peaceful conduct."[37] Convinced that they had no other choice given their belief that the core identity of the people was Mvskoke and they should remain *este-cate*, Harjo and the Snakes decided to resist allotment and go on their own.

When the spring weather came in 1900, allowing the holding of stomp dances, Chitto Harjo traveled to various *tvlofvs* with a copy of the Cusseta Treaty to talk about the Mvskokes' legal right to have their own government. He urged support for a government made up of a council of the *tvlofvs* led by traditionalists, like the one at old Ocmulgee before removal. In October the Snake leader and his followers formed their Mvskoke government, with a new constitution to establish the lawmaking power in a council consisting of two houses, the House of Kings and the House of Warriors. Worried, Chief Porter asked the federal government to keep a watchful eye on Snake activities. In establishing their own government, Porter alleged, the Snakes and Harjo had gone too far. And maybe they had.[38]

In January 1901 the Lighthorse police of Chitto Harjo's government began putting up signs announcing the new laws that the Snakes had passed. In response, the federal government took action in support of Porter. On January 17, U.S. Deputy Marshal Grant Johnson, an African American, ran into a force of fifty Snake Lighthorse a few miles west of Eufaula. Badly outnumbered, Johnson wisely backed down. But the Snake movement was growing. By the end of the month more than five thousand men, women, and children had joined the Crazy Snake traditionalist movement, worrying whites and everyone else. On January 24, U.S. Marshal Leo Bennett sent a posse of thirty officers to arrest Harjo and other Snake leaders. Rumor placed them at a cabin along the Canadian River. Although no guns were fired, the Snakes drove the posse away. Feeling extremely

THE SNAKES

anxious about the large and growing number of Indians and freedmen gathering at Hickory Ground, Agent J. B. Shoenfelt requested five hundred soldiers from the War Department in Washington. He waited for an answer.[39]

Tense feelings between Indians and whites elsewhere did not help, and they were compounded by rumors of war between the Mvskoke traditionalists and the federal government. Chitto Harjo wanted to avoid Indians and whites fighting; he was a White Stick and hoped for peace to prevail. On January 25, 1901, Lieutenant H. B. Dixon led sixty-five soldiers of Troop A of the Eighth U.S. Cavalry to camp near Henryetta. Two days later, close to noon on Sunday, Leo Bennett sent his deputy marshals to arrest Chitto Harjo. They woke the Snake leader from a nap, and he went peacefully with them, shocking Bennett and Dixon, who had expected trouble. The authorities arrested Crazy Snake on the charge of "conspiracy" according to Section 5440 of the Revised Statutes of the United States. The next day, without firing a shot, Dixon's soldiers arrested all the main Snake leaders.[40]

Still, calm prevailed.

On the night of February 4, Marshal Bennett and a number of his men escorted Chitto Harjo from the military camp and detained twenty more Snakes. In total, ninety-six Snakes were arrested, but the court released sixteen on bonds, fined two, and released five on their personal recognizance as government witnesses. Those arrested ranged in age from fourteen (Ben Harjo) to eighty-eight (Oktayache Micco and Katcha Micco).[41] The Snakes were scheduled to go before a grand jury.[42]

Crazy Snake said "he saw no reason for his arrest and felt confident that when the Indians were given a trial before the Great White Father's Court they would be released. He said they were acting in good faith and had papers from Washington that gave them the right

THE SNAKES

to establish their old government." When asked about killing whites, Harjo replied that "it was never their intention, and they expected finally to get all the whites out." Judge John R. Thomas lectured Harjo and the other arrested Snakes, then he sentenced them to two years at the U.S. penitentiary at Leavenworth in Kansas.[43] In addition, Judge Thomas fined Harjo and each Snake five thousand dollars for conspiracy plus 364 days in jail at Fort Smith, Arkansas, with a fine of two hundred dollars for assault and battery. Before being sent to Leavenworth, Harjo persisted in speaking out against allotments, but despite his actions, Judge Thomas accepted a plea bargain to suspend the two-year sentence. But he ordered Harjo to be rearrested on April 16. In the end, Harjo and the other Snakes served only a part of their sentences due to good behavior and acceptance of allotments.[44]

While Chitto Harjo and the others were serving their sentences, the press exploited the divisions in the community. On March 1, 1901, the assimilationist Mvskokes (and then the Semvnoles) reached an agreement with the Dawes Commission. Two days later the Mvskokes and Semvnoles became citizens of the United States as a part of the assimilation process opposed by Chitto Harjo. Crazy Snake made a last appeal to the Mvskokes in a speech on April 1. He warned, "Do not give away your birthrights. No white man can take it away from you." The Snake leader urged, "Never sign the allotment roll for there's no power on earth that can compel you to give up your homes to the white man, nor turn over your fields to the renters who are occupying the prairies, driving our game away and troubling the last remnant of the noble descendants of those who fought on the Hickory ground in Alabama." After his release Harjo went into hiding for ten months. During this time he kept meeting discreetly with others to refrain from being enrolled for allotments.[45] In March 1901, the *Indian Advocate* reported, "Crazy Snake now finds himself more

THE SNAKES

condemned by the Indians than by the whites, not because the Indians have no sympathy with his national aspirations, but because they feel keenly that he has lowered the prestige of Creek arms in what practically all of them realized from the beginning, was a hopeless undertaking." The publication promoted Christian doctrine, denouncing all Native traditionalism, including the Mvskoke Medicine Way. "The Indians want it understood that the so-called 'rebellion' was in no sense one of the tribe or 'nation' of Creeks, and they would like to impress it upon the Caucasian mind that, if the 'nation' had made common cause with the Snake band, their defeat, while inevitable, would have made another glorious page in Creek history." The Porter government wanted the newspaper to know that it was the legitimate Mvskoke Nation and that the Snake band was a minority.[46]

The Snakes had armed themselves three times—in 1901, 1902, and 1909—to fight against land allotment, and the thought of another Snake incident lingered. In 1911, during the administration of Governor Lee Cruce, the state legislature considered a special session to address certain matters of importance, including a pension to those who served against Chitto Harjo and the Snakes or, as Walter Ferguson, editor of the *Cherokee Republican*, called them, "the first heroes in the history of our new state."[47]

Black Gold

Taking an enormous gamble in 1896, Edwin B. Foster filed a request to lease as much land as he could on the Osage reservation in Indian Territory. The Department of the Interior granted Foster a blanket ten-year lease to drill for oil anywhere on the reservation. Several years later, the department renewed the lease for another ten years.[48] But the lease did not garner much attention until June 1901.

THE SNAKES

In spring 1901 two enterprising men from the Pennsylvania oil fields, John S. Wick and Jesse Heydrick, arrived in the Mvskoke Nation and negotiated leases for thousands of acres from Mvskoke allottees; Susan Bland was one of them. It did not take long until Wick and Heydrick ran out of money, but Susan Bland's white husband and a friend of his worked out an agreement with the two want-to-be oil men. In the wee hours of June 25, a gusher hit, shaking the ground and ushering in the Sue A. Bland No. 1 oil field. Suddenly oil rushers poured into tiny Red Fork, a town of three stores and a dozen houses, by every means of transportation.

People were convinced more gushers would follow the Sue Bland No. 1, and the oil rush overwhelmed the Tulsa area. Applications for allotments poured in for the land that had until recently been considered worthless.[49] Wildcatters used water witching methods and quackery, then gambled and guessed by drilling dry holes where new oil pools might be. About a dozen miles south of Tulsa, the Ida Glenn No. 1 erupted like a volcano at daybreak on November 22, 1905, making it rain oil. With the oil rush led by Robert F. Galbreath, the Glenn Pool quickly became the first major oil field on Mvskoke land in the Indian Territory.[50] As the oil strikes and gushers added to the excitement and enticed more outsiders, the Enabling Act of June 16, 1906, paved the way for Oklahoma to become the forty-sixth state the following year. By the end of 1907, roughly 1.5 million people populated the new state.[51]

The northeast quarter of Indian Territory yielded more underground oil pools, transforming the Cross Timbers into the largest oil-producing entity in the world. Uncontrolled wildcatting and lucky guessing produced twenty-one oil fields that reached their highest production in 1927, two years before the Great Crash on Wall Street.[52]

The oil found under Mvskoke lands and those of the Osage and other tribes invited numerous problems and unwanted trouble along

125

with windfall wealth. Swindles and even cold-blooded murders made victims of those simultaneously blessed and cursed with quarterly royalty payments of $3,350.[53] The most noted Mvskoke victim was Jackson Barnett, sometimes called the world's richest Indian, who possessed $24 million when he died at ninety-two years of age in 1934. A quiet elderly man who enjoyed hunting and fishing as well as tending to his horses, Jackson Barnett was exploited for his oil wealth by a raven-haired prostitute from Kansas City who married him twice and absconded with him to Los Angeles.[54] The Mvskokes could never adjust to the debauchery, graft, and corruption that came as white people rushed in to profit from the oil fields.[55]

During these years, rather than depending completely on farming, Mvskoke people began to find jobs in towns like Muskogee, Okmulgee, and Tulsa. These day jobs called for speaking English and coming into contact with whites, Blacks, and Indians of other tribes on a daily basis. In the days following statehood, from the outside it seemed roughly 95 percent of the Mvskokes worked "in factories, shops, and on the farms," and others became professionals, such as "lawyers, doctors, teachers, and nurses." Some Mvskokes owned large farms, and others benefited from the oil pumped from their allotments.[56] But within Mvskoke communities, the *tvlofvs* still functioned and people danced at the Green Corn ceremonies as they used to. *Poyvfekcv yekcetv,* the Spirit Power, persisted.

President Theodore Roosevelt delivered his first official message to Congress on December 3, 1901, soon after the first hostilities of the Crazy Snake movement. In his lengthy address, he stated, "In my judgement the time has arrived when we should definitely make up our minds to recognize the Indian as an individual and not as a member of a tribe. The General Allotment Act is a mighty pulverizing engine to break up the tribal mass. It acts directly upon the family and the individual. Under its provisions some sixty thousand Indians have already become citizens of the United States."[57] The Indian Base Line and Meridian had been authorized by an act of Congress on April 8, 1864.[58] This historic intersection laid the foundation for the Indian Territory to be surveyed and organized in the same way as public lands. All thirty-six remaining tribes in Indian Territory at the creation of the Dawes Commission received allotted lands, and on the Dawes rolls over 101,000 Indians were assigned lands.[59] The continual process kept both the Dawes Commission and the Cherokee Commission, also known as the Jerome Commission, busy. The Dawes Commission continued its work until every inch of the Mvskoke reservation and the rest of Indian Territory was surveyed and accounted for. The "pulverizing engine" of the Indian allotment system yielded a surplus of 90 million acres.

Hickory Ground

Early spring rains gave no indication of what lay ahead. Hickory Ground and the many other grounds among the Five Nations celebrated the corn harvest by holding their Green Corn ceremonies. Yet the prophets suspected something was not right. Hot days in July turned to scorching days in August. The summer of 1901 witnessed days with temperatures over 110 degrees, and any wind blew only hot air making life unbearable for humans, plants, and animals. Were the elemental powers in discord? Relief finally arrived with the fall months, then winter and a new year.[60]

While he was in prison Crazy Snake was cut off from many of his supporters in Indian Territory, but they continued to agitate against allotment, ridiculing what was going on, circulating anti-allotment petitions, and retaining lobbyists in Washington. They stoked the ceremonial fires and continued to resist white culture and practice the Green Corn Ceremony, inspiring new recruits who

THE SNAKES

arrived at Hickory Ground. One of Harjo's sons, Thomas Wilson, became a lobbyist and went to Washington to assist in representing the Snakes.[61]

Frank Jones remembered that by 1902 the Snakes had been "reduced now to about two hundred at the old Hickory Stomping Ground—same reign of terror followed—arrests followed."[62] During the latter part of February 1902, as two to three hundred Snakes and fifty Cherokee sympathizers camped at Hickory Ground, the *Weekly-Times Journal* reported with alarm that they were "trying to reorganize the ancient Creek government here and expel the white people by reviving an old law under the operation of which . . . Indians may lease or rent land to a white man or employ a white laborer." Chitto Harjo wanted to exclude whites completely. The incarcerated Snakes were going to be paroled, and, anticipating trouble, the newspaper reported, "The Snakes are again disturbed and there are 'doings' at old Hickory Ground."[63] Leaving Eufaula, Grant Johnson, a Black U.S. deputy marshal, and his men stopped at Harjo's house, again arrested him and twenty Snakes, and brought them to the camp on February 22, 1902. Frank recalled, "There was no resistance at this time, no loss of life."[64] Harjo and his followers were escorted by the military and placed in a federal jail in Muskogee until being sentenced for two years at Leavenworth Federal Prison in Kansas.[65]

Eight months later, on November 4, 1902, the Snakes were released after they promised to enroll for their land allotments. When Chitto Harjo and the Snakes returned to Henryetta on the Frisco train they were "greeted warmly by hundreds of Indians, as well as white onlookers. There were people all in the streets, on top of the buildings, on top of the wagons, anywhere they thought they might get a view."[66] It seemed a Native son had returned a hero. By now even Pleasant Porter had begun to have his doubts about allotment: "I was compelled under the advance of civilization to sign the paper that I (now) know took the lifeblood of my people." He was starting to sound like Chitto Harjo: "If we had our own way, we would be living with the lands in common, and we would have these prairies all open, (and we would have) our little bunches of cattle, and bands of deer that would jump up from the head of every hollow, and flocks of turkeys running up every hillside, and every stream would be full of sun perch."[67] In 1903 the Mvskoke voters reelected him as principal chief.[68]

Harjo lived with his wife and two children in a log cabin made from walnut trees several miles east and south of Hickory Ground, in a clearing at the bottom of Tiger Mountain.[69] Tiger Mountain resembled a wooded tall hill about one hundred feet high. A creek meandered behind the Harjo farm toward the southeast to the North Fork of the Canadian River. The farm, on five or ten acres, had a small separate kitchen, a barn with blacksmith tools, and a smokehouse for meat. In addition to his self-taught skills as a blacksmith, Harjo liked to do silver work, making rings and ornaments that he often gifted to relatives and friends. The family had the usual crops planted—corn, wheat, and oats. They raised chickens, pigs, and kept cattle, and Chitto loved horses.[70]

A niece of Chitto Harjo, Ada Roach, said, "I remember when they were taking the followers of Crazy Snake to Muskogee. There would be one Snake and one soldier. They cut their hair off there. I heard that Chitto Harjo nearly cried when he lost his hair. My uncle was a Snake Indian, that is he didn't wish to be allotted land. He, like the others called Snake Indians, wanted to be free to move anywhere he wished [to be] on the land owned by the Creek Nation."[71]

A white farmer, Andrew Willhite, encountered the Snakes, recalling, "I was not afraid of the Indians but if I met six of them on the trail, they usually came in groups like that, I knew enough to pull out of the trail and let them pass." The farmer also said, "I've

THE SNAKES

seen Crazy Snake spread a blanket on the ground and preach to them and have seen them throw their money on the blanket. . . . The money was supposed to go to lawyers who were getting the land for them. Anyway Crazy Snake took money from them."[72] Lee Hawkins described further details. Hawkins, a Mvskoke, said, "I made several trips down to the Hickory Ground Town. I had several relatives down there. . . . They paid $1.00 a head, each member, to join Chitto Harjo, who led the Snake Uprising. They tried to get me to join but I didn't do it. I saw many pay their $1.00 to Sol Haggty who was the collector." Hawkins explained, "It was their understanding that if they followed Chitto Harjo they would get the country back from the white people and that each of the ones who followed him would have their share, the same as if they were Indians."[73] Harjo was cautious against infiltrators and wanted only the most loyal of the traditionalists because he needed to depend on them.

Hawkins claimed, "Nobody was allowed on the Chitto camp ground except the members, neither white, black nor Indians. When anyone came they were met at the edge of the ground and asked their business."[74] He added, "These negro followers of Chitto Harjo were from Muskogee, Haskell and all around. Henry Jacobs of Holdenville was one of them."[75] Other freedmen traveled from afar to help the traditionalists because they had been good to the former slaves.

"Crazy Snake and his followers began roaming around over the country armed with Winchesters, arresting and punishing all of the Indians who had accepted their allotment," said Henry Jacobs, a freedman. He stressed, "It was also a heavy fine for any of the Indians to hire a white man to work for them and sometimes Indians hiring such white men would be severely punished."[76] While the Mvskoke Medicine Way was inclusive, the Mvskoke national government following the Reconstruction years decided to become "exclusive" in order to maintain political control over the reservations and

THE SNAKES

their residents. The Mvskokes feared white intruders—settlers, cattlemen, railroad workers, outlaws, missionaries, and basic white labor—would soon outnumber them. The general situation was getting out of control and the old order needed to be restored.

Mrs. Willie Blair witnessed the Snakes whipping Mvskokes who broke the law and said, "The Indians punished the law violators in their own way which seemed brutal to the white people. Once three of their men had stolen a hog and hogs were plentiful so they were being whipped for stealing. . . . I was working for [a doctor], watching his stock for him as he always wanted a fresh team when he came in. [John] Likowski had a post office at Sonora and the doctor's wife and I rode right through the Ground when going to the post office." Mrs. Blair explained, "They had camps, shacks and arbors and we didn't pass between them but through the ground. These [guilty] men were being whipped and we didn't want to see it at close range but watch[ed] it from a distance." She stressed, "It wasn't Chitto Harjo's nor any Full Blood's way to steal for they had stricter laws and punishments for stealing than white people have."[77] Honor was stressed among the Mvskokes, and wrongdoing brought disgrace to one's family and clan.

A Mvskoke elder, Agnes Kelley, described the Snake Indians as being unusual: "They were called Snakes after Chitto Harjo and are a very peculiar people. They won't talk to you for they do not speak to each other. If I, or another Indian that they know, meets one and speaks to him or her, the other Snake Indian might speak but is not likely to. He would just look at you and go on. Indians are funny that way."[78] Agnes Kelley's opinion was a part of the increasing problem in Indian-white relations. The division between Indians and whites widened with the increasing number of whites, the Boomers, cattlemen, and outlaws, and mixed-bloods acting less *este-cate.*

THE SNAKES

The growing problem of intruders threatened the Mvskoke Nation and the rest of Indian Territory; and racial relations became strained. There were now many more whites in Indian Territory than Indians. Newcomers were strangers, but instead of trying to get along, Indians and whites held each other at arm's length. At the same time, many Indians disagreed with Chitto Harjo and his Snake traditionalists, adding to *etekvlkē*, the old chasm dividing Indians.

Jim Guin recalled an incident that occurred when he was a ten-year-old white lad: "One day in the late Summer of 1903, Dad and Uncle Bill decided to cut the tall grass to be found on Uncle Bill's son's allotment. Uncle Bill's son was named Ivory. This grass was to be used as hay." Guin explained, "It so happened that Ivory's allotment was near Hickory Ground. This ground was situated near the small town of Salem and was at that time headquarters for the 'Crazy Snake' Chitto Harjo." Remembering one incident, Guin said, "Uncle and Dad, after making the trip had but little time that first day to mow hay. They made camp in a small woodland and used their wagon to sleep under." Jim Guin described the Snakes firing at his father and uncle, stating, "The first night they were startled to hear the zing of buckshot uncomfortably near, in fact a bullet went into their camp fire. They jumped to their feet, ran a short distance and hid behind trees."[79]

"Soon about ten negro 'Snake' Indians on horses entered the circle of their camp fire," said Guin. "One of these negroes sang out: 'Hello, white man! We burn you before day.' The savages started dancing about the fire, yelling and gobbling as they did so. This commotion summoned other 'Crazy Snake' Indians from Hickory Ground. My dad and uncle heard them swiftly approach on horses." The two men expected trouble. Guin described, "They didn't have anything but an old muzzle loaded gun to stand off their foes, so they decided the best thing to do was to retreat. This they did. They went

132

THE SNAKES

to the home of a friendly Indian of the name of Billy Cheeks. He lived on the North [Fork of the] Canadian about four miles from the place of attack. The next morning Dad and Uncle Bill returned to their camp, got their wagon and team and came back home."[80]

In August 1903 Oklahoma City's *Weekly-Times Journal* warned of possible violence near Eufaula. An election in Cherokee country set the Keetoowahs against the national government trying to exercise authority over them, fueling rumors that Crazy Snake and some of his followers had conspired with the Keetoowahs.[81] The alarmist reporting, vilifying Chitto Harjo and the Snakes as wild Indians ready to go to war, caught the attention of Frederick T. Cummins of New York, who wanted to exhibit Chitto Harjo and some of his Snakes at the World's Fair in St. Louis in 1904. In a letter to U.S. Marshal E. H. Hubbard, Cummins proposed hiring Chitto Harjo for thirty dollars per month, plus twenty-five dollars per month for Snake men, fifteen dollars for Snake women, and five dollars per month for children, free room, board, and transportation to and from St. Louis.[82] The arrangement did not happen.

The Dawes Commission was close to winding up its work when Alexander Posey, the Mvskoke newspaper editor, and Drennan C. Skaggs traveled to the home of Chitto Harjo to try to enroll him for an allotment. Late Wednesday afternoon on September 27, the two men arrived at the Harjo farmstead. Seeing them approaching, Harjo took two chairs from inside and met them on the front porch. Harjo knew why they were there; Posey stated their business in Mvskoke. Chitto Harjo listened then responded, "The agreement between the white man and the Indian gave the Indian the right of undisturbed possession and enjoyment of this country as long as grass grows and rivers run." After a brief pause, Harjo continued, "I notice the grass is still growing, that the water in the North [Fork of the] Canadian is still flowing toward the sea . . . the Indian has not changed

THE SNAKES

very materially, he still tills his softkypatch, his color remains the same and he attends to his business and has asked for no change. I shall never hold up my right arm and swear that I take my allotment of land in good faith."[83]

In 1905 Chitto Harjo made a second trip to Washington hoping to see President Roosevelt, but he returned home discouraged. A year later, spring arrived and on March 6, the Curtis Act dissolved the governments of the Five Nations. Then news arrived that representatives of the congressional Select Committee to Investigate Matters Connected with Affairs in the Indian Territory were coming to Tulsa in November. In 1902 Congress had voted to withdraw from allotment millions of acres from the holdings of Indian Territory tribes after the discovery of oil, natural gas, and coal on reservation lands. The tribes were to be compensated for this land, and the committee's task was to hear testimony from any party—including tribes and their representatives, oil companies, railroads—with a financial interest in the matter. Chitto Harjo addressed them.

The meeting on November 23, 1906, was held in the old Elks Lodge hall in the Seaman Building at 16 West Third Street in Tulsa. The room was packed to capacity.[84] Chitto Harjo's wife Nokeche and his children Salina, Thomas, and Legus sat in the front row. Chitto Harjo rose when the committee invited him to speak. His many experiences of giving long talks at Hickory Ground empowered him. Although some of the people understood the Mvskoke language, the interpreter translated the spoken words with the same sincerity that Chitto expressed them. Crazy Snake went on for almost an hour, his heart taking over his voice, producing ten pages of testimony. He finished with this request:

> All that I am begging of you, honorable Senators, is that these ancient agreements and treaties wherein you promised to take care

THE SNAKES

of me and my people be fulfilled, and that you will remove all the difficulties that have been raised in reference to my people and their country, and I ask you to see that these promises are faithfully kept. I understand you are the representatives of the Government sent here to look into these things, and I hope you will relieve us. That is all I desire to say.[85]

Chairman Clarence D. Clark, who was overseeing the meeting, asked Harjo who did he represent? Harjo replied, "I am here representing myself and my people." The chairman, who was a senator from Wyoming, asked, "Who are you people?" Harjo replied, "I am not representing anyone here. I am the speaker here for my people. They have delegated me to make a talk to you and tell you what we want, and I am doing it at their request. I am here as the official spokesman of all the people." Kansas senator Chester Long inserted: "That is, a faction—he has a party or faction, has he not?" Harjo clarified, "I mean all the full bloods who want to retain their tribal relation as of old, and do not want their land in severalty."[86]

After his speech, Chitto Harjo sat down with his family. Cornelius Perryman, a mixed-blood in the House of Kings, spoke, and when he finished, Harjo stood up to address the senators. David Hodge hurried to the front of the room to stand by Harjo to translate. Harjo wanted to know their senators' views on allotment. He explained that as a speaker to his *tvlofv* and to other Mvskokes he needed to know what to tell them. The senators replied that the Treaty of Cusseta of 1832 had been changed since the Mvskoke Nation had accepted allotments. Harjo replied, "I think I have the privilege of appealing to the other tribes and notifying them in reference to the disagreement between you and me in reference to this matter. . . . That is all I have to say."[87] Afterwards, Chitto Harjo left with his family and about a

THE SNAKES

dozen of his supporters who had accompanied him. They wanted the senators to witness that Crazy Snake did not stand alone.

In November 1907 Oklahoma Territory and Indian Territory together became the forty-sixth state, Oklahoma. Chitto Harjo was no longer fighting only against the allotting of his tribe's lands; he was now trying to help save Mvskoke sovereignty.

CHITTO HARJO'S NEPHEW
DANIEL STARR

Crazy Snake, known also as Chitto Harjo, was my uncle belonging to the Alligator clan. He was the leader of an old treaty band. He had established council grounds southeast of Henryetta known as the Hickory Ground busk grounds where he camped for days at a time to attend to the business councils with his people. Not only Indians made up his people at this particular time as many negroes had been included or had joined in his band. I was constantly urged and reminded by my uncle [Chitto Harjo] that I must cherish and keep on the stand for the old Indian rights as he was. Many a time I would go in his company to the home of Isphecha where I would listen for hours at a time to their lengthy discussions on matters dear to the hearts of the Older Indians who were maintaining strong beliefs and stand for the continued existence of the old Indian laws. It seemed to me that those old cherished Indian laws could not be in existence for long although all the older Indians had either sided in for the new ways or for the old tribal laws which the Indians had great faith and love. There were too many white people coming into the Indian Territory to even think that the Indians could keep on with the tribal laws. When I expressed my opposition against my uncle's views, he finally gave up trying to win me to his side so that he went so far as to disown me.[1]

6

"Snake War"

One of the tragic things that can happen to a person is to fall under the deep spell of *ehosa*. Among Mvskokes and Semvnoles this is a state of confusion that can lead to feelings of panic and fear. The degree of confusion or *ehosa* can become so great that a person forgets where he or she is, not know what time it is, or what day, or not even being able to remember his or her name. Self-identity and knowing who you are related to and where you are from are critical. This is important since the human mind can be overpowered.

Hvmmaketv (that's what they used to say)

From 1906 to 1908 the Snakes joined with many of the traditional Keetoowah Cherokees, Choctaws, and Chickasaws to form the Four Mothers Society to speak openly against land allotments.[1] Traditionalists in each group blamed mainly the mixed-bloods for acting like white men and going away from the traditional ways. The society focused more on restoring the old ways of their cultures. The danger of allotments dividing their reservations and separating family members on different parcels of lands established common ground among the Four Mothers. The members of the Four Mothers hoped for legislation that would undo the Dawes Act of individualizing their tribal lands. One lobbyist, L. C. Moore, wrote to the organization: "But I now see the sunlight of justice and the silver moon of peace rising and dispelling the dark clouds that have so long shrouded the Four Mothers. . . . Stand together; trust in God, and all will be well. We called on the Secretary of the Interior, Commissioner of Indian Affairs and Congress, and a bill will be introduced in the next Congress, the passage of which will be of lasting joy to all Indians sheltered by the Creek Nation who signed the original treaty of 1832."[2] Unfortunately the Four Mothers Society lacked lobbying power, and Washington's attention was focused on Oklahoma Territory pressing for statehood.

The State of Sequoyah

Realizing that statehood was coming to Oklahoma Territory, Native leaders of Indian Territory, seeking to preserve their autonomy against certain white domination, began to push hard for their own state, the State of Sequoyah. Leaders of the Five Nations served as vice presidents of the convention and the delegates elected Pleasant Porter as president.[3] The delegates chose thirty to forty members to draft the constitution and subcommittees to draw a map of future counties for the proposed State of Sequoyah.[4]

One Mvskoke elder recalled, "In 1905 the tribes called a convention at the Muskogee, Indian Territory (and, while I think of it, we used to call Muskogee Arkansas Town) on August 21, to form a constitution for a state composed of Indian Territory separate to that of the Oklahoma Territory." The elder fondly remembered, "Our Creek Chief, Pleasant Porter, a neighbor of mine for years and with whom I had been deer hunting many times, was selected and elected president of that convention, and we had a Creek poet by the name of Alex Posey who was elected secretary. Out of the five tribes I believe that the one absent was the Chickasaw tribe." You can imagine the elder shrugging his shoulders. Then he added, "Of course Sequoyah was a Cherokee, and it was he who composed the Cherokee alphabet and, in order to pay tribute to him, they voted to call the Indian Territory the State of Sequoyah, and it was to have forty-eight counties. The results of this convention was brought by representatives of the five tribes before Congress, but for some reason they never acted" on it.[5] This was because Oklahoma Territory also wanted statehood and President Theodore Roosevelt did not want two new states. Oklahoma Territory and Indian Territory merged to become the State of Oklahoma.

Pleasant Porter called the convention to order on August 22, 1905. One of the delegates, Chinnubbie Harjo, the pen name of Alexander Posey, suggested the name for the proposed state to honor the work of the Cherokee genius.[6] The delegates "selected Fort Gibson, [the] Cherokee town on the line between Creek and Cherokee Nations, as the state capital city of Sequoyah for a period of six years."[7]

On August 23 the convention selected a committee to draft the constitution. The committee of fifty members chose William Wirt Hastings, a prominent Cherokee who later represented Oklahoma in the House of Representatives, to serve as the chairman. The committee created a lot of excitement in the eastern half of Indian Territory when it drafted the Sequoyah Constitution on September 8, 1905, for consideration by the voters. In an election on November 7 the residents of Indian Territory accepted the constitution by a six-to-one majority of 56,279 to 9,073. The next step, presenting the desire of the convention to the U.S. Congress, proved not to be so easy. In Congress on December 4, 1905, a bill to admit the State of Sequoyah was introduced in the House of Representatives. The bill was tabled. A Senate bill, introduced by Porter McCumber of South Dakota, was also tabled.[8] At the same time, Oklahoma Territory lobbied Congress for statehood.

"SNAKE WAR"

In 1908 Harjo and the Snakes called for a council to gather at Hickory Ground. Lobbyists hired by the Snakes arrived from Washington, and newspapers sensationalized the meeting, calling it another "Snake War." Panicked whites felt threatened by the gatherings of full-bloods, mixed-blood traditionalists, and freedmen. In a climate of fear the rush of emotions developed into an us-versus-them situation, whites against people of color, causing racial violence to spiral out of control. As far as the Snakes and freedmen were concerned it was the whites who were causing the trouble.

Many freedmen from the campground were accused of stealing chickens and small livestock from settlers and farmers, causing authorities to be asked to stop the thievery.[9] Local people complained, but what caught the most attention was when "someone ran off with a thousand pounds of smoked bacon" belonging to Morey Springs, a white farmer.[10]

Deputy W. H. Morey of McIntosh County rode to Hickory Ground to find who had stolen the meat. Against the advice from others who had fought the Snakes, Adjutant General Frank Canton, who was later dubbed a one-man army, traveled alone to Hickory Ground to learn what was going on. Canton aimed to talk man-to-man with Chitto Harjo and work out a peaceful solution to the rumored Indian war.[11] Heavily armed with hunting rifles and shotguns, the Indians and their freedmen allies drew their guns to protect their women and children from Canton, who was said to be a man hunter. During his talk with the adjutant general, Chitto Harjo agreed to tell his followers to put their guns away, but they kept them close by just in case. When the council ended, the Indians returned to their homes. Peace prevailed.

Although Mvskokes and freedmen had very good friendships, even intermarriage, Blacks could not be adopted into Mvskoke clans. Racial bigotry was being promoted by whites to discriminate against people of color, and it was learned by the Mvskokes and other Indian groups during slavery, especially during Jim Crowism after the Civil War. Due to the increasing amount of violence after the war and during the first great depression of 1873 to 1879, Indians and whites did not trust each other. Outlaws and cattle drives moving from Texas to Kansas and passing through Indian Territory only accentuated these problems, making it difficult for Indians, whites, Blacks, and mixed-bloods to get along.

According to one early settler, Andrew Willhite, "The whites got scared and some of them went to Henryetta and others camped on the North Canadian River." It was customary for farmers to graze their cattle where there were no fences, so the livestock grazed where they wanted to. Bluestem grass, gramma, and Indiangrass were common to the Henryetta area and known to grow tall due to thirty to forty inches of annual rain and provided effective hiding. The bottom land of the North Fork of the Canadian River also allowed lots of mosquitoes that farmers and cows had to deal with, especially with the summer humidity. He added, "We boys had to stay with the cattle, and they [Snakes] were right in the pasture. Everyone carried six-shooters but it was not on account of these followers of Chitto. It was natural for a cowboy to put his gun on as to put his clothes on. One reason was that a steer might attack him. They could kill a person on foot." Then the shooting began. Willhite and his wife lived about three miles away. He said, "My wife heard the shooting from our home. Some of the Indians left horses and cows and scattered like quail but others loaded their dead and wounded into wagons and took them away. When I got home two days later there were soldiers here, about three hundred."[12] Wild rumors spread citing Indian uprisings everywhere. Naturally all the blame pointed towards the Snakes who became the scapegoats of gossip and newspapers.

"SNAKE WAR"

Crazy Snake continued to argue that the Mvskokes had the legal right to maintain their traditional government based on the treaties that his people had signed with the United States. His critics, even those among the Mvskokes, called him a rebel, but his supporters called him a Native patriot seeking justice. In February 1909 Chitto Harjo traveled to Washington to try to get lawyers to undo the allotment process by going to court. He hoped to convince Robert G. Valentine, the assistant commissioner of Indian Affairs, that the Mvskokes had been wronged and that the 1832 Cusseta Treaty and Treaty of 1866 should be upheld. Valentine, a thirty-six-year-old progressive politician from Massachusetts, sent the full-blood traditionalist away with a stern declaration, "It is impossible for the old times and manners of life to return."[13] One can only imagine the older man thinking the younger man had a lot to learn and wishing that he could have talked to the commissioner, Francis Leupp, who was not available.

At the end of February 1909, no one was really sure where Chitto Harjo was. The situation remained tense between whites and traditionalists. Troops gathered about Henryetta searching for the Snake Indians and their African American allies. On the morning of Monday, March 22, 1909, A. Y. Patty, a constable from Eufaula, and two others with arrest warrants rode to Hickory Ground. Mostly freedmen and some Mvskokes watched them approach then cautiously reached for their guns. Patty had expected only a few, but now he and his two partners found themselves being surrounded by the Snakes. Patty was thinking what to say to the armed group when one of the Snakes told the three white men to get out "and never come back." Patty attempted to argue, but the sounds of guns cocking persuaded the men to ride away. Patty called over his shoulder that he would be back as the three men rode five miles to Henryetta to round up a posse.[14]

"SNAKE WAR"

A little over twenty-five miles east of Hickory Ground lay the gem of the prairie, or that was what early boosters called Checotah, founded in 1893. It was formerly a rest stop along the old Texas Road, then it became a depot for the Katy railroad. Not too far from the Gentry Hotel at Broadway and Gentry in downtown Checotah, "standing on the side walk, [was] an old man, an old grey bearded, grey haired man. And young men would come up to him and raise their hands and he'd give them some kind of oath of office." The elderly man was Larkin Ryal who as a justice of the peace swore in the "young men as deputies to the sheriff."[15]

Everyone living around Hickory Ground grew tense in anticipation of a war. Larkin Ryal and his wife lived two miles south of Hickory Ground. Ryal said, "A man came to me for a Search Warrant, . . . I issued it and went with him to see that the searching was done right. The Sheriff and some others were in the tents searching for the meat when the negroes overpowered them and made them leave. As he was leaving, Deputy Patty turned in his saddle and said, 'I'll see you again.'"[16]

Laurel Pittman, a mixed-blood Mvskoke, lived in the troubled area. Sheriff Doc Odom asked Pittman to join his posse to raid Chitto Harjo's home, but Pittman refused, telling Odom that perhaps he was "too hasty in taking any such action as the rumor of the various depredations in the community could possibly be false or at least exaggerated." Pittman added, "They had no positive proof that Chitto Harjo and his clan were responsible for the crimes which only rumors had charged them with." Pittman proposed that "if he [Odom] would delay his intended raid on Chitto Harjo's home, I would take Punch Marshell, a Creek Indian who lived three miles southwest of Checotah and to go to Harjo's home, and as we were both friendly with Harjo, we could stay over night with them and in that way investigate and ascertain if there were any evidence to substantiate the

"SNAKE WAR"

rumors." Odom refused the proposal, saying that he had a posse ready and was ready to act that night. "I saw he was determined and I could not change his mind, so I washed my hands of the whole affair."[17]

It took two days to organize a posse of fourteen men consisting of lawmen and citizens, to be led by Patty and his deputy, Frank Jones. These men set out on horseback for the Snake camp. Patty and the posse tied their horses some distance away, then divided up into three groups to surprise the Snake camp. At least two dozen Snakes were counted. The Snakes seemed unaware that they were being surrounded. The posse decided to dig trenches to catch the camp in a crossfire at daybreak. But when two or three of the posse left to go to Edwards's store, a couple of Snakes saw them leaving.

One of the Snakes, Leo Pinehill, described what happened next, "As the meeting was under way, some of the lookouts reported that some party was approaching the meeting; just coming over the hill were some men. They were officials and government men sent to stop Harjo's men and subdue them into accepting allotments."[18] Pinehill added, "When the approaching men were seen, those at the meeting began to get restless and two or three of the men began to plead that no one shoot." Harjo ordered the men to shoot only if necessary, but some of "the Snake men didn't wait to carry out the orders" and had already started shooting.[19]

In near darkness, both sides sporadically shot at each other out of panic during the cold night hours of March. At daylight, Joe Ferguson left for Eufaula to recruit more men for the final gun battle. Sixty-year-old Reverend Timothy Fowler stood up to bid Ferguson good luck! At that moment, one of the Snakes shot at Ferguson, and some of the buckshot hit the preacher in the forehead and chest; he began bleeding profusely. The posse fired at the camp, but most of the Snakes managed to hide behind bushes and trees. For over an hour, both sides fired at each other. Running low on ammunition, forty-two of the Snakes surrendered, while about fifteen escaped into the woods. A banker from Henryetta who joined the posse claimed a half dozen Snakes had been killed, but a later report put the number at more than a dozen.[20] Two members of the posse were killed, one being Timothy Fowler, who bled to death from buckshot wounds.

A white settler, Joe Merrick, who knew Chitto Harjo, recalled:

> He wanted this country to stay as the tribes had it. Old man Patty and a bunch went out and nobody knows how many they killed and a lot were brought back as prisoners. They said they had been stealing meat but I don't believe they were any worse than the ones who claimed they were stolen from. I stayed out of it for I didn't think the white folks had any business out there and I thought that surely there would be an indictment and somebody would have to answer for the happenings of that day.[21]

Stolen meat may not have been the real issue compelling authorities to be called to the area. Someone said a dog had chased a rabbit into the smoked meat house causing a commotion and accusations alleged of meat being stolen.[22]

David Starr, a Mvskoke from Arbeka Deep Fork and nephew of Chitto Harjo, commented on the hostilities. "The councils were repeatedly held with Chitto Harjo as the leader," said Starr. "These councils were continued until some of the members of Harjo's band began to commit thievery of meats and any other things. They were requested by officials to cease these acts but when they didn't stop, the officials with other interested people took steps to stop them."[23]

On Saturday, March 27, 1909, a new posse of twenty-one deputies led by A. Y. Patty and Bill Ransome headed for Hickory Ground. The intention was to order the Snakes to disperse once and for all, and to arrest those who refused. The lawmen expected a gun battle, but to their disbelief no one was at Hickory Ground. The Snakes had decided to desert rather than fight. Searching the tents, the posse found "a magic lantern, cooking utensils, and a phonograph." The posse set fire to all the tents and any buildings in sight. In the blackened scene, the only thing standing was a stone chimney here and there, and an American flag.[24] The Snakes flew the American flag because the Mvskokes had signed nearly twenty treaties with the United States. The Treaty of 1866 promised to protect the Mvskokes so that they could start their own autonomous government. This guarantee was also an article of the Cusseta Treaty of 1832.

In late March 1909, the morning front page of the *Shawnee Daily Herald* incorrectly reported, "Word has come from here that the troops effected the capture of Crazy Snake, the chief of the turbulent Creeks, and that he is held a prisoner on the Johnson farm, eighteen miles of Checotah." The erroneous article added, "With this same news comes the report that the chief sustained a wound in the head from a bullet in the fight of Saturday night, and that he is in serious condition."[25]

Reportedly one law officer returned to search the charred remains at Hickory Ground, but some freedmen appeared and stopped him from doing anything. The next morning, a posse that was large enough to take control arrived and arrested about forty freedmen, one half Indian, and a white man.[26] An additional seventy-five local volunteers arrived, creating a show of overwhelming force and thus preventing a gun battle.

A Mvskoke, Lee Hawkins, recalled, "I believe it was early the next morning when these white men came back. No one knows exactly how many of the Chitto Harjo followers were killed but they captured many and took them to Eufaula to jail. My uncle was there and he said the jail was full. They were kept in jail for quite a while, then turned loose. My uncle was sixty-seven years old and it was his first time in jail. He said the jail was the lousiest place he had ever seen and he had a job of getting rid of the lice."[27]

Discouraged about not finding Chitto Harjo at Hickory Ground, six lawmen were appointed by Doc Odom to go to Harjo's house. These intrepid men included Lee Bateman of Checotah, Marshal Edward Baum of Checotah, Deputy Herman Odom, the twenty-two-year-old son of Sheriff Odom, Marshal Bill Carr from Checotah, the famed man hunter Deputy William Frank Jones, and Frank Swift, a friend of Jones. Sheriff Odom had issued a warrant for Chitto Harjo on the charge of inciting a riot.[28]

Chitto Harjo's house faced east, compelling the lawmen to approach from the south, following a ravine to keep from being seen. The sun hung low behind the hills to the west. At a distance the hidden lawmen saw two Indians with Winchesters running from an old shack toward Harjo's house. The posse yelled at them to halt, but the two kept running. Charlie Coker, an Afro-Semvnole, was shot and fell to the ground, and Sa-Pa-Ye, a Mvskoke medicine maker, surrendered. While the lawmen chained the medicine maker to a tree, Coker escaped; the posse had assumed he had been shot to death when he fell, but in fact he had only a slight wound. From nowhere, a third Indian emerged to help Coker warn Chitto Harjo.

While Frank Swift stayed to guard the chained prisoner, Baum and young Odom led the rest of the lawmen along the edge of some trees; and they had to risk crossing a barbed wire fence to reach a position in front of the cabin. Smoke filled the air from brush being burned across the ravine. At a distance, the lawmen could see several saddles on the porch of the house and some horses tied nearby. At once several Indians ran from the cabin toward the woods. Baum yelled at them to halt and he stood up to fire a couple of warning shots over their heads, but they did not stop. Nearby, north of the cabin, a marksman waited in hiding. He shot Baum. Young Odom hurried to help Baum, but as soon as he moved, the marksman shot and killed the young lawman. The rest of the lawmen opened fire on the Indians in the woods, shooting randomly because one of theirs had been killed. The sun was setting in its sacred way of light giving way to darkness. The three remaining lawmen counted the remaining ammunition in their hands: only three cartridges among them. For a moment they thought one cartridge for each of them, if the Snakes attacked and took them prisoner. The worried men realized if they waited until nightfall, they would be surrounded by the Indians and killed. They decided to return to Swift and his prisoner chained to the tree; they left the two bodies of their friends. The humbled posse rode to the one-store town of Pierce, which had the only telephone for miles around. Swift cranked the phone to call Sheriff Odom in Checotah and half hoped he would not answer. Swift sighed while the phone rang, knowing he had to tell Odom the bad news that his son had been killed by the Snakes.[29]

In Checotah by happenstance some deputies had captured the young son of Chitto Harjo, Thomas, who had gone to school and spoke English.[30] Thomas was about eighteen or nineteen years old at the time. The Mvskoke cursed the deputies "vehemently, and refused to tell them anything about his [father's] where abouts." Deputy Frank Jones brought out a heavy rope, exclaiming, "Maybe this will help you." The deputies tied the rope around young Harjo's neck and proceeded to hang him. Deputy Jones yelled, "Tell us where your father is, or you'll hang there till you die." The boy struggled but refused. Seconds before death and choking for breath, the boy, who could hardly talk, finally said: "Let me down and I will tell you all you want to know." While holding his throat he uttered: "My father is with the Indians. He was with them in the house last night, and he left the house with them after the battle. It was Charles Coker, the Seminole, and I who shadowed the officers as they approached our home yesterday evening. Coker covered their path before they reached the house, and as the officers followed he turned and fired. He is an expert shot, and was fully 300 yards distance when he made the targets of the bodies of the officers."[31]

Why was the son of Chitto Harjo in Checotah? Was he buying guns? Ammunition or supplies? Trying to collect information to help the Snakes? Or was it just happenstance? After getting the information they wanted from young Harjo, the authorities surprisingly let him go free. Oscar V. Watson, a young settler at the time, told his version of the incident. Watson said, "There were a number of Freedman Negroes and only one Creek Indian in the Hickory Ground Camp at the time of the battle, which lasted but one hour."[32] Oscar Watson described how "the Indians gathered on the Ground in a large number, and a negro man dressed in [a] soldier's clothing advised the people that he was working to move out, that there would be trouble." Watson surmised, "Most all of the people of that district went to Henryetta. Finally the Indians all returned to their homes. The negroes stayed on, they were a trifling bunch. As they didn't have any work to do, they had to take anything they could get to eat." They had no choice. Watson said, "They entered people's homes and took food stuff to eat, and killed the farms' calves."[33]

Oscar Watson continued, "We, the citizens and the Deputy Sheriff, stayed all night at the Salem Store. The next day just after daylight, we entered the camp on the south side, down Wolf Creek. Dr. [John Henderson] Perkins, a Henryetta Doctor, led our squad. There were a number of shots fired by both sides but it's a mistake when they say how many negroes were killed." Watson was there, and he explained, "I know of one that was killed by Cope and his son away from camp, the negro who had a little store held out his white flag and advised us that his people had had enough. He was asked to come to us and he did so." Watson admitted, "We used him to run the camps or tents where the negroes lived. We captured several guns and rounded them all up."[34] "One of them made the remark, 'What do you expect to do with us?' And Mr. W. M. Morey advised him, 'We will hang every damn one of you to a limb.' But this was not done. All of them were taken to jail and held there for a time and did not return to the camp anymore." "Mr. Timothy Fowler was the only one of the white men that suffered a wound," said Watson, "he got his eye shot out by one of the negroes that was in camp."[35]

Doc Odom wanted revenge and telegrammed the Oklahoma governor, Charles Haskell, in the late hours of March 27, requesting state troops to suppress the Snakes. Odom claimed sixty-five armed Negroes had killed three deputies, and he blamed Chitto Harjo. In response, Haskell instructed Roy Hoffman to lead five companies of the newly organized National Guard to suppress the Indians. With Hoffman rode Fred Cook, the Mvskoke Indian agent; surprisingly Crazy Snake's own son, Legus Jones (perhaps acting as a spy for his father), and Thomas Tiger as interpreters; plus Fred Barde, the noted Oklahoman who wrote for the *Kansas City Star*.[36] Very early on Sunday, March 28, 1909, Governor Haskell ordered the requested five companies of the Oklahoma National Guard to the Hickory Ground area in a manhunt for Crazy Snake and anyone helping him.

Hoffman later recalled, "I was awakened one morning about 1 o'clock by the receipt of a telegraphic message from Governor Haskell announcing the substance that the son of Sheriff Odom of McIntosh County and two other deputies had been killed in a pitched fight between deputies and Crazy Snake." According to Hoffman the Snakes had retreated and Sheriff Odom ordered for Harjo's cabin to be set on fire. Hoffman arranged for special trains from Muskogee and Oklahoma to transport 125 men to go to Henryetta, the closest railroad point to the fighting. "There we detrained and marched out for Hickory camp ground, which had been the old stomp dance and pow wow ground of the Crazy Snake band of Indians." Hoffman's men camped at the ground that night. He said, "I heard rumors of several [men] having been killed here, but could confirm nothing except that I found one white man in an Indian hut about a mile away suffering from a gunshot wound in the arm, and I found one newly made grave, in which they informed me a Creek negro, killed during the fight, had been buried." Search parties scouted in every direction, but found no Indians or freedmen. "The parties [of possible suspects] arrested were all promptly turned over to the authorities either of McIntosh, Muskogee or Okmulgee counties." Hoffman found the burned home of Chitto Harjo or what was left of it. "From the wife and daughter of Snake, we learned, through interpreters that he had been shot in the fight and had gone off south with some members of his tribe." Hoffman and his men followed a trail for about twenty miles to the North Fork of the Canadian River. They met a Mvskoke woman who admitted that she had fed breakfast to Chitto Harjo and his friends, who included Pin Harjo, a dwarf who was a known killer of at least twenty men. With the trail going cold, authorities indicted Chitto Harjo "for murder in McIntosh county, but he had never been taken into custody" for this charge.[37]

Chitto Harjo was never seen again in the Mvskoke Nation. After he and his companions fled, lawmen seized about two thousand pounds of smoked meat from Harjo's smokehouse, then burned it down. Most likely Harjo's wife and children escaped to Polly Davis's house nearby. Sonny Jackson, a Mvskoke elder, said, "Crazy Snake, who was a medicine man and who believed in his medicine, depended on his medicine; they fought bravely and were winning the battle when Crazy Snake was shot down." In detail, Jackson explained, "When he was shot down, his friend came to where he had fallen, started to carry him from the battle but the enemy came on trying to reach him before he was carried to safety as they wanted him alive;

"SNAKE WAR"

but they had no luck for the Indian, standing over his fallen master, shot down four men who were quite a distance away. He was known to be a good shot with a gun, so unmolested he carried his chief away from the battle." Jackson added, "Seeing the fallen leader the others gave up; some escaped as did Crazy Snake and about thirteen or fourteen of Snake's men were arrested and taken to Muskogee for trial."[38]

Polly Jones Davis was Chitto Harjo's older sister and lived close to his farmhouse. She was at home when the attack occurred. She said, "I was at home, which was a short distance from the home of Chitto Harjo when a posse of white people approached his home and opened fire at the house or at any one they could see. There were three negroes and Charley Coker, a full-blood [Semvnole]," at her brother's cabin when the posse approached with their guns raised. Polly Davis said, "The three negroes immediately ran away and had it not been for Charley Coker remaining at the house with Chitto Harjo and aiding in his defense of the home, there is no doubt but that they would have killed Chitto Harjo."[39]

A white settler who lived during these years said, "Frank Harris, a white man, who lived close to the Ryal school, confessed to me that he stole the meat that caused all that trouble."[40] Lee Hawkins said the same thing, that "I have heard that a white man who lived close to the camp later confessed he had stolen the meat, but he didn't say anything about it then."[41] Polly Jones surmised, "The cause of the battle was a personal enmity which some white people held toward my brother. They circulated a false report to the effect that some of their smoke houses in the community had been robbed of meat and accused Chitto Harjo and his friends of doing it." The sister reiterated, "Of course, such reports were resented by him and his friends. Chitto was convinced that the posse that approached his home that day did not come for the purpose of arresting him but to murder him in cold blood and his actions were only in self-defense."[42]

"SNAKE WAR"

Leo Pinehill, a Snake, recalled, "It was during the shooting that Harjo was wounded in the hip. I wanted to help the man I knew, and I did finally get him to a horse and help him mount while I found my horse. We managed to ride away from the scene of the shooting before there was any capture."[43] Unsure of what to do, Pinehill said, "I didn't know where to take him but we just rode on until we reached the Choctaw country. In the time we traveled, we had to stop along the way and doctor the wound and we sometimes stopped at some friendly Indian home where we stayed until the wound seemed to be getting better." The small group had to keep moving. Pinehill explained, "I could have hastened the healing of the wound if we had stopped in one place long enough but we were anxious to make further progress as we would go on. We were stopping one place when I knew that we could go no farther as the wound seemed to be getting bad and, even though I tried in every way I knew, Chitto Harjo died." The end of Pinehill's statement is not true because there is overwhelming evidence that Harjo died at Daniel Bob's place much later.[44] This was one version of what happened, and there were others.

Chitto Harjo and his friends managed to escape with their lives from Sheriff Doc Odom and his posse who desperately wanted to capture them and kill the leader of the Snakes. The small Snake group was in bad shape, but it disappeared into the night. No one really knew the whereabouts of Crazy Snake, and his absence mystified local authorities. Wild rumors spread about where he might be, even a legend that he lived on in Mexico. "All of his followers think that he drifted to old Mexico and died there," recalled one freedman, and another insisted that "Crazy Snake or Chitto Harjo, who did not die when he was shot down, recovered and escaped to Mexico and has never been apprehended. It is said that he is still alive although he has become an old man."[45]

"SNAKE WAR"

The Last Handshake

Chitto Harjo never fully healed from his gunshot wound. The leader of the Crazy Snake movement died during mid-morning on April 11, 1911, in the rural Kiamichi Mountains.[46] Daniel Bob made sure that Crazy Snake was buried according to Mvskoke tradition. Everyone at the graveside took a fistful of earth and one at a time dropped it into the grave while they told Chitto Harjo that they would see him later. There is no word for "goodbye" in the Mvskoke language. This tradition is called the "last handshake." In preparation, Daniel Bob and others built a spirit house, which they placed over the grave, facing East. According to custom, a medicine maker and Daniel Bob made a small fire at the head of the spirit house like a beacon for the spirit to return from visiting individuals for four days and nights. As the fourth day ended with the twilight ushering in night, the medicine maker blew an antler horn four times to announce that Chitto Harjo had begun his journey sun-wise across the sky to the West. When the door opened between light and dark at dusk, he embarked along the Milky Way to the Other Side to join the spirits.[47]

No one was sure about what happened to Chitto Harjo until much later. The newspapers and local rumor, including critics of Native traditionalism and those who knew nothing about Indians, held to their racist views. The majority of *este-hvtkes* cast Harjo as a troublemaker and even went as far as labeling him a murderer of whites.

Rumors of a savage killer on the loose fed the imaginations of gullible ticket buyers who went to see the Buffalo Bill Cody copycat shows, for example, the Signal Corps Cowboys at Bedford Riding Academy in 1909, where one of the three performances portrayed Crazy Snake and his band of "savages." White riders pretending to be Snakes waved make-believe scalps above their heads and cowboys came to the rescue.[48] In another version, an after-dinner club presented a "'Mellow Drammer' in All Its Gory Hideousness." It was described as "Crazy Snake, Shot-in-the-pants, and their band of Creeks, negroes, Highbinders and squawomen [*sic*] met their finish yesterday. They were rounded up and their capture and last agonies made a fine entertainment for the members of the Club at their weekly lunch at the Iroquois [restaurant]."[49] Racism became a daily part of the tense interactions among Indians, whites, African Americans, and mixed-bloods.

REDBIRD SMITH'S GRANDSON
CROSSLIN FIELDS SMITH

My grandfather, Redbird [Smith], used to talk about the Keetoowah faith as one that is larger than anything that you can imagine. A faith that is for all mankind. One that is used to render services to others; to uplift life. This means you can't have any prejudice. All the negative feelings have got to go, all the hate and false pride. You have to get to the core of life. It takes intellect to be able to broaden that to a worldwide, or even universal level. It's that big. The idea that we are just little specks way down here that gives you humbleness. So, the basis of this healing is humbleness. It is an internal development, and no one can teach you except the Spirit, if you know how to commune with it.[1]

7

Legacy

Spirits are all around us, day and night. We need to simply acknowledge them and respect them. You might hear an unusual sound, or your name being called in the wind. To not believe in spirits and ghosts is not being Mvskoke. This is why when you finish dinner in the evening, leave a tiny amount of food outside in the same place or even pour a little bit of what you were drinking on the ground. This is to let the spirits know you have not forgotten them, and they will leave you alone.

Hvmmaketv (that's what they used to say)

Chitto Harjo's legacy carried on. The Snakes continued to have their meetings, under the leadership of Nocus Fixico, and some were certain that they were making future plans "as they still want to be free citizens and live as they did in the early days of the Indian Territory."[1] The years from Oklahoma statehood to the beginning of the Great War were not peaceful ones. The drafting of roughly sixty Mvskoke young men for service in the Great War provoked enough opposition to require the Henryetta Home Guards to be called into action.[2] Roughly one hundred civilians accompanied the home guard to suppress protests led mostly by white and Black tenant farmers and socialists in the Green Corn Rebellion in August 1917.[3] Two months later, on October 5, Eufaula Harjo wrote the secretary of war,

LEGACY

Newton D. Baker, on behalf of the Four Mothers Society, reminding him that the U.S. made the Cusseta Treaty with the Mvskokes and that he had the authority to recognize their legal rights. Harjo wrote, "We stand by the treaty of 1832, say as long as grass grew, water run and sun rises."[4]

The sudden death of Redbird Smith in 1918 did not end the spiritual power of the Keetoowahs. Smith was a Keetoowah Cherokee medicine maker who, like Chitto Harjo, opposed tribal land allotment. He was the most outspoken traditionalist of the Cherokees. Close relatives and friends buried Smith according to the death ceremony of the Nighthawk Keetoowahs. On the morning of the funeral a large white crane flew from the East and spent the entire day at the stomp ground. The crane flew to the graveyard, landed in a tree, and cried out. After the funeral, the white crane sat until sunset then flew to the West.[5] With the death of their leader, many Keetoowahs joined the Four Mothers and held membership in both groups.

On June 14, 1922, the Four Mothers Society wrote to President Warren Harding: "We, the four civilized nations of Indians of the State of Oklahoma, formerly Indian Territory, do hereby present to you our complaint, as follows: . . . Thru this complaint, we the full blooded Indians are asking that you recover all of our treaty rights. We make our complaints on recorded facts."[6] Harding had campaigned in 1920 with the slogan "Return to Normalcy," delivered during a speech in Boston on May 19, but he did not respond to the Four Mothers Society's request, to their desire to return to the normalcy of traditionalism. Instead, the allotment process continued: that same year 246 allotments were assigned on reservations in Arizona, California, Minnesota, Montana, Nevada, Oregon, South Dakota, Washington, and Wisconsin.[7]

LEGACY

The Snake faction continued to meet until as late as 1930, and the Four Mothers Society carried on.[8] Many Mvskoke traditionalists, like my relatives, continued the old ways. The Indian Reorganization Act (IRA) of 1934 was one of the most significant legislative measures to affect American Indians, but it initially excluded Indians in Oklahoma. The new law called for the restoration of tribal governments, preservation of Indian arts and crafts, and federal programs to improve reservation conditions for American Indian livelihood.[9] The IRA of 1934 ended the allotment policy as implemented by the General Allotment Act of 1887, though the Alaska Native Allotment Act of 1906 continued to allot Alaska Natives until the 1906 law was repealed by the Alaska Native Claims Settlement Act of 1971.[10]

In 1936 Congress enacted the Alaska Native Reorganization Act and Oklahoma Indian Welfare Act (OIWA). These two measures had essentially the same provisions as in the IRA. The OIWA provided for restructuring tribal governments, funding for economic development, loans for land purchases, and tribal options for participating or not in the New Deal programs to reorganize tribal governments in exchange for funding assistance. The act also permitted tribal towns and communities to form cooperative associations.[11] Originally the Oklahoma tribes, with a population of 140,000, had been excluded from the IRA because of their progress in assimilating. Senator Elmer Thomas reported, "The Oklahoma Indians having made progress beyond the reservation plan, it was thought best not to encourage a return to the reservation." Federal officials believed Oklahoma tribes like the Mvskokes had little need of services compared to tribes farther west.

The traditional towns or stomp grounds shifted or changed as some were more active than others, but all together there were forty-four Mvskoke *tvlofvs*.[12] A Mvskoke elder, Nafa Butcher, recalled that "Okfuske, Nuyaka, and Arbeka desired to be their own towns with their own separate busk grounds. In fact, Nuyaka had been well organized and was considered to be a strong *tvlofv* because of its many people. Some people from there left to organize Okfuskee, and started their town under Bunner Hicks as the town chief or *mēkko* and Sparney Harjo was the town medicine man."[13]

Of the Mvskoke *tvlofvs* interested in reorganizing under the OIWA, only three followed through: Thlopthlocco, Alabama-Quassarte, and Kialegee. Later in the year, the Keetoowah Society, Inc., divided, and one of the two parties became the United Keetoowah Band of Cherokee Indians. Differences were resolved and the two parties merged and became federally recognized in 1950, based on the Oklahoma Indian Welfare Act of 1936.[14]

Although the remaining towns wanted the credit unions offered under the Indian New Deal, they refused to have county lines separating their towns, fearing that new boundaries would group together unfriendly members of the different towns. In 1944 the Mvskokes held a convention and adopted a new constitution and bylaws. Under this new governing document, the executive and legislative branches of the government were combined into the Creek Indian Council.[15]

Following the Depression, Tom Christie served as the leader of the Keetoowahs in northeast Oklahoma. Keetoowah elder Calvin Naked Head recalled:

> They wanted the government go out and buy them a piece of land, where they could all move into, the whole 400, 500 how many they had. To move on that place there and as the government promised them all years ago, "You shall be provided for, as long as the river flows and the grass grow." They wanted the government to keep that promise yet. And be fed by the government you'll never be in

LEGACY

want. Because we're moving you away from your own grounds in North Carolina. Back to what is now Oklahoma. . . . Now that was their understanding as it has been handed down.[16]

The Keetoowahs felt ignored by the government, and they ignored the government.

The Inter-Tribal Council of the Five Civilized Tribes reemerged in 1949. Not to be confused with the traditionalist Four Mothers Society, the inter-tribal council consisted of the leaders of the Five Civilized Tribes who started to hold quarterly meetings about political issues held in common. But despite efforts at unity the old curse of *etekvlkē* returned in 1950, when Chief John Davis refused to recognize the newly created Creek Indian Council, claiming it was not elected according to tradition. Taking matters into his own hands, he appointed the *mēkkvke* of the *tvlofv* to be the new council. He also changed the procedure by which the *tvlofvs* elected their chief.[17] For the next two decades, the Bureau of Indian Affairs appointed the chiefs of the Mvskokes, Semvnoles, Cherokees, Choctaws, and Chickasaws.

Such federal paternalism compelled traditionalists of the Cherokees and Mvskokes to come together. In late November 1954, six Cherokees and twenty-six Mvskokes of the Four Mothers Society met with officials of the Bureau of Indian Affairs (BIA) in Muskogee, citing five issues of concern: "continued tax exemption of Indian lands. Retention of old 'stomp grounds.' Continued Indian customs and patterns of living. Reservations not wanted; the land could be called 'public domain.' Restoration of the provisions of the 1832 Treaty with the Creeks."[18]

A year later BIA area director Paul L. Fickinger and his administrative assistant, Marie L. Hayes, once again met with members of the Four Mothers Society. "The Four Mothers opposed in every way

163

possible the dissolution of tribal government and the allotting of land; they want public domain set aside for their exclusive use in order that the landless children born may have homes and the lands on which to make a living." Fickinger felt the Four Mothers Society members were "unprogressive and retarded" and was frustrated that "it will take tedious and repetitious discussions and meetings to assist them toward their absorption into the life of the community and State."[19] Meanwhile, Utah senator Arthur Watkins led Congress to approve House Concurrent Resolution 108 to dissolve federal trust relations with tribes, bands, and communities on a case-by-case basis.[20]

The termination policy of the 1950s, which resulted in 109 cases of termination of trust, proved difficult across Indian Country. But federal-Indian relations improved under the John F. Kennedy administration, and the administration of Lyndon Johnson continued to favor Native people. In the late 1960s the traditionalists of the turn of the century were still remembered and celebrated. Locally an elderly Cherokee, Sam Chewey, who was eighty-two years old in 1969, said the Keetoowahs celebrated Redbird Smith's birthday by holding a stomp dance at the ground named after him. The leader of the ground was Stoke Smith, the son of Redbird Smith. Chewey said, "July nineteenth, they're going to have a big stomp dance over there. They have [it] every year, you know. That's Chief Redbird Smith's birthday, you know. Yeah, Stoke Smith is getting to be quite an old man, but they sure—everybody respects him though. They look to him. Well, his daddy, Redbird Smith told him all about the stomp dance ritual and program."[21]

In 1970 Congress passed Public Law 91–495, also known as the Principal Chiefs Act. This law enabled the Five Nations to elect their own leaders.[22] For the Mvskokes of Oklahoma, an election was held for principal chief. A lifetime resident of Okmulgee, Claude Cox, ran for the position and was elected by voting tribal members. My father knew Claude Cox very well and drove with him to communities to help campaign. My dad, who enjoyed talking to people, would greet tribal members in Mvskoke and encourage them to vote for Claude, a mixed-blood who could not speak the language. Cox was reelected in the next election and served for twenty years. Chief Cox established the modern Mvskoke government under Indian self-determination.

This was the beginning of the modern tribal government, implemented under the new federal Indian policy of 1975, that called for Indian self-determination.[23] In addition, a major court case, *Harjo v. Kleppe* in 1976, ruled that the Mvskokes had the right to self-government, thus allowing the Mvskokes to create the Creek National Legislature.[24] From the Cox administration, the Mvskokes began to move forward in preserving their history and investing in tribal programs to help their members. Another important court case in 1988, *Muscogee (Creek) Nation v. Hodel,* ruled in favor of the Mvskokes, allowing them to establish a judiciary branch of government based on the Oklahoma Indian Welfare Act of 1946. This law amended the Curtis Act of 1898.[25] The Mvskokes reestablished a tribal court system and in the following years reintroduced the Lighthorse police.

Following the federal policy of self-determination, the revised constitution of 1979 differed from the one in 1867. It installed a national council to replace the House of Kings and House of Warriors. In addition, the principal chief formed a third of the modern government, with the remaining third being a justice system of a six-member supreme court appointed by the principal chief.[26]

In 1992 the Mvskoke Nation completed a renovation of the Council House located on Sixth Street in downtown Okmulgee, Oklahoma. On May 29, 1993, on an unusually warm day, I had the honor of speaking at the Council House rededication. The outdoor audience included a handful of original allottees, now in their late years, standing in the shade of an enormous elm tree in the back of the Council House. When it was my turn to speak from the back porch roof, I talked about Chitto Harjo and described the devastating impact of the Dawes Act on our Mvskoke people. The original allottees nodded their heads in agreement. I mentioned that my Semvnole grandfather, Jonas Fixico, had received allotment No. 945, and my dad, John Fixico, nodded in agreement as he rested in his lawn chair in the shade of the great elm. It was a somber but calm afternoon being on the hallowed capital ground where Crazy Snake, Eufaula Harjo, and many other Mvskokes had walked and voiced their concerns about allotment.[27]

On December 18, 2010, the last original Mvskoke allottee, No. 2035, Martha Berryhill, passed away at the age of 110. She had lived in Okmulgee all her life.[28] Martha lived a Christian life, although she knew of the Medicine Way of her people. Many Mvskokes chose the Christian way over the Medicine Way of traditionalism: by the end of the twentieth century, sixty to sixty-five Native churches dotted the Muscogee landscape, including the oldest ones: Believers Baptist, Davis Chapel, Deep Fork Hillibi, New Joy Baptist, Tuskegee Baptist, and Weogufkee Baptist. Other churches included Bemo Baptist, Belvin Baptist, Butler Baptist, and Grave Creek Baptist. Additional oldest churches consisted of Hickory Ground No. 1, Hickory Ground No. 2, Little Cussetah, Little Quarsarty, Many Springs, Randall Baptist, Snake Creek, and Concharty.[29] Other Mvskokes felt pulled between the old and the new ways. David Proctor, the *mēkko* of Tulahassee Wvkokaye ceremonial ground, said that as a young person he "was always interested in it because you could hear it from where we lived." His aunts and cousins talked about going to the stomp grounds and dancing. Proctor was going to follow in his father's footsteps and become a minister, and so, he

LEGACY

said, "I always wanted to go but I never had the opportunity." But his father opened up his mother's old camp at Tallahassee and he has been going ever since. Proctor said, "I guess you can say it's just in your blood. You want to follow in the footsteps of your elders."[30]

The reconciliation between traditionalists and churchgoing Indians that was developing in the late twentieth century was the calm before a storm. In 2004 the Poarch Band of Creeks in Wetumka, Alabama, wanted to build a casino over the graves of tribal members belonging to the original Hickory Ground. The Muscogee Nation of Oklahoma disagreed and wanted to negotiate with the Poarch Band to stop the construction out of respect to the ancestors buried there. The Poarch Band had three tribal casinos already operating. The Mvskoke National Council passed a law protecting Hickory Ground as a site of cultural and historical significance and allocating funds to protect it and "cause commercial and gaming activity to cease."[31] The Poarch Band began to remove human remains and funerary objects from the original Hickory Ground, and in 2013 it held a grand opening for the Wind Creek Casino and Resort in Wetumpka. The Muscogee Nation filed a lawsuit claiming the Poarch Band of Creeks and the U.S. government "violated federal laws including the Native American Graves Protection and Reparation Act, the National Historic Preservation Act, the Religious Freedom Restoration Act and the Indian Reorganization Act." George Thompson, *mēkko* of Hickory Ground, said, "No amount of money is worth betraying our faith and disrespecting our ancestors. That land is sacred ground and it needs to be returned to its sacred condition."[32] Mēkko Thompson could not believe the graves of some of the oldest Mvskokes were going to be plowed up for the sake of greed. No doubt *Botha* was among the Poarch Band. On March 15, 2021, Judge Myron H. Thompson of U.S. district court dismissed the lawsuit filed by the Muscogee Creeks of Oklahoma against the Poarch Band.[33]

LEGACY

In 2019 the Muscogee Nation passed a law to create an ambassador's position to represent the tribe in Washington, D.C., on a permanent basis. In the legislation, Chitto Harjo was described as an example of dignified representation for the Mvskoke people. "The requirements for the position include being a Muscogee (Creek) citizen, possess no felonies, and to be of high, public regarding and moral standing." The position started on January 19, 2019.[34]

The Muscogee Nation appointed Jonodev Osceola Chaudhuri as its official ambassador to the U.S. Congress. Chaudhuri is the son of Joyotpaul Chaudhuri and the late Jean Hill Chaudhuri, a full-blood Mvskoke born on her father's allotment in Okfuskee County, Oklahoma. In his Broken Promises Report on November 19, 2019, he reminded the Subcommittee on Indigenous Peoples in an oversight hearing that "the Muscogee (Creek) Nation Reservation that exists today was created in a treaty my Nation signed with the United States in 1866, stating that our lands in what is today Oklahoma would be 'forever set apart as a home for said Creek Nation,'" as guaranteed in the Treaty of 1866.[35] This was a part of the cycle of life and rebuilding in the *Poyvfekcv* "Spirit" way. Rebuilding included renewed interest.

As of this writing, there are 191,000 enrolled Mvskoke tribal members living in and outside of Oklahoma. There are about sixteen active stomp grounds and eighty-one Mvskoke churches scattered throughout the Mvskoke Nation.[36] The tribe continues to be economically self-sustaining on its reservation. In the twenty-first century, the Mvskokes are a hybrid of what they once were, although this is reality to even the remaining traditionalists. In the twenty-first century *Poyvekcv yekcetv Emeyoksicetv seko* remains embedded in the people who continue the Medicine Way.

Chitto Harjo believed in a cause. He was a kindred spirit of Native patriots like Pontiac, Black Hawk, Tecumseh, and Wovoka,

LEGACY

who led movements to defend the best interests of their people against the United States. They sought to preserve the Medicine Way of their people that began with the origins of their tribal communities dating back centuries.

Some progressive Mvskokes praised Chitto Harjo because they understood what he was trying to do, but they also criticized him for being unrealistic. George Looney said, "He was quite a prominent man who wanted things to stay as they had been in the past. He didn't understand it [allotment] would be a benefit to his people, who would have their own business[es] to transact, didn't observe deep enough but just saw the bright side he had been accustomed to."[37]

The tensions between traditionalism and progressivism continued for the rest of the twentieth century and persist into the twenty-first. During a mid-July day in 2021 my wife Michelle and I drove along I-40 searching for Tiger Mountain and Hickory Ground where Chitto Harjo had held many of his meetings. Tiger Mountain Road exit trails north into a small mountain area packed with so many trees that you can hardly see anything that might have been there during the Crazy Snake years. We had better luck finding a rural church where we saw a man cleaning the graveyard. We stopped, got out of our small rental car, and I greeted him in Mvskoke. He responded and we shook hands. He was Deacon Wendell Wayne Harjo of Hickory Ground No. 1 Church. We spent the good part of an hour in a wonderful conversation talking about our relatives, Mvskoke history, and what the deacon knew about Chitto Harjo. With the good deacon's permission my talented wife went about taking photographs of the church, camp houses, and other interesting things. I had hoped Deacon Harjo might be related to Crazy Snake, but Harjo or Fixico among the Mvskokes and Semvnoles is like Smith or Jones. The good deacon was certain that he was not related to Chitto Harjo. As we swapped stories and tales, the deacon said the area around the church

169

was haunted and not a good place to be at night because of the mosquitos and ticks, but also because of other things more spiritual than human.

This deep spiritualism of *Poyvfekcv* is the metaphysical energy of *Epohfvnkv,* the old Medicine Way of the Mvskokes. The Spirit Power remained within the Hickory Ground; you could feel it. The same everlasting feeling rested in Hickory Ground Stomp Ground, which Michelle and I visited the following summer. We paid our respect to Hickory Ground, the *tvlofv* where Chitto Harjo spoke passionately and patriotically to Msvkokes and other traditionalists about embracing the Medicine Way of *Poyvfekcv.* I left respectfully remembering that I had danced at Hickory Ground as a young *cēpvnē.*

Notes

Preface

1. Walter Pierce Interview by Grace Kelley, March 15, 1938, Interview 13241, 392–393, Henryetta, Oklahoma, Indian-Pioneer Papers, Western History Collections, University of Oklahoma, Norman (henceforth Indian-Pioneer Papers); Agnes Kelley Interview by Grace Kelley, August 19, 1937, Okmulgee, Oklahoma, Second Interview 7229, 149, Indian-Pioneer Papers; Charley Snakeys Interview by Jefferson Berryhill, June 17, 1937, Interview 6492, 376, Okmulgee, Oklahoma, Indian-Pioneer Papers.

2. Sarah Deer and Cecilia Knapp, "Muscogee Constitutional Jurisprudence: Vhakv Em Pvtakv (The Carpet under the Law)," *Tulsa Law Review* 49, no. 125 (2013), 137–138. The Mvskoke Confederacy has been referred to as a loose association of towns and a war league developing in the mid-1700s to about 1763, Steven C. Hahn, *The Invention of the Creek Nation, 1670–1763* (Lincoln: University of Nebraska Press, 2004), 5–8.

3. Robbie Ethridge, *Creek Country: The Creek Indians and Their World* (Chapel Hill: University of North Carolina Press, 2003), 22–31.

4. March Monday Interview by Jerome M. Emmons, July 9, 1937, Interview 6592, 83, Morris, Oklahoma, Indian-Pioneer Papers, and Chelsie Rich, "Citizen Makes First Set of Turtle Shell Shakers," *Muscogee Nation News,* September 1, 2014, vol. 44, issue 17, 6, Okmulgee, Oklahoma.

5. J. Leitch Wright Jr., *Creek and Seminoles: Destruction and Regeneration of the Muscogulge People* (Lincoln: University of Nebraska Press, 1986), 6.

6. Siah Hicks Interview by Billie Byrd, November 17, 1937, Interview 12167, 180, Mason, Oklahoma, Indian-Pioneer Papers.

7. Jean Chaudhuri and Joyotpaul Chaudhuri, *A Sacred Path: The Way of the Muscogee Creeks* (Los Angeles: UCLA American Indian Studies Center, 2001), 8, 53, and 75; and Donald L. Fixico, "From the Seventh Direction: Writing Indian History from the Heart," *Journal of the West* 49, no. 4 (Fall 2010), 45.

NOTES TO PAGES xxii–4

8. Jerry H. Gill, *Native American Worldviews: An Introduction* (New York: Humanity Books, 2002), 137.

9. Donald L. Fixico, *The American Indian Mind in a Linear World: American Indian Studies and Traditional Knowledge* (New York: Routledge, 2003), 175–176.

10. "Jonas Fixico," *Daily Oklahoman*, August 26, 1958.

11. James H. Howard in collaboration with Willie Lena, *Oklahoma Seminoles, Medicine, Magic and Religion* (Norman: University of Oklahoma Press, 1990), 107.

12. Ted Isham, "Este Mvskokevlke Today," *Muscogee Nation News*, October 2006, vol. 36, issue 10, section C, 2, Okmulgee, Oklahoma.

Chitto Harjo's Testimony

1. Statement of Mr. Wilson Jones (Indian name, Chitto Harjo; "Crazy Snake"), November 23, 1906, *Report of the Select Committee to Investigate Matters Connected with Affairs in the Indian Territory,* vol. 2 (Washington, DC: U.S. Government Printing Office, 1907), 1252.

Introduction

1. Mel H. Bolster, "The Smoked Meat Rebellion: Early Oklahoma and Creek Unrest," *Chronicles of Oklahoma* 31, no. 1 (Spring 1953), 38.

2. "Facts about Crazy Snake and His Band of Indians," *Dallas Morning News,* April 4, 1909.

3. "Chitto" means "snake" and "Harjo"—pronounced "Had-jo," (the *r* is actually a *d*)—means "brave, reckless, or crazy." Throughout the book, I will use Chitto Harjo and Crazy Snake interchangeably.

4. Howard, *Oklahoma Seminoles,* 124.

5. Chaudhuri and Chaudhuri, *Sacred Path,* 114.

6. J. B. Campbell, *Campbell's Abstract of Creek Freedman Census Cards and Index* (Muskogee, OK: Phoenix Job Printing Company, 1915), 168, Oklahoma Heritage Center; and Bolster, "Smoked Meat Rebellion," 39.

7. Allotment of land and homestead designations, Chitto Harjo, Roll No. 7934, Certificate No. 19045, September 4, 1903, texa0007d, creek-by-blood, Oklahoma Heritage Center, Oklahoma City.

8. Donald L. Fixico, ed., *Indian Treaties in the United States: An Encyclopedia and Documents Collection* (Santa Barbara: ABC-CLIO Press, 2018), xv.

9. Mieke Van Der Linden, *The Acquisition of Africa, 1870–1914: The Nature of International Law* (Leiden: Brill and Martinus Nijhoff, 2016), 293–300.

NOTES TO PAGES 5–8

10. "Indigenous Peoples," World Bank, last updated March 19, 2021, https://www.worldbank.org/en/topic/indigenouspeoples#1, accessed January 22, 2022.

11. Brett L. Walker, *The Conquest of Ainu Lands: Ecology and Culture in Japanese Expansion, 1590–1800* (Berkeley: University of California Press, 2003), 49–72.

12. Joanna Crow, *The Mapuche in Modern Chile: A Cultural History* (Gainesville: University Press of Florida, 2013), 31.

13. Michael King, *Whina: A Biography of Whina Cooper* (London: Hooder and Stoughton, 1983).

14. "An Impossible Dream Come True," Amnesty International, June 12, 2014, https://www.amnesty.org/en/latest/campaigns/2014/06/an-impossible-dream-come-true/, accessed March 4, 2022.

15. Tom Holm, J. Diane Pearson, and Ben Chavis, "Peoplehood: A Model for the Extension of Sovereignty in American Indian Studies," *Wicazo Sa Review* 18, no. 1 (Spring 2003), 7–24.

16. Vine Deloria Jr., *The Metaphysics of Modern Existence* (Golden, CO: Fulcrum Publishers, 2012), 2.

17. Taiaiake Alfred, *Peace, Power, Righteousness: An Indigenous Manifesto* (New York: Oxford University Press, 1999); Roxane Dunbar Ortiz, *An Indigenous Peoples' History of the United States* (New York: Beacon Press, 2014); Kevin Bruyneel, *The Third Space of Sovereignty: The Postcolonial Politics of U.S.-Indigenous Relations* (Minneapolis: University of Minnesota Press, 2007); Michael Witgen, *An Infinity of Nations: How the Native New World Shaped Early North America* (Philadelphia: University of Pennsylvania Press, 2012); and Ned Blackhawk, *The Rediscovery of America: Native Peoples and the Unmaking of U.S. History* (New Haven: Yale University Press, 2023).

18. Patrick Wolfe, "Settler Colonialism and the Elimination of the Native," *Journal of Genocide Research* 8, no. 4 (December 2006), 387–409.

19. Fixico, *Indian Treaties in the United States*, xix.

20. Paola Giuliano and Nathan Nunn, "Understanding Cultural Persistence and Change," *Review of Economics* 88, no. 4 (2021), 1543 and 1573–1578.

21. Stephanie A. Quezada, Moira P. Shaw, and Michael A. Zarate, "Cultural Inertia: The Relationship between Ethnic Identity and Reactions to Cultural Change," *Social Psychology* 43, no. 4 (2012), 245.

22. Fixico, *American Indian Mind in a Linear World*, 2, 27, and 42.

23. James Eder, *On the Road to Tribal Extinction: Depopulation, Deculturation, and Adaptive Well-Being among the Batak of the Philippines* (Berkeley: University of California Press, 1987), x.

NOTES TO PAGES 9-15

24. Henry Dobyns, "Indian Extinction in the Middle Santa Cruz River Valley," *New Mexico Historical Review* 38, no. 2 (1963), 163–181.

25. Angie Debo, *The Road to Disappearance: A History of the Creek Indians* (Norman: University of Oklahoma Press, 1941), 376. See also Richard Slotkin, *Regeneration through Violence: The Mythology of the American Frontier, 1600–1860* (Middletown, CT: Wesleyan University Press, 1973); Stuart Banner, *How the Indians Lost Their Land: Law and Power on the Frontier* (Cambridge: Belknap Press, 2007); and David E. Stannard, *American Holocaust: The Conquest of the New World* (New York: Oxford University Press, 1992).

26. Michael Overall, "The Muscogee Nation Is Dropping 'Creek' from Its Name. Here's Why," *Tulsa World*, May 5, 2021. The Papago changed their name to Tohono O'odham in 1986, the Navajo to Diné in 1993, and the Winnebago to Ho-Chunk in 1993.

27. Duane Kendall Hale, *Researching and Writing Tribal Histories* (Grand Rapids: Michigan Indian Press, 1991), 1–83.

The Importance of the East

1. Siah Hicks interview by Billie Byrd, November 17, 1937, Interview 12167, 179–180, Mason, Oklahoma, Indian-Pioneer Papers.

Chapter 1. The Medicine Way

1. Although *Hesaketvmesē* and *Epohfvnkv* are both timeless, they are not to be confused with each other. *Epohfvnkv* is limitless, containing all that is known and all that is unknown, such that there is nothing else. It has no boundaries and it includes absolutely everything, including enemies and contradictions. This inclusion is a fundamental part of the Mvskoke worldview. *Hesaketvmesē* (the Maker of Breath) is not a supreme god but is a supreme power, providing breath and wind in various forms from a whisper or a song to a raging tornado or hurricane driven by dangerous winds.

2. H. R. Antle, "The Legend of Abuska," 256.

3. Antle, "Legend of Abuska," *Chronicles of Oklahoma* 20, no. 3 (September 1942), 256.

4. Christopher Columbus Choate Interview by Don Moon Jr., March 28, 1938, Interview 10386, 9, Guthrie, Oklahoma, Indian-Pioneer Papers.

5. Donald L. Fixico, *Call for Change: The Medicine Way of American Indian History, Ethos & Reality* (Lincoln: University of Nebraska Press, 2013), 5.

NOTES TO PAGES 15-19

6. Fred Johnson Interview by Grace Kelley, January 14, 1938, Interview 12668, 236, Henryetta, Oklahoma, Indian-Pioneer Papers.

7. D. O. Gillis Interview by Effie S. Jackson, June 30, 1937, Interview 6466, 110, Tulsa, Oklahoma, Indian-Pioneer Papers.

8. Fred Johnson Interview, 236.

9. Chaudhuri and Chaudhuri, *Sacred Path,* 183.

10. Charles Hudson, *The Southeastern Indians* (Knoxville: University of Tennessee Press, 1976), 226.

11. Ada M. Roach Interview by Jerome Emmons, June 28, 1837, Schulter, Oklahoma, Second Interview 6490, 348, Indian-Pioneer Papers.

12. Rolla Canard Interview by Grace Kelley, September 14, 1937, Interview 7512, 273, Wetumka, Oklahoma, Indian-Pioneer Papers.

13. Claudio Saunt, *A New Order of Things: Property, Power, and the Transformation of the Creek Indians, 1733–1816* (Cambridge: Cambridge University Press, 1999), 14–16, and Douglas A. Hurt, "The Shaping of a Creek (Muscogee) Homeland in Indian Territory, 1828–1907" (Ph.D. diss., Department of Geography, University of Oklahoma, 2000), 38.

14. Albert S. Gatschet, *A Migration Legend of the Creek Indians,* vol. 1 (Philadelphia: D. G. Brinton, 1884), 234, and Bill Grantham, *Creation Myths and Legends of the Creek Indians* (Gainesville: University Press of Florida, 2002), 106–108.

15. Debo, *Road to Disappearance,* 15.

16. John R. Swanton, "Social Organization and Social Usages of the Indians of the Creek Confederacy," *Forty-Second Annual Report of the Bureau of American Ethnology to the Secretary of the Smithsonian Institution 1924–1925* (Washington, DC: U.S. Government Printing Office, 1928), 107–170.

17. Swanton, "Social Organization," 145.

18. Chaudhuri and Chaudhuri, *Sacred Path,* 25–27, 44.

19. For the origin of the Muscogee Creeks, see John R. Swanton, *Early History of the Creek Indians and Their Neighbors,* Bureau of American Ethnology Bulletin 73 (Washington, DC: U.S. Government Printing Office, 1922), 11–16, and John R. Swanton, "The Social History and Usages of the Creek Confederacy," *Forty-Second Annual Report of the Bureau of American Ethnology* (Washington, DC: U.S. Government Printing Office, 1928), 33–34.

20. Chaudhuri and Chaudhuri, *Sacred Path,* 76, and David Lewis Jr. and Ann T. Jordan, *Creek Indian Medicine Ways: The Enduring Power of Mvskoke Religion* (Albuquerque: University of New Mexico Press, 2002), 42–43.

NOTES TO PAGES 19-21

21. Around the mid-1700s, Mvskokes began to develop towns in the panhandle and then in present-day central Florida. The Mvskokes called the people who lived there Semvnoles, referring to those who camp at a distance. Fixico, *Call for Change*, 6–7.

22. The *tvlofv* (town community) system of more than sixty town communities divided into Upper traditional Mvskokes and Lower progressive Mvskokes to form the Mvskoke Confederacy is in Fixico, *Call for Change*, 6–7; Hurt, "Shaping of a Creek (Muscogee) Homeland," 49; Ross Hassig, "Internal Conflict in the Creek War of 1813–1814," *Ethnohistory* 21, no. 3 (Summer 1974), 265; Swanton, "Social Organization," 307; "Preliminary Sketch of Thlopthlocco Tribal Town," *Muscogee Nation News,* April 2009, vol. 39, issue 4, Okmulgee, Oklahoma; March Monday Interview by Jerome M. Emmons, July 9, 1937, Interview 6592, 77–78, Morris, Oklahoma, Indian-Pioneer Papers. The spelling of "Arbeka" is used according to its identification on the Muscogee Nation website; it is sometimes spelled "Arbeca" or "Arbecca." There was also a Little Arbeka (Abiehka) town identified by South Carolina trader Charlesworth Glover in 1725, who described Little Arbeka with 120 people as the northernmost of eight towns known collectively as Arbeka, Amos J. Wright Jr., *Historic Indian Towns of Alabama, 1540–1838* (Tuscaloosa: University of Alabama Press, 2003), 1, and Hurt, "Shaping of a Creek (Muscogee) Homeland," 49.

23. Patrick E. Moore, "Native American History Series: Muscogee Confederacy," *Muscogee Nation News,* August 2006, vol. 36, issue 8, section B, 1, Okmulgee, Oklahoma.

24. The peoplehood matrix was introduced by Robert Thomas in the 1980s and developed with Tom Holm, J. Diane Pearson, and Ben Chavis, "Peoplehood: A Model for the Extension of Sovereignty in American Indian Studies," *Wicazo Sa Review* 18, no. 1 (Spring 2003), 12.

25. Chaudhuri and Chaudhuri, *Sacred Path,* 86–88.

26. W. O. Williams Interview by Grace Kelley, April 26–27, 1937, [no interview number], 502, Henryetta, Oklahoma, Indian-Pioneer Papers.

27. Chaudhuri and Chaudhuri, *Sacred Path,* 48–49.

28. David A. Chang, *The Color of the Land: Race, Nation, and the Politics of Landownership in Oklahoma, 1832–1929* (Chapel Hill: University of North Carolina Press, 2010), 20.

29. Hurt, "Shaping of a Creek (Muscogee) Homeland," 99.

30. Howard, *Oklahoma Seminoles,* 123–156.

NOTES TO PAGES 22-25

31. Betty Fussell, *The Story of Corn: The Myth and History, the Culture and Agriculture, the Art and Science of America's Quintessential Crop* (New York: Alfred A. Knopf, 1992), 15–21.

32. Theda Perdue, ed., *Nations Remembered: An Oral History of the Five Civilized Tribes, 1865–1907* (Westport, CT: Greenwood, 1980), 54.

33. Hurt, "Shaping of a Creek (Muscogee) Homeland," 38.

34. Alexander Spoehr, "Oklahoma Seminole Towns," *Chronicles of Oklahoma* 19, no. 4 (December 1941), 378–379, and David Lewis Jr. and Ann T. Jordan, *Creek Indian Medicine Ways: The Enduring Power of Mvskoke Religion* (Albuquerque: University of New Mexico Press, 2002), xix.

35. For discussion of Muscogee Creek traditions and other members of the Five Civilized Tribes in the late nineteenth century, see Perdue, *Nations Remembered,* 87–115. For history and cultural information about the Creeks, see Angie Debo, *Road to Disappearance: A History of the Creek Indians* (Norman: University of Oklahoma Press, 1941); Michael Green, *The Politics of Indian Removal: Creek Government and Society* (Lincoln: University of Nebraska Press, 1982); J. Leitch Wright Jr., *Creeks and Seminoles, The Destruction and Regeneration of the Muscogulgee People* (Lincoln: University of Nebraska Press, 1986). For cultural information on the Seminoles of Oklahoma, refer to James H. Howard in collaboration with Willie Lena, *Oklahoma Seminoles: Medicine, Magic and Religion* (Norman: University of Oklahoma Press, 1990).

36. Hurt, "Shaping of a Creek (Muscogee) Homeland," 73.

37. Swanton, "Social Organization," 276–298; and "Notes on the Creek Indians," Bureau of American Ethnology Bulletin no. 123 (Washington, DC: U.S. Government Printing Office, 1939), 132–136, 139–141. Leitch Wright listed fox and potato clans among non-Muscogee towns, which belonged to the Creek Confederacy, see J. Leitch Wright Jr., *Creeks and Seminoles: Destruction and Regeneration of the Muscogulgee People* (Lincoln: University of Nebraska Press, 1986), 18–19.

38. Mary R. Haas, "Creek Inter-Town Relations," *American Anthropologist* 42 (1940), 479.

39. Swanton, "Social Organization," 482.

40. Chaudhuri and Chaudhuri, *Sacred Path,* 23–27.

41. More information about the cultural traditions the Five Nations is in Perdue, *Nations Remembered,* 87–115. For information about the Mvskokes, see Debo, *Road to Disappearance;* Green, *Politics of Indian Removal;* Wright, *Creeks and*

NOTES TO PAGES 25-31

Seminoles. For information about the Seminoles of Oklahoma, see Howard, *Oklahoma Seminoles.*

42. Walter Gray Interview by James Russell Gray, January 20, 1938, Interview 13865, 358, Hartshorne, Oklahoma, Indian-Pioneer Papers.

43. Sharon A. Fife, "Baptist Indian Church: Thlewarle," *Chronicles of Oklahoma* 48, no. 4 (Winter 1970–1971), 452.

44. Larkin Ryal Interview by Grace Kelley, March 10, 1937, [no interview number], 297, Henryetta, Oklahoma, Indian-Pioneer Papers.

45. Matthew 3:14, Holy Bible, King James Version (Wichita: DeVore and Sons, 1991).

46. Howard, *Oklahoma Seminoles,* 242–243.

47. Karen Shade, "From Greek to Creek: Man Publishes Mvskoke Language Bible," *Native Times,* December 12, 2011, https://www.nativetimes.com/life/people /6516-from-greek-to-creek-man-publishes-mvskoke-language-bible, accessed December 26, 2021.

48. Henry M. Teller, Secretary of the Interior, to Hiram Price, Commissioner of Indian Affairs, December 2, 1882, Executive Document, Office of Indian Affairs, Legislative and Executive Publications, Proquest Congressional, https:// congressional-proquest-com.ezproxy1.lib.asu.edu/congressional/search/basic/ba sicsearch, accessed February 16, 2022.

49. Rules Governing the Court of Indian Offenses, Department letter, Hiram Price, Commissioner of Indian Affairs, March 30, 1883, Executive Document, Office of Indian Affairs, Legislative and Executive Publications, Proquest Congressional, https://congressional-proquest-com.ezproxy1.lib.asu.edu/congressional /search/basic/basicsearch, accessed February 16, 2022.

50. Order by Commissioner of Indian Affairs John D. C. Atkins, February 2, 1887, *Annual Report of the Commissioner of Indian Affairs* (Washington, DC: U.S. Government Printing Office, 1888), 20–23.

51. Michael C. Coleman, *Presbyterian Missionary Attitudes toward American Indians, 1837–1893* (Jackson: University Press of Mississippi, 1985), 12.

52. Guy Logsdon, "Oklahoma's First Book: Istutsi in Naktsoku," *Chronicles of Oklahoma* 54, no. 2 (Summer 1976), 179.

53. Bookshelf, Muscogee (Seminole/Creek) Documentation Project, 1, http:// muskogee.blogs.wm.edu/bookshelf/, accessed December 26, 2021.

54. Mvskoke History: A Short Course for Muscogee Nation Employees, Muscogee Nation website, https://sde.ok.gov/sites/ok.gov.sde/files/Mvskoke_His tory_Powerpoint.pdf, accessed December 31, 2021.

NOTES TO PAGES 32-38

55. Claudio Saunt, "Telling Stories: The Political Uses of Myth and History in the Cherokee and Creek Nations," *Journal of American History* 93, no. 3 (December 2006), 688–689.

56. Daniel F. Littlefield Jr., *Africans and Creeks: From the Colonial Period to the Civil War* (Westport, CT: Greenwood, 1979), 142, and Debo, *Road to Disappearance,* 120.

57. Hurt, "Shaping of a Creek (Muscogee) Homeland," 95.

58. W. O. Williams Interview by Grace Kelley, April 26–27, 1937, [no interview number], 508, Henryetta, Oklahoma, Indian-Pioneer Papers.

59. Debo, *Road to Disappearance,* 120.

60. Carolyn Thomas Foreman, "August Robertson Moore: A Sketch of Her Life and Times," *Chronicles of Oklahoma* 13, no. 4 (December 1935), 399–400.

61. R. L. Nichols Interview by Maurice R. Anderson, December 22, 1937, Interview 9585, 53, Pauls Valley, Oklahoma, Indian-Pioneer Papers.

62. Chaudhuri and Chaudhuri, *Sacred Path,* 10–11.

63. Carolyn Thomas Foreman, "Two Notable Women of the Creek Nation," *Chronicles of Oklahoma* 35, no. 3 (Fall 1956), 318.

64. Mvskoke History: A Short Course for Muscogee Nation Employees, Muscogee Nation website, https://sde.ok.gov/sites/ok.gov.sde/files/Mvskoke_History_Powerpoint.pdf, accessed December 31, 2021.

65. "The Fourth at Tulsa," *Indian Chieftain,* July 8, 1888, 2, Vinita, Indian Territory.

66. Donald N. Brown, "The Ghost Dance Religion among the Oklahoma Cheyenne," *Chronicles of Oklahoma* 30, no. 4 (Winter 1952), 400.

67. Brown, "Ghost Dance Religion," 411.

A Black Preacher Punished by the Creek Lighthorse in 1845

1. E. C. Routh, "The Story of Oklahoma Baptists" (1932), 36, Baptist History homepage, http://baptisthistoryhomepage.com/ok.bapt.routh.ch4.buckner.html, accessed July 11, 2020.

Chapter 2. Moving Fire

Epigraph: Chaudhuri and Chaudhuri, *Sacred Path,* 86–88.

1. Chaudhuri and Chaudhuri, *Sacred Path,* 3.

2. Ohland Morton, "Confederate Government Relations with the Five Civilized Tribes," *Chronicles of Oklahoma* 31, no. 2 (Summer 1953), 197.

NOTES TO PAGES 39-45

3. The final battle of the Red Stick or Mvskoke War of 2,500 Red Sticks against Andrew Jackson's combined force of 15,000 occurred on March 27, 1814, at Horseshoe Bend on the Tallapoosa River in eastern Alabama Territory. Alabama became a state in 1819.

4. Ross Hassig, "Internal Conflict in the Creek War of 1813–1814," *Ethnohistory* 21, no. 3 (Summer 1974), 259–263.

5. David Williams, *Georgia Gold Rush: Twenty-Niners, Cherokees, and Gold Fever* (Columbia: University of South Carolina Press, 1993), 21–36.

6. President Andrew Jackson addressing the Creek Nation, 1829, https://www.presidency.ucsb.edu/documents/letter-the-creek-indians, accessed June 15, 2024.

7. Anthony F. C. Wallace, *The Long, Bitter Trail: Andrew Jackson and the Indians* (New York: Hill and Wang, 1993), 41–45.

8. David Crocket to Charles Shultz, December 25, 1834, Washington, DC, Davy Crocket on the removal of the Cherokees, 1834, Gilder Lehrman Collection, Gilder Lehrman Institute of American History, AP U.S. History Study Guide, https://www.gilderlehrman.org/sites/default/files/inline-pdfs/t-01162.pdf, accessed December 25, 2021.

9. Michael Cassity and Danney Goble, *Divided Hearts: The Presbyterian Journey through Oklahoma History* (Norman: University of Oklahoma Press, 2009), 11.

10. "Speech of Mr. [Theodore] Frelinghuysen of New Jersey, Delivered in the Senate of the United States, April 6, 1830, On the Bill for an Exchange of Lands with the Indians Residing in Any of the States or Territories, and for Their Removal West of the Mississippi" (Washington, DC: Office of the National Journal, 1830), 9, https://babel.hathitrust.org/cgi/pt?id=wu.89077033439&view=1up&seq=9, accessed March 8, 2021.

11. "Indian Removal Act," May 28, 1830, *U.S. Statutes at Large,* vol. 4, 411.

12. "Treaty with the Creeks, 1832," March 24, 1832, in Charles J. Kappler, comp. and ed., *Indian Affairs, 1778–1883* (New York: Interland Publishing, 1972), 341–343.

13. [no title], *New York Evening Post,* November 13, 1833, in "The Great Meteor Storm of 1833," https://www.pigeonroost.net/the-great-meteor-storm-of-1833/, accessed December 27, 2021.

14. Revelation 6:12–14, Holy Bible, King James Version (Wichita: DeVore and Sons, Inc., 1991), 1259–1260.

NOTES TO PAGES 45–49

15. Candace S. Greene and Russell Thornton, eds., *The Year the Stars Fell: Lakota Winter Counts at the Smithsonian* (Lincoln: University of Nebraska Press, 2007), viii.

16. Christopher D. Haveman, *Rivers of Sand: Creek Indian Emigration, Relocation, & Ethnic Cleansing in the American South* (Lincoln: University of Nebraska Press, 2016), 176.

17. Gloria Jahoda, *The Trail of Tears: The Story of the American Indian Removals, 1813–1855* (New York: Holt, Rinehart and Winston, 1975), 153.

18. John T. Ellisor, *The Second Creek War: Interethnic Conflict and Collusion on a Collapsing Frontier* (Lincoln: University of Nebraska Press, 2010), 140–144.

19. Jahoda, *Trail of Tears,* 154.

20. Ellisor, *Second Creek War,* 371–376.

21. Jahoda, *Trail of Tears,* 122.

22. Haveman, *Rivers of Sand,* 126 and 233.

23. Deer and Knapp, "Muscogee Constitutional Jurisprudence," 143.

24. Swanton, "Social Organization," 485.

25. Lela J. McBride, *Opothleyahola and the Loyal Muskogee: Their Flight to Kansas in the Civil War* (Jefferson, NC: McFarland, 2000), 16.

26. Simon Jackson Interview by Billie Byrd, August 31, 1937, Interview 7385, 175, Welty, Oklahoma, Indian-Pioneer Papers.

27. Mose Wiley Interview by Grace Kelley, November 22, 1937, Interview 12262, 18, Dustin, Oklahoma, Indian-Pioneer Papers.

28. Howard, *Oklahoma Seminoles,* 106.

29. The black drink is made from red root with water and called "taking medicine" during the four days of the Green Corn Dance ceremony. Opothleyahola is quoted in Debo, *Road to Disappearance,* 100–102. In this version, Opothleyahola led Kialegee, Hillibi, Assilanpi, and Fish Pond, and Tuckabatchee arrived later, "Preliminary Sketch of the Kialegee Tribal Town," *Muscogee Nation News,* August 2009, vol. 39, issue 8, section B, 2, Okmulgee, Oklahoma.

30. Haveman, *Rivers of Sand,* 182.

31. McBride, *Opothleyahola and the Loyal Muskogee,* 93.

32. John R. Swanton, "The Green Corn Dance," *Chronicles of Oklahoma* 10, no. 2 (June 1932), 172.

33. Albert S. Gatschet, *A Migration Legend of the Creek Indians: With a Linguistic, Historic and Ethnographic Introduction,* vol. 1 (Philadelphia: D. G. Brinton,

NOTES TO PAGES 49–52

1884), 234, and Bill Grantham, *Creation Myths and Legends of the Creek Indians* (Gainesville: University Press of Florida, 2002), 106–108.

34. This hymn was sung on the Trail of Suffering and is still sung in churches today. A recording can be found at Muscogee (Creek) Hymn, produced and edited by Elisa Harkins, https://vimeo.com/326497446, accessed December 25, 2021.

35. Chaudhuri and Chaudhuri, *Sacred Path*, 62.

36. Haveman, *Rivers of Sand*, 193.

37. Beth W. Heimann Collection 2008.125, box 3, Charles Hicks, Index Cards Creek, American Board of Commissioners for Foreign Missions (AFCFM), Papers of Missionaries and Teachers A–W, 1820–1860, Oklahoma History Center, Oklahoma City.

38. Daniel Starr Interview by Billie Byrd, October 18, 1937, Interview 7850, 111, Henryetta, Oklahoma, Indian-Pioneer Papers.

39. Joe Simmers Interview by Billie Byrd, November 24, 1937, Interview 12219, 169, Bearden, Oklahoma, Indian-Pioneer Papers.

40. Daniel F. Littlefield Jr., *Africans and Creeks: From the Colonial Period to the Civil War* (Westport, CT: Greenwood, 1979), 135, and Hurt, "Shaping of a Creek (Muscogee) Homeland," 93.

41. Nancy Grayson Barnett Interview by Grace Kelley, November 11, 1937, Interview 12128, 395, Bryant, Oklahoma, Indian-Pioneer Papers.

42. Kent Carter, "Snakes and Scribes: The Dawes Commission and the Enrollment of the Creeks," *Chronicles of Oklahoma* 75, no. 4 (Winter 1997–1998), 386. Andre Paul DuChateau, "Creek Nation on the Eve of the Civil War," *Chronicles of Oklahoma* 52, no. 3 (Fall 1974), 292. Littlefield, *Africans and Creeks*, 136. It has also been suggested that from the 1840s to 1867 there were about forty-five to fifty towns, Hurt, "Shaping of a Creek (Muscogee) Homeland," 90.

43. David A. Chang, *The Color of the Land: Race, Nation, and the Politics of Landownership in Oklahoma, 1832–1929* (University of North Carolina Press, 2010), 23.

44. Gary Zellar, "Occupying the Middle Ground: African Creeks in the First Indian Home Guard, 1862–1865," *Chronicles of Oklahoma* 76, no. 1 (Spring 1998), 49.

45. Haveman, *Rivers of Sand*, 89.

46. Christopher Columbus Choate Interview by Don Moon Jr., March 28, 1938, Interview 10386, 6, Guthrie, Oklahoma, Indian-Pioneer Papers.

47. LeRoy Ward Interview by Grace Kelley, October 9, 1937, Interview 7781, 201, Henryetta, Oklahoma, Indian-Pioneer Papers.

NOTES TO PAGES 53-61

48. By the end of the Civil War, the twenty-five Semvnole towns were reduced to fourteen and two of them were freedman towns. Alexander Spoehr, "Oklahoma Seminole Towns," *Chronicles of Oklahoma* 19, no. 4 (December 1941), 377.

49. See Jeffrey Ostler, *Surviving Genocide: Native Nations and the United States from the American Revolution to Bleeding Kansas* (New Haven: Yale University Press, 2019), and Claudio Saunt, *Unworthy Republic: The Dispossession of Native Americans and the Road to Indian Territory* (New York: W. W. Norton, 2020).

A White Boy's First Stomp Dance

1. Walter Gary (teenage white settler) Interview by James Russell Gray, December 18, 1937, Interview 12442, 320–230, Hartshorne, Oklahoma, Indian-Pioneer Papers.

Chapter 3. The White Man's War

Epigraph: Chaudhuri and Chaudhuri, *Sacred Path,* 69.

1. Andre Paul DuChateau, "Creek Nation on the Eve of the Civil War," *Chronicles of Oklahoma* 52, no. 3 (Fall 1974), 296–297.

2. Larkin Ryal Interview by Grace Kelley, March 10, 1937 [no interview number], 296, Henryetta, Oklahoma, Indian-Pioneer Papers.

3. Hurt, "Shaping of a Creek (Muscogee) Homeland," 139 and 141.

4. W. A. Carleton, *Not Yours, but You* (Berkeley, CA: [s.n.], ca. 1954), 30.

5. Sterling Cosper, "MCN in Context around the 1866 Treaty Signing," *Muscogee Nation News,* September 15, 2018, vol. 48, issue 18, 7, Okmulgee, Oklahoma.

6. Hurt, "Shaping of a Creek (Muscogee) Homeland," 110–111.

7. Andre Paul DuChateau, "Creek Nation on the Eve of the Civil War," *Chronicles of Oklahoma* 52, no. 3 (Fall 1974), 296.

8. Muriel H. Wright, "General Douglas H. Cooper, C.S.A.," *Chronicles of Oklahoma* 32, no. 2 (Summer 1954), 165.

9. "Treaty with the Creeks, 1838," November 23, 1838, in Charles J. Kappler, comp. and ed., *Indian Affairs 1778–1883* (New York: Interland Publishing, 1972), 524–525.

10. Wright, "General Douglas H. Cooper, C.S.A.," 157.

11. Walter Lee Brown, *A Life of Albert Pike* (Fayetteville: University of Arkansas Press, 1997), 358–359.

183

NOTES TO PAGES 61-64

12. T. Paul Wilson, "Confederate Delegates of the Five Civilized Tribes," *Chronicles of Oklahoma* 53, no. 3 (Fall 1975), 354–356.

13. Charles R. Freeman, "The Battle of Honey Springs," *Chronicles of Oklahoma* 13, no. 2 (June 1935), 154.

14. Lela J. McBride, *Opothleyahola and the Loyal Muskogee: Their Flight to Kansas in the Civil War* (Jefferson, NC: McFarland, 2000), 141.

15. Brown, *Life of Albert Pike*, 363.

16. Kenny A. Franks, "An Analysis of the Confederate Treaties with the Five Civilized Tribes," *Chronicles of Oklahoma* 51, no. 4 (Winter 1972), 458–473, and "The Implementation of the Confederate Treaties with the Five Civilized Tribes," *Chronicles of Oklahoma* 51, no. 1 (Spring 1973), 21–33; and Kinneth McNeil, "Confederate Treaties with the Tribes of Indian Territory," *Chronicles of Oklahoma* 42, no. 4 (Winter 1964–1965), 408–420.

17. McBride, *Opothleyahola and the Loyal Muskogee*, 150.

18. Mēkko Hutko and Opothleyahola's letter is quoted in Patrick N. Minges, *Slavery in the Cherokee Nation: The Keetoowah Society and the Defining of a People, 1855–1867* (New York: Routledge, 2003), 107.

19. President Abraham Lincoln finally responded to Mēkko Hutko and Opothleyahola on September 10, 1861.

20. McBride, *Opothleyahola and the Loyal Muskogee*, 151.

21. Wright, "General Douglas H. Cooper, C.S.A.," 143.

22. Fred Johnson Interview by Grace Kelley, January 14, 1938, Interview 12668, 237, Henryetta, Oklahoma, Indian-Pioneer Papers.

23. Don Diehl, "The Civil War Ripped Creek Nation: part 2," *Muscogee Nation News,* April 1, 2016, vol. 46, issue 7, 2, Okmulgee, Oklahoma.

24. McBride, *Opothleyahola and the Loyal Muskogee,* 166.

25. Joseph Bruner Interview by Effie S. Jackson, February 28, 1938, Interview 13105, 321, Sapulpa, Oklahoma, Indian-Pioneer Papers.

26. James H. Howard in collaboration with Willie Lena, *Oklahoma Seminoles: Medicine, Magic and Religion* (Norman: University of Oklahoma Press, 1990), 15.

27. Don Diehl, "The Civil War Ripped Creek Nation: Part 3," *Muscogee Creek Nation* (Okmulgee, OK), April 15, 2016, vol. 46, issue 8, 6.

28. McBride, *Opothleyahola and the Loyal Muskogee,* 167.

29. Dean Trickett, "The Civil War in Indian Territory 1862 (Continued)," *Chronicles of Oklahoma* 19, no. 4 (December 1941), 385, and Wright, "General Douglas H. Cooper, C.S.A.," 165.

NOTES TO PAGES 65-68

30. McBride, *Opothleyahola and the Loyal Muskogee,* 169.

31. McBride, *Opothleyahola and the Loyal Muskogee,* 170.

32. Arthur Shoemaker, "The Battle of Chustenahlah," *Chronicles of Oklahoma* 38, no. 2 (Summer 1960), 181.

33. Phoebe Banks in George P. Rawick, ed., *The American Slave: A Composite Autobiography: Oklahoma and Mississippi Narratives,* vol. 7 (Westport, CT: Greenwood, 1941), 10, and Wright, "General Douglas H. Cooper, C.S.A," 166.

34. Carter Blue Clark, "Opothleyahola and the Creeks during the Civil War," in H. Glenn Jordan and Thomas M. Holm, eds., *Indian Leaders: Oklahoma's First Statesmen* (Oklahoma City: Oklahoma Historical Society, 1979), 59, and Debo, *Road to Disappearance,* 152.

35. Don Cook Interview by Nettie Cain, August 9, 1937, Interview 7450, 173, Holdenville, Oklahoma, Indian-Pioneer Papers.

36. John Harrison Interview by L. W. Wilson, n.d., Interview 5145, 328, no place given, Indian-Pioneer Papers.

37. Dean Banks, "Civil War Refugees from Indian Territory," *Chronicles of Oklahoma* 41, no. 3 (Autumn 1963), 292.

38. Clark, "Opothleyahola and the Creeks during the Civil War," in Jordan and Holm, eds., *Indian Leaders,* 61.

39. John Bartlett Meserve, "The Perrymans," *Chronicles of Oklahoma* 15, no. 2 (June 1937), 173.

40. Angie Debo, *A History of the Indians of the United States* (Norman: University of Oklahoma Press, 1970), 176. Unpublished Chitto Harjo biographical essay by Salina Harjo, n.d., Chitto Harjo binder, 4, Historical and Cultural Preservation Archives and Records, Muscogee Nation, Okmulgee, Oklahoma.

41. John Bartlett Meserve, "The Plea of Crazy Snake (Chitto Harjo)," *Chronicles of Oklahoma* 11, no. 3 (September 1933), 905–906.

42. Wright, "General Douglas H. Cooper, C.S.A," 179.

43. Kenny A. Franks, *Stand Watie and the Agony of the Cherokee Nation* (Memphis: Memphis State University Press, 1979), 180.

44. Franks, *Stand Watie,* 180.

45. Treaty with the Creeks, 1866, https://treaties.okstate.edu/treaties/treaty -with-the-creeks-1866-0931, accessed February 15, 2024.

46. Carl Coke Rister, *Land Hunger: David L. Payne and the Oklahoma Boomers* (Norman: University of Oklahoma Press, 1942), 37–38. The drive of Manifest Destiny is argued by Reginald Horsman in *Race and Manifest Destiny:*

NOTES TO PAGES 69-73

The Origins of American Racial Anglo-Saxonism (Cambridge: Harvard University Press, 1981), 7–178, and supported by Patrick Wolfe, "Settler Colonialism and the Elimination of the Native," *Journal of Genocidal Research* 8, no. 4 (2006), 387–409; and Patrick Wolfe, *Settler Colonialism and the Transformation of Anthropology: The Politics and Poetics of an Ethnographic Event* (London: Cassell, 1999), 1–42; and Lorenzo Veracini, *Settler Colonialism: A Theoretical Overview* (London: Palgrave, 2010), 1–15.

47. Hurt, "Shaping of a Creek (Muscogee) Homeland," 113.

48. Sam J. Haynes Interview, 330–331.

49. "Creek Government," *Indian Advocate,* March, n.d., 1901, 75, Shawnee, Oklahoma Territory. See also the Mvskoke Creek Constitution of 1867, in *Constitution and Laws of the Muskogee Nation* as compiled and codified by A. P. McKellop, under Act of October 15, 1892 (Muskogee, Indian Territory: F. C. Hubbard, Printer, 1893).

50. Muriel H. Wright, "Official Seals of the Five Civilized Tribes," *Chronicles of Oklahoma* 18, no. 4 (December 1940), 366.

51. Alex Blackston Interview by L. W. Wilson, October 14, 1937, Interview 7826, 299–300, Porter, Oklahoma, Indian-Pioneer Papers.

52. Christopher Columbus Smith Interview by Robert J. Boatman, June 28, 1937, Interview 4701, 372, Cole, Oklahoma, Indian-Pioneer Papers.

53. Andrew Willhite Interview by Grace Kelley, January 11, 1938, Henryetta, Oklahoma, Second Interview 12650, 110, Indian-Pioneer Papers.

54. Emma Haun Whipple Interview by Nora L. Lorrin, April 15, 1938, Interview 10472, 63, El Reno, Oklahoma, Indian-Pioneer Papers.

55. William T. Grant Interview by Ida B. Lankford, July 9, 1937, Interview 4768, 230, Bessie, Oklahoma, Indian-Pioneer Papers.

56. Elmer Hill Interview by Billie Byrd, March 23, 1939, [no interview number], 311, Okemah, Oklahoma, Indian-Pioneer Papers.

57. I have used *cepan,* meaning "boy," and it is pronounced as "cha bon" in the Mvskoke language.

58. Kenneth McIntosh, "Chitto Harjo, the Crazy Snake and the Birth of Indian Political Activism in the Twentieth Century" (Ph.D. diss., Department of History, Texas Christian University, Fort Worth, 1993), 37.

59. Salina Harjo, unpub. Chitto Harjo essay, 4.

60. Donald L. Fixico, "The Spiritual Balance of Peace in the Red Stick War, 1813–1814," in Yasmin Saikia and Chad Haines, eds., *People's Peace: Prospects for a Human Future* (Syracuse: Syracuse University Press, 2019), 70.

NOTES TO PAGES 73-80

61. Debo, *History of the Indians,* 14.

62. Chaudhuri and Chaudhuri, *Sacred Path,* 94 and 121.

The Green Peach War

1. Agnes Kelley Interview by Grace Kelley, August 19, 1937, 145–154, Okmulgee, Oklahoma, Second Interview 7229, Indian-Pioneer Papers.

Chapter 4. The Sands Uprising and the Green Peach War

1. Debo, *Road to Disappearance,* 246.

2. John Bartlett Meserve, "Chief Pleasant Porter," *Chronicles of Oklahoma* 9, no. 3 (September 1931), 322.

3. "Pleasant Porter," in *The Encyclopedia of Oklahoma History and Culture,* https://www.okhistory.org/publications/enc/entry?entry=PO032, accessed February 15, 2024.

4. Carleton, *Not Yours, but You,* 30.

5. O. A. Lambert, "Historical Sketch of Col. Samuel Checote, Once Chief of the Creek Nation," *Chronicles of Oklahoma* 4, no. 3 (September 1926), 275.

6. John Bartlett Meserve, "Chief Samuel Checote, with Sketches of Chiefs Locher Harjo and Ward Coachman," *Chronicles of Oklahoma* 16, no. 4 (December 1938), 403.

7. Ohland Morton, "The Government of the Creek Indians: Earliest Forms," *Chronicles of Oklahoma* 8, no. 1 (March 1930), 55.

8. Morton, "Government of the Creek Indians," 55.

9. Muscogee Creek Constitution of 1867 in *Constitution and Laws of the Muskogee Nation* as compiled and codified by A. P. McKellop, under Act of October 15, 1892 (Muskogee, Indian Territory: F. C. Hubbard, Printer, 1893).

10. Berlin B. Chapman, "Unratified Treaty with the Creeks, 1868," *Chronicles of Oklahoma* 16, no. 3 (September 1938), 337–338 and 343–345.

11. Chapman, "Unratified Treaty with the Creeks, 1868," 339.

12. Morton, "Government of the Creek Indians," 56.

13. C. W. Turner, "Events among the Muskogees during Sixty Years," *Chronicles of Oklahoma* 10, no. 1 (March 1932), 28.

14. Turner, "Events among the Muskogees," 29.

15. Morton, "Government of the Creek Indians," 57; Meserve, "Chief Pleasant Porter," 324; and Meserve, "Chief Samuel Checote," 403.

16. The term "Boomer" likely started with newspapers calling out unscrupulous individuals who aggressively promoted opening Indian Territory. On May 29,

NOTES TO PAGES 80-83

1879, the *Atchison Champion* labeled the Unappropriated Lands "Oklahoma" (see Notices, *Atchison Champion,* May 29, 1879). The *Columbus Courier* in Kansas went as far as calling the land-hungry promoters "Oklahoma Boomers" (*Columbus Courier,* December 4, 1879). The Oklahoma "boom," as a land opportunity like "Oregon or Bust," appeared in the *Kansas City Times* as early as May 15, 1879. "Boom" and "Boomers" have also been attributed to Dr. Morrison Munford, editor of the *Kansas City Times,* who used the two terms for the first time in association with the push to settle the Unappropriated Lands. (See Stan Hoig, "Boomer Movement," in Dianna Everett, ed., *The Encyclopedia of Oklahoma History and Culture,* vol. 1 [Oklahoma City: Oklahoma Historical Society, 2009], 154–155.)

17. "An Act to Secure Homesteads to Actual Settlers on the Public Domain," P.L. 37–64, May 20, 1862, ch. 75, *U.S. Statutes at Large,* vol. 12, 392.

18. Carl Coke Rister, *Land Hunger: David L. Payne and the Oklahoma Boomers* (Norman: University of Oklahoma Press, 1942), 41.

19. Dede Weldon Casad, *The Governor's Stake: The Parallel Lives of Two Texas Governors: Richard Coke and Lawrence Sullivan Ross* (Fort Worth: Eaken Press, 2003), 167.

20. From Report of October 24, 1881, in *House Executive Document,* no. 1, part 5, vol. 2, 47 Cong., 1st Sess., serial 2018, 17–19, and Report of November 1, 1880, in *House Executive Document,* no. 1, part 5, vol. 1, 46th Cong., 3d Sess., serial 1959, 5–6 and 11–13, quoted in Francis Paul Prucha, ed., *Americanizing the American Indians: Writings by the "Friends of the Indian," 1880–1900* (Lincoln: University of Nebraska Press, 1973), 88, and Frederick E. Hoxie, *A Final Promise: The Campaign to Assimilate the Indians, 1880–1920* (Lincoln: University of Nebraska Press, 1984), 71.

21. "Protest of the Representatives of the Indian Territory," To the Congress of the United States, no date, introduced to the Senate by Senator Henry M. Teller, *Congressional Record-Senate,* 1881, part 1, vol. 11, page 875.

22. *House Report* No. 1876, 40th Cong., 2d Sess., serial 1938, 7–10, quoted in Prucha, *Americanizing the American Indians,* 128.

23. *Congressional Record,* vol. 11, part 1 (46th Cong., 3d Sess.), 780–781 and 934–936, quoted in Prucha, *Americanizing the American Indians,* 123–124.

24. Jo Lea Wetherilt Behrens, "Forgotten Challengers to Severalty: The National Indian Defense Association and Council Fire," *Chronicles of Oklahoma* 75, no. 2 (Summer 1997), 132.

NOTES TO PAGES 83-88

25. Fifteenth Annual Report of the Board of Indian Commissioners, February 1, 1884, H.R. Exec. Doc. No. 1, 48th Cong., 1st Sess. (1883), 69–70, quoted in Prucha, *Americanizing the American Indians,* 28 and 30.

26. Prucha, *Americanizing the American Indians,* 27–30, 100–110, and 317–328.

27. Janey B. Hendrix, "Redbird Smith and the Nighthawk Keetoowahs," *Journal of Cherokee Studies* 8, no. 1 (1993), 32, and Proceedings of the Third Annual Meeting of the Lake Mohonk Conference of Friends of the Indian Held October 7 to 9, 1885 (Philadelphia: Sherman, 1886), 1.

28. Francis Paul Prucha, *The Great Father: The United States Government and the American Indian* (Lincoln: University of Nebraska Press, 1984, 1986 abridged edition), 222–223; Hoxie, *Final Promise,* 71; and D. S. Otis, *The Dawes Act and the Allotment of Indian Lands* (Norman: University of Oklahoma Press, 1973), 29, 428–489.

29. Wilcomb Washburn, *The Assault on Indian Tribalism: The General Allotment Law (Dawes Act) of 1887* (Philadelphia: J. B. Lippincott, 1975), 17.

30. See Helen Hunt Jackson, *A Century of Dishonor: A Sketch of the U.S. Government's Dealings with Some of the Indian Tribes* (Boston: Roberts Brothers, 1881).

31. Otis, *Dawes Act,* 21.

32. Hoxie, *Final Promise,* 71.

33. "General Allotment Act," February 8, 1887, *U.S. Statutes at Large,* vol. 24, 388–391.

34. Hurt, "Shaping of a Creek (Muscogee) Homeland," 145–146.

35. H. F. O'Beirne and E. S. O'Beirne, *The Indian Territory: Its Chiefs, Legislators and Leading Men* (Saint Louis: C. B. Woodward, 1892), 41.

36. Kent Carter, "Snakes and Scribes: The Dawes Commission and the Enrollment of the Creeks," *Chronicles of Oklahoma* 75, no. 4 (Winter 1997–1998), 388.

37. "Biographical Sketch of Isparhecher," January 1, 1903, *South McAlester Capital* 10, no. 6, South McAlester, Indian Territory, Isparhechar Collection, box 1, folder 44, Western History Collections, University of Oklahoma, Norman.

38. Debo, *Road to Disappearance,* 251, 265.

39. McIntosh, "Chitto Harjo, the Crazy Snake and the Birth of Indian Political Activism in the Twentieth Century," 24.

40. O'Beirne and O'Beirne, *Indian Territory,* 43.

41. Alex Blackston Interview by L. W. Wilson, October 14, 1937, Interview 7826, 300–301, Porter, Oklahoma, Indian-Pioneer Papers.

NOTES TO PAGES 88-94

42. Janey B. Hendrix, *Redbird Smith and the Nighthawk Keetoowahs* (Park Hill, OK: Cross-Cultural Education Center, 1983), 62.

43. John Harrison Interview by L. W. Wilson, n.d., Interview 5145, [no place given], 346, Indian-Pioneer Papers.

44. John B. Meserve, "Chief Isparhecher," *Chronicles of Oklahoma* 10, no. 1 (March 1932), 60.

45. Katja May, *African Americans and Native Americans in the Cherokee and Creek Nations, 1830s to 1920s: Collision and Collusion* (London: Routledge, 1996), 141–142. In another account, Sleeping Rabbit was arrested in Muskogee and shot to death trying to escape, Hendrix, *Redbird Smith and the Nighthawk Keetoowahs*, 28.

46. Alex Blackston Interview by L. W. Wilson, October 14, 1937, Interview 7826, 301, Porter, Oklahoma, Indian-Pioneer Papers.

47. Don Cook Interview by Nettie Cain, August 9, 1937, Interview 7450, 175, Holdenville, Oklahoma, Indian-Pioneer Papers, and Meserve, "Chief Isparhecher," 53.

48. "The Creek Trouble," *Indian Chieftain*, February 16, 1883, 2, Vinita, Indian Territory.

49. Meserve, "Chief Pleasant Porter," 326.

50. Samuel Checote to G. W. Grayson and L. C. Perryman, January 2, 1883, Grayson Family Collection, box 5, folder 8, Western History Collections, University of Oklahoma, Norman.

51. Notices, *Cheyenne Transporter*, February 26, 1883, 1, Darlington, Indian Territory.

52. "The Creek Trouble," *Indian Chieftain*, February 16, 1883, 2, Vinita, Indian Territory.

53. "Sac and Fox Agency News," *Cheyenne Transporter*, March 12, 1883, 1, Darlington, Indian Territory.

54. "Sac and Fox Agency News," *Cheyenne Transporter*, March 12, 1883, 1, Darlington, Indian Territory.

55. O'Beirne and O'Beirne, *Indian Territory*, 43.

56. "The Agreement and Recommendations between the Muskogee Gov't and Epishishee Party," *Indian Chieftain*, August 17, 1883, 2, Vinita, Indian Territory.

57. Sebron Miller Interview by Jefferson Berryhill, June 8, 1937, Interview 6235, n.p., 252. Indian-Pioneer Papers.

58. John Bartlett Meserve, "The Perrymans," *Chronicles of Oklahoma* 15, no. 2 (June 1937), 169–170, 166–184.

NOTES TO PAGES 94–109

59. Debo, *Road to Disappearance,* 268–281, and "Election of Isparhechar as Principal Chief," *Wagoner Record,* September 20, 1895, vol. 3, no. 51, Wagoner, Indian Territory, Isparhecher Collection, box 1, folder 4, Western History Collections, University of Oklahoma, Norman.

60. "Late Indian News from Washington," *Indian Chieftain,* July 8, 1888, 2, Vinita, Indian Territory.

61. "The Number of Colored," *Indian Chieftain,* July 8, 1888, 2, Vinita, Indian Territory.

62. Orpha B. Russell, "William G. Bruner, Member of the House of Kings, Creek Nation," *Chronicles of Oklahoma* 30, no. 4 (Winter 2013), 400.

63. William Bruner Interview by Nettie Cain, October 29, 1937, Interview 12051, 332, Calvin, Oklahoma, Indian-Pioneer Papers.

64. John McGilbray Interview by Jas. S. Buchanan, July 28, 1937, Interview 6943, 185, Yahola, Oklahoma, Indian-Pioneer Papers, and "Isparhecher's Message," *Daily Chieftain,* December 17, 1898, Vinita, Indian Territory.

65. John McGilbray Interview, 187.

66. Eliza Palmer Interview by Grace Kelley, September 20, 1937, Interview 7561, 71, Okmulgee, Oklahoma, Indian-Pioneer Papers.

67. David A. Chang, *The Color of the Land: Race, Nation, and the Politics of Landownership in Oklahoma, 1832–1929* (Chapel Hill: University of North Carolina Press, 2010), 96.

68. Obituary of Isparharcher, *Tulsa Democrat,* January 9, 1903, vol. 9, no. 2, Tulsa, Indian Territory, Isparhechar Collection, Western History Collections, University of Oklahoma, Norman.

69. Chaudhuri and Chaudhuri, *Sacred Path,* 76.

Fus Fixico's Letter to Pleasant Porter about Allotments, 1905

1. "Letter of Fus Fixico" by Alex Posey, *Sturm's Magazine* (Tulsa, Indian Territory), 1, no. 2 (October 1905), 90–92, Mrs. Alfred Mitchell Collection, box M-24, folder 24, Western History Collections, University of Oklahoma, Norman.

Chapter 5. The Snakes

Epigraph: Jerry H. Gill, *Native American Worldviews: An Introduction* (New York: Humanity Books, 2002), 137.

1. Stan Hoig, *The Oklahoma Land Rush* (Oklahoma City: Oklahoma Historical Society, 1984), ix–xi, and Michael J. Hightower, *1889: The Boomer Movement,*

NOTES TO PAGES 109-112

the Land Run, and Early Oklahoma City (Norman: University of Oklahoma Press, 2018), 168–179.

2. Hurt, "Shaping of a Creek (Muscogee) Homeland," 171.

3. "Congressional Visitors," *Daily Chieftain,* September 26, 1889, 1, Vinita, Indian Territory.

4. "Memorial of the Muscogee Nation by Its National Council to the President and Congress of the United States," October 1889, Western History Collections, University of Oklahoma Library, Norman.

5. Edwin C. McReynolds, *Oklahoma: A History of the Sooner State* (Norman: University of Oklahoma Press, 1954), 292–293, and S. N. D. North, Director, Department of Commerce and U.S. Bureau of the Census, *Population of Oklahoma and Indian Territory 1907,* Bulletin 89 (Washington, DC: U.S. Government Printing Office, 1907); United States Census Bureau, Oklahoma, https://www.census .gov/geographies/reference-files/2010/geo/state-local-geo-guides-2010/oklahoma .html, accessed June 11, 2024.

6. Charles Curtis, *In His Own Words: Kansan, Native American, Jockey, Attorney, Senator and Vice President of the United States of America* (Topeka: Kitty Frank, 2019), 5–10.

7. Richard Williams, "The Part-Cherokee President," *New York Times,* July 16, 1998.

8. "Act for the Protection of the People of Indian Territory," June 28, 1898, *U.S. Statutes at Large,* vol. 30, 497–498, 502, and Circe Sturm, "Blood Politics, Racial Classification, and Cherokee National Identity: The Trials and Tribulations of the Cherokee Freedmen," *American Indian Quarterly* 22, no. 1/2 (Winter–Spring 1998), 236.

9. Debo, *Road to Disappearance,* 369.

10. "Isparhecher's Message," *Daily Chieftain,* December 17, 1898, 1, Vinita, Indian Territory.

11. "An Act Making Appropriations for Current and Contingent Expenses, and Fulfilling Treaty Stipulations with Indian Tribes, for Fiscal Year Ending June Thirtieth, Eighteen Hundred and Ninety-Five, and for Other Purposes," August 15, 1894, https://www.govinfo.gov/app/details/STATUTE-28/STATUTE-28-Pg286-2, accessed June 11, 2024, Amendment Intended to Be Proposed by Mr. [Bishop W.] Perkins to the Bill (H.R. 10415), 44–45, 52d Cong., 2d Sess.

12. Ena Herrington Burnett Interview by Mary D. Dorward, April 26, 1937, Interview 13827, 277, Tulsa, Oklahoma, Indian-Pioneer Papers.

NOTES TO PAGES 112-119

13. Rebecca M. Tiger Interview by Billy Byrd, January 13, 1938, Interview 12662, 87, Okemah, Oklahoma, Indian-Pioneer Papers.

14. Salina Harjo, unpub. Chitto Harjo essay, 19.

15. Henry Jacobs Interview by Otis Hume, July 24, 1937, Interview 7014, 228, Sasakwa, Oklahoma, Indian-Pioneer Papers.

16. Joe Grayson Interview by Grace Kelley, October 10, 1937, Interview 7780, 449, Henryetta, Oklahoma, Indian-Pioneer Papers.

17. Joe Simmers Interview by Billie Byrd, November 24, 1937, Interview 12219, 171, Bearden, Oklahoma, Indian-Pioneer Papers.

18. Winey Lewis Interview by Grace Kelley, August 12, 1937, Henryetta, Oklahoma, Interview 7142, [no page number], addendum to Indian-Pioneer Interviews, Indian-Pioneer Papers.

19. Salina Harjo, unpub. Chitto Harjo essay, 16.

20. LeRoy Ward Interview by Grace Kelley, October 9, 1937, Interview 7781, 204, Henryetta, Oklahoma, Indian-Pioneer Papers.

21. William Frank Jones Interview by Effie S. Jackson, April 19, 1937, Interview 5358, 409–10, Tulsa, Oklahoma, Indian-Pioneer Papers.

22. Ralph Marsh, "Crazy Snake's Rebellion, How Chitto Harjo Lived, and Died, by a Treaty's Promise," *Oklahoma Today* (May–June 1992), 31.

23. McIntosh, "Chitto Harjo, the Crazy Snake and the Birth of Indian Political Activism in the Twentieth Century," 22, 46.

24. Mrs. Artie Potts Interview by Gomer Gower, April 25, 1938, Interview 13715, 305–306, Talihina, Oklahoma, Indian-Pioneer Papers.

25. Mrs. Willie Blair Interview by Grace Kelley, April 22, 1938, Interview 13714, 358, Calvin, Oklahoma, Indian-Pioneer Papers.

26. Benjamin Knight Interview by Gus Hummingbird, July 23, 1937, Interview 6878, 271, Goingsnake District, Indian-Pioneer Papers.

27. Tabatha Toney, "'Until We Fall to The Ground United': Cherokee Resilience and Interfactional Cooperation in the Early Twentieth Century" (Ph.D. diss., Department of History, Oklahoma State University, Stillwater, 2018), 78.

28. Toney, "'Until We Fall to The Ground United,'" 143.

29. Wilcomb Washburn, *The Assault on Indian Tribalism: The General Allotment Law (Dawes Act) of 1887* (Philadelphia: J. B. Lippincott, 1975), 17.

30. See Margaret Mead, *The Changing Culture of an Indian Tribe* (New York: Capricorn Books, 1966). See also James O. Young, *Cultural Appropriation and the Arts* (Hoboken: Wiley-Blackwell, 2010).

NOTES TO PAGES 119–125

31. Prucha, *Great Father*, 260, and Lyman S. Tyler, *History of Indian Policy* (Washington: United States Department of the Interior, Bureau of Indian Affairs, 1973), 97.

32. Debo, *Road to Disappearance*, 376.

33. "Mvskoke History: Pleasant Porter," *Muscogee Nation News*, July 2007, vol. 37, issue 7, section B, 1.

34. "Rebellious Indians in Jail," *Chickasaw Daily Express*, February 7, 1901, 1.

35. Salina Harjo, unpub. Chitto Harjo essay, 25.

36. "Treaty with the Creeks, 1832," March 24, 1832, in Charles J. Kappler, comp. and ed., *Indian Affairs 1778–1883* (Interland Publishing, 1972), 341–343.

37. Salina Harjo, unpub. Chitto Harjo essay, 25.

38. Kent Carter, *The Dawes Commission and the Allotment of the Five Civilized Tribes, 1893–1914* (Orem, UT: Ancestry.com, 1999), 55; John B. Meserve, "Chief Pleasant Porter," *Chronicles of Oklahoma* 9, no. 3 (September 1931), 331.

39. McIntosh, "Chitto Harjo, the Crazy Snake and the Birth of Indian Political Activism in the Twentieth Century," 53; Carter, *Dawes Commission*, 56, and McIntosh, 67. Interestingly, after his job as Indian agent, Shoenfelt and Harjo became friends. "Crazy Snake Is Curious Type," *Herald Democrat*, April 26, 1909.

40. Carter, *Dawes Commission*, 57, and McIntosh, "Chitto Harjo, the Crazy Snake and the Birth of Indian Political Activism in the Twentieth Century," 60.

41. Salina Harjo, unpub. Chitto Harjo essay, 25, and McIntosh, "Chitto Harjo, the Crazy Snake and the Birth of Indian Political Activism in the Twentieth Century," 64–65.

42. "Rebellious Indians in Jail," *Chickasaw Daily Express*, February 7, 1901, 1.

43. Meserve, "Chief Pleasant Porter," 331.

44. Meserve, "Chief Pleasant Porter," 331; McIntosh, "Chitto Harjo, the Crazy Snake and the Birth of Indian Political Activism in the Twentieth Century," 67; Carter, *Dawes Commission*, 57 and 66.

45. "Rise to Battle for Royal Rights of Olden Day," *Oklahoma News*, March 29, 1909.

46. "An Indian Aristocracy," *Indian Advocate*, March, n.d., 1901, 70.

47. "Special Session? Sure, Says Editor Walter Ferguson," *Shawnee Daily News*, September 1, 1911, 3, Shawnee, Oklahoma.

48. David C. Boles, "Prairie Oil & Gas Company," *Chronicles of Oklahoma* 46, no. 2 (Summer 1968), 197.

49. "Porter Speaks Expects Trouble," *Indian Chieftain*, July 4, 1901, Vinita, Indian Territory, Pleasant Porter Papers, box 2, folder 70, Western History Collections, University of Oklahoma Libraries.

NOTES TO PAGES 125–129

50. Robert Gregory, *Oil in Oklahoma* (Muskogee, OK: James C. Leake, 1976), 1.

51. Commissioner of Indian Affairs W. A. Jones to Secretary of Interior Cornelius N. Bless, September 26, 1897, Annual Report of the Commissioner of Indian Affairs 1898 (Washington, DC: U.S. Government Printing Office, 1898), 111, https://babel.hathitrust.org/cgi/pt?id=nyp.33433081678900&view=1up&seq=6, accessed April 6, 2020.

52. Dan T. Boyd, "Oklahoma: The Ultimate Oil Opportunity," *Shale Shaker* (May–June 2008), 1.

53. Anna Webb-Storey, "Culture Clash: A Case Study of Three Osage Native American Families" (Ph.D. diss., Department of Education, Oklahoma State University, Stillwater, 1998), 3.

54. George Windes, "And Still the Waters Run: Jackson Barnett," *Muscogee Nation News,* May 1, 2012, vol. 12, issue 9, 9, Okmulgee, Oklahoma.

55. Angie Debo, *The Road to Disappearance: A History of the Creek Indians* (Norman: University of Oklahoma Press, 1967), 376, originally published 1941.

56. Ohland Morton, "Reconstruction in the Creek Nation," *Chronicles of Oklahoma* 9, no. 2 (June 1931), 179.

57. Theodore Roosevelt, "First Annual Message to Congress," December 3, 1901, *Congressional Record,* vol. 35, 57th Cong., 1st Sess., part 1, 90.

58. "Act Authorizing the Survey of Indian and Other Reservations, under the Direction and Control of the General Land Office, and in Conformity to the Rules and Regulations under Which Other Public Lands Are Surveyed," April 8, 1864, *U.S. Statutes at Large,* vol. 14, 774.

59. "Allotment Records for Indigenous Peoples of the United States," https://www.familysearch.org/wiki/en/Allotment_Records_for_Indigenous_Peoples_of_the_United_States, accessed March 12, 2021.

60. "Scorching All Over Land Oklahoma Has Hottest Day," *Oklahoma State Capital,* August 17, 1909, Guthrie, Oklahoma.

61. "Crazy Snake Is Curious Type," *Herald Democrat,* April 26, 1909.

62. William Frank Jones Interview, 413, Indian-Pioneer Papers.

63. "That Indian Uprising," *Weekly-Times Journal,* February 28, 1902, 4.

64. William Frank Jones Interview, 412–413, Indian-Pioneer Papers.

65. "The Plea of Crazy Snake (Chitto Harjo)," *Muscogee Nation News,* October 2007, vol. 37, issue 10, section B, 2, and Marsh, "Crazy Snake's Rebellion," 33.

66. Salina Harjo, unpub. Chitto Harjo essay, 21–32.

67. Marsh, "Crazy Snake's Rebellion," 32.

NOTES TO PAGES 129-135

68. "Mvskoke History: Pleasant Porter," *Muscogee Nation News,* July 2007, vol. 37, issue 7, section B, 1.

69. Marsh, "Crazy Snake's Rebellion," 31, and "Facts about Crazy Snake and His Band of Indians; Stand by Treaty of 1832 with Government; Do Not Believe United States Has the Right to Force Allotment upon Them; People Loyal to Chief," *Dallas Morning News,* April 4, 1909.

70. Debo, *History of the Indians,* 310.

71. Ada M. Roach Interview by Jerome Emmons, June 28, 1837, Schulter, Oklahoma, Second Interview 6490, 352, Indian-Pioneer Papers.

72. Andrew Willhite Interview by Grace Kelley, January 11, 1938, Henryetta, Oklahoma, Second Interview 12650, 111, Indian-Pioneer Papers.

73. Lee Hawkins Interview by Grace Kelley, August 30, 1937, Interview 7304, 310, Henryetta, Oklahoma, Indian-Pioneer Papers.

74. Lee Hawkins Interview by Grace Kelley, August 30, 1937, Interview 7304, 213, Henryetta, Oklahoma, Indian-Pioneer Papers.

75. Lee Hawkins Interview by Grace Kelley, August 30, 1937, Interview 7304, 214, Henryetta, Oklahoma, Indian-Pioneer Papers.

76. Henry Jacobs Interview by Otis Hume, July 24, 1937, Interview 7014, 229, Sasakwa, Oklahoma, Indian-Pioneer Papers.

77. Mrs. Willie Blair Interview by Grace Kelley, April 22, 1938, Interview 13714, 359, Calvin, Oklahoma, Indian-Pioneer Papers.

78. Agnes Kelley Interview by Grace Kelley, August 19, 1937, Okmulgee, Oklahoma, Second Interview 7229, 146, Indian-Pioneer Papers.

79. Jim Guin Interview by Melvin Stites, May 8, 1938, Interview 13806, 338, Hanna, Oklahoma, Indian-Pioneer Papers.

80. Jim Guin Interview, 338–339.

81. "Outbreak Is Feared," *Weekly-Times Journal,* August 14, 1903, 4, Oklahoma City, Oklahoma Territory, and "Visit of Crazy Snake," *Weekly-Times Journal,* August 13, 1903, 5, Oklahoma City, Oklahoma Territory.

82. "Want to Exhibit Snake Indians," *Perkins Journal,* February 19, 1904, n.p.

83. McIntosh, "Chitto Harjo, the Crazy Snake and the Birth of Indian Political Activism in the Twentieth Century," 82.

84. Salina Harjo, unpub. Chitto Harjo essay, 32.

85. Statement of Mr. Wilson Jones (Indian name, Chitto Harjo; "Crazy Snake"), November 23, 1906, *Report of the Select Committee to Investigate Matters Connected with Affairs in the Indian Territory,* vol. 2 (Washington, DC: U.S. Government Printing Office, 1907), 1252.

NOTES TO PAGES 135-144

86. Statement of Mr. Wilson Jones, 1252.

87. Statement of Mr. Wilson Jones, 1258–1259.

Chitto Harjo's Nephew

1. Daniel Starr Interview by Billie Byrd, October 18, 1937, Interview 7850, 11–113, Henryetta, Oklahoma, Indian-Pioneer Papers.

Chapter 6. "Snake War"

Epigraph: Donald L. Fixico, *"That's What They Used to Say": Reflections on American Indian Oral Traditions* (Norman: University of Oklahoma Press, 2017), 4–5.

1. McIntosh, "Chitto Harjo, the Crazy Snake and the Birth of Indian Political Activism in the Twentieth Century," 23.

2. L. C. Moore to the Leaders and Members of the Four Mothers Nation, June 1910, G. N. Belvin Collection, box 1, folder 12, Western History Collections, University of Oklahoma, Norman.

3. Edwin C. McReynolds, *Oklahoma: A History of the Sooner State* (Norman: University of Oklahoma Press, 1954), 313, and *Sequoyah Convention Wasn't in Vain* (5), from Constitutional Convention Reunion–Souvenir Edition, September 22, 1929, William H. Murray Papers, box 5, folder 51, Carl Albert Center Congressional and Political Collections, University of Oklahoma, Norman.

4. William H. Murray, "The Constitutional Convention," *Chronicles of Oklahoma* 9, no. 2 (June 1931), 129–130.

5. Creek Interview, 9:368–72, in Theda Perdue, ed. *Nations Remembered: An Oral History of the Five Civilized Tribes, 1865–1907* (Westport, CT: Greenwood, 1980), 194.

6. Deer and Knapp, "Muscogee Constitutional Jurisprudence," 161–162.

7. *Sequoyah Convention Wasn't in Vain* (5).

8. McReynolds, *Oklahoma*, 314, and *Sequoyah Convention Wasn't in Vain* (5).

9. Estelle Conklin Hoffman, *Our Family and Early Oklahoma* (unknown publisher, 1952), 30.

10. Bolster, "Smoked Meat Rebellion," 37 and 39.

11. Edward Everett Dale, ed., *Frontier Trails: The Autobiography of Frank M. Canton* (Norman: University of Oklahoma Press, 1966), 237.

12. Andrew Willhite Interview by Grace Kelley, January 11, 1938, Henryetta, Oklahoma, Second Interview 12650, 112, Indian-Pioneer Papers.

13. McIntosh, "Chitto Harjo, the Crazy Snake and the Birth of Indian Political Activism in the Twentieth Century," 117.

NOTES TO PAGES 144-152

14. Bolster, "Smoked Meat Rebellion," 37 and 39.

15. Mrs. John Mitchell interviewed by Bill Savage, June 9, 1967, T-180–1, No. 3636, pp. 3–4, Doris Duke Indian Oral History Interviews, Western History Collections, University of Oklahoma, Norman.

16. Larkin Ryal Interview by Grace Kelley, March 10, 1937, [no interview number], 295–296, Henryetta, Oklahoma, Indian-Pioneer Papers.

17. Laurel Pitman Interview by Jas. S. Buchanan, October 25, 1937, 514–515, Interview 7930, Muskogee, Oklahoma, Indian-Pioneer Papers.

18. Leo Pinehill Interview by Billie Byrd, February 14, 1938, Interview 12960, 442, Bristow, Oklahoma, Indian-Pioneer Papers.

19. Leo Pinehill Interview, 443.

20. Bolster, "Smoked Meat Rebellion," 42.

21. Joe Merrick Interview by Grace Kelley, October 12, 1937, Interview 7802, 203, Henryetta, Oklahoma, Indian-Pioneer Papers.

22. Marsh, "Crazy Snake's Rebellion," 33.

23. Daniel Starr Interview, 113.

24. Bolster, "Smoked Meat Rebellion," 44.

25. "Crazy Snake Reported Caught," *Shawnee Daily Herald,* March 31, 1909, 1, Shawnee, Oklahoma.

26. Marsh, "Crazy Snake's Rebellion," 33.

27. Lee Hawkins Interview by Grace Kelley, August 30, 1937, Interview 7304, 214, Henryetta, Oklahoma, Indian-Pioneer Papers.

28. Marsh, "Crazy Snake's Rebellion," 33.

29. Bolster, "Smoked Meat Rebellion," 45.

30. Chitto Harjo's son, Thomas Jones, went to school in Washington for several years, "Facts about Crazy Snake and His Band of Indians; Stand by Treaty of 1832 with Government; Do Not Believe United States Has the Right to Force Allotment upon Them; People Loyal to Chief," *Dallas Morning News,* April 4, 1909. See also "News Worth Remembering," *La Follette's Weekly Magazine* 1, no. 13 (April 3, 1909), 12.

31. "Young Harjo Forced to Confess with Rope about Neck," *Guthrie Daily Leader,* March 29, 1909, Guthrie, Oklahoma.

32. Oscar V. Watson Interview by Grace Kelley, n.d., ca. 1937, Interview 5272, n.p., 506, Indian-Pioneer Papers.

33. Oscar V. Watson Interview, 507.

34. Oscar V. Watson Interview, 507–508.

35. Oscar V. Watson Interview, 507–508.

36. Hoffman, *Our Family and Early Oklahoma,* 29 and 31.

NOTES TO PAGES 153-159

37. "For First Time True Story of the Last Oklahoma Indian Uprising Is Told by Man Who Put It Down," *Tulsa Daily World,* June 13, 1915, 11.

38. Sonny Jackson Interview by Jefferson Berryhill, July 28, 1937, Interview 7566, 178, Okmulgee, Oklahoma, Indian-Pioneer Papers.

39. In the interview, Davis said Charley Coker was a full-blood Creek, Polly Jones Davis Interview by Jas. S. Buchanan, October 26, 1937, Interview 7945, 334, Hoffman, Oklahoma, Indian-Pioneer Papers.

40. Larkin Ryal Interview, 303.

41. Lee Hawkins Interview by Grace Kelley, August 30, 1937, Interview 7304, 214, Henryetta, Oklahoma, Indian-Pioneer Papers.

42. Polly Jones Davis Interview by Jas. S. Buchanan, October 26, 1937, Interview 7945, 335, Hoffman, Oklahoma, Indian-Pioneer Papers.

43. Leo Pinehill Interview by Billie Byrd, February 14, 1938, Interview 12960, 442, Bristow, Oklahoma, Indian-Pioneer Papers.

44. Leo Pinehill Interview.

45. Sonny Jackson Interview, 178–179.

46. Hoffman, *Our Family and Early Oklahoma,* 31.

47. John Bartlett Meserve, "The Plea of Crazy Snake (Chitto Harjo)," *Chronicles of Oklahoma* 11, no. 3 (September 1933), 911; Mrs. Irwin A. Watson, "Creek Indian Burial Customs Today," *Chronicles of Oklahoma* 28, no. 3 (Spring 1950), 95–102; and Amanda Rutland, "An Examination of Traditional Mvskoke Funerary Practices," *Muscogee Nation News,* October 1, 2015, vol. 45, issue 19, 7, Okmulgee, Oklahoma.

48. "Signal Corps Cowboys Slay Crazy Snake Band," *Brooklyn Daily Eagle,* April 1, 1909, 1, Brooklyn, New York.

49. "Crazy Snake Rounded Up by the Ad. Club," *Buffalo Illustrated Times,* April 11, 1909, 1, Buffalo, New York.

Redbird Smith's Grandson

1. Crosslin Fields Smith, *Stand as One: Spiritual Teachings of Keetoowah* (Taos, NM: Dog Soldier Press, 2018), 5.

Chapter 7. Legacy

1. William Bruner Interview by Nettie Cain, October 29, 1937, Interview 12051, 333, Calvin, Oklahoma, Indian-Pioneer Collection, Western History Collections, University of Oklahoma, Norman.

2. Chief Redbird Smith, Chief of the Nighthawk Keetoowahs (Cherokee), last updated October 18, 2021, https://www.geni.com/people/Chief-Redbird-Smith

NOTES TO PAGES 159-162

-Chief-of-the-Nighthawk-Keetoowahs-Cherokee/600000001172542948 9, accessed February 2, 2022.

3. Nigel Anthony Sellars, "Treasonous Tenant Farmers and Seditious Sharecroppers: The 1917 Green Corn Rebellion Trials," *Oklahoma City University Law Review* 27 (2002), 1097–1100.

4. Letter from Eufaula Harjo to Secretary of War, October 5, 1917, *Over There: Missouri and the Great War,* Missouri Digital Heritage Hosted Collections, https://mdh.contentdm.oclc.org/digital/collection/overthere/id/10522/, accessed February 20, 2021.

5. Janey B. Hendrix, *Redbird Smith and the Nighthawk Keetoowahs* (Park Hill, OK: Cross-Cultural Education Center, 1983), 78.

6. Cherokee Indians Executive Committee Meeting with Four Mothers Nations Society, October 1, 1955–October 1, 1955, folder 002121–011–0354, Collection: Major Council Meetings of American Indian Tribes, part 1, section 1: Navajo, Five Civilized Tribes, Pueblo, Cheyenne and Arapaho, and Ute, 1914–1956, Series: Five Civilized Tribes: Cherokee Nation, National Archives, Washington, DC, Record Group 75, Bureau of Indian Affairs, Central Classified Files, Decimal 054, https://congressional.proquest.com/histvault?q=002121–011–0354&accountid =4485, accessed February 1, 2022.

7. "Allotments," Report of the Commissioner of Indian Affairs, Fiscal Year Ended June 30, 1922 (Washington, DC: U.S. Government Printing Office, 1922), 14–15.

8. Deer and Knapp, "Muscogee Constitutional Jurisprudence," 163, and Debo, *Road to Disappearance,* 295–296.

9. "Indian Reorganization Act," June 18, 1934, *U.S. Statutes at Large,* vol. 48, pt. 1:984–988.

10. "An Act Authorizing the Secretary of the Interior to Allot Homesteads to the Natives of Alaska," P.L. 59–171, May 17, 1906, *U.S. Statutes at Large,* vol. 34, 197, and "Alaska Native Claims Settlement Act," P.L. 92–203, December 18, 1971, *U.S. Statutes at Large,* vol. 85, 688.

11. "Oklahoma Indian Welfare Act," June 26, 1936, *U.S. Statutes at Large,* vol. 49, 1967–68.

12. Morris Opler, "The Creek Tribal Towns of Oklahoma in 1937," *Papers in Anthropology* 13, no. 1 (1972), 1–116, and Hurt, "Shaping of a Creek (Muscogee) Homeland," 191.

13. Nafa Butcher Interview by Billie Byrd, May 28, 1937, Interview 6037, 71, Okemah, Oklahoma, Indian-Pioneer Papers.

NOTES TO PAGES 162–165

14. "Oklahoma Indian Welfare Act," June 26, 1936, *U.S. Statutes at Large,* vol. 49, 1967–68.

15. Mvskoke History: A Short Course for Muscogee Nation Employees, Muscogee Nation website, https://sde.ok.gov/sites/ok.gov.sde/files/Mvskoke_History_Powerpoint.pdf, accessed December 31, 2021.

16. Calvin Naked Head interviewed by Boyce Timmons, August 14, 1967, T-136, No. 2706, p. A4, Doris Duke Indian Oral History Interview.

17. Mvskoke History: A Short Course for Muscogee Nation Employees, Muscogee Nation website, https://sde.ok.gov/sites/ok.gov.sde/files/Mvskoke_History_Powerpoint.pdf, accessed December 31, 2021.

18. Cherokee Indians Executive Committee Meeting with Four Mothers Nations Society, November 27, 1954–November 27, 1954, folder 002121–011–0333, Collection: Major Council Meetings of American Indian Tribes, part 1, section 1: Navajo, Five Civilized Tribes, Pueblo, Cheyenne and Arapaho, and Ute, 1914–1956, Series: Five Civilized Tribes, National Archives, Washington, DC, Record Group 75, Bureau of Indian Affairs, Central Classified Files, Decimal 054, https://congressional.proquest.com/histvault?q=002121–011–0333&accountid=4485, accessed February 1, 2022.

19. Cherokee Indians Executive Committee Meeting with Four Mothers Nations Society, October 1, 1955–October 1, 1955, folder 002121–011–0354, Collection: Major Council Meetings of American Indian Tribes, part 1, section 1: Navajo, Five Civilized Tribes, Pueblo, Cheyenne and Arapaho, and Ute, 1914–1956, Series: Five Civilized Tribes: Cherokee Nation, National Archives, Washington, DC, Record Group 75, Bureau of Indian Affairs, Central Classified Files, Decimal 054, https://congressional.proquest.com/histvault?q=002121–011–0354&accountid=4485, accessed February 1, 2022.

20. Donald L. Fixico, *Termination and Relocation: Federal Indian Policy, 1945–1960* (Albuquerque: University of New Mexico Press, 1986), 91–107.

21. Sam Chewey interviewed by J. W. Tyner, May 14, 1969, T-431-2, No. 10788, p. 10, Doris Duke Indian Oral History Interviews, Western History Collections, University of Oklahoma, Norman.

22. "An Act to Authorize Each of the Five Civilized Tribes of Oklahoma to Select Their Principal Chief, and for Other Purposes," P.L. 91–495 (S. 3116), October 22, 1970, *U.S. Statutes at Large,* vol. 84, 1091.

23. "Indian Self-Determination and Education Assistance Act," P.L. 93–638, *U.S. Statutes at Large,* vol. 88, 2203–2217.

NOTES TO PAGES 165–169

24. *Allen Harjo et al., v. Thomas S. Kleppe et al.*, September 2, 1976, 420 F. Supp. 1110 (D.D.C. 1976).

25. *Muscogee (Creek) Nation v. Hodel*, 670 F. Supp. 434 (D.D.C. 1987). Donald Hodel was secretary of the Interior at the time.

26. Deer and Knapp, "Muscogee Constitutional Jurisprudence," 169.

27. Sara Plummer, "Tribe Regains Historic Council House," *Tulsa World*, November 15, 2010.

28. "Berryhill Passes at 110," *Muscogee Nation News*, January 1, 2010, vol. 41, issue 11, 1, Okmulgee, Oklahoma.

29. "Hymn Singing," *Muscogee Nation News*, July 2007, vol. 37, issue 7, Section C, 5, Okmulgee, Oklahoma, and Hurt, "Shaping of a Creek (Muscogee) Homeland," 199.

30. Liz Gray, "I Am Muscogee," *Muscogee Nation News*, June 15, 2017, vol. 47, issue 12, 2, Okmulgee, Oklahoma.

31. Rita Williams, "National Council approves bill to preserve and protect Hickory Ground near Wetumka, Ala.," *Muscogee Nation News*, October 2008, vol. 38, issue 10, 4, Okmulgee, Oklahoma.

32. Liz Gray, "The Fight for Hickory Ground Continues," *Muscogee Nation News*, June 15, 2019, vol. 49, issue 12, 1, and Rita Williams, "Hickory Ground Ceremonial Members/Poarch Creek Indians Meetings," *Muscogee Nation News*, May 2007, vol. 37, issue 5, section A, 4, Okmulgee, Oklahoma.

33. *Muscogee Creek Nation, Hickory Ground, and Mēkko George Thompson v. Poarch Band of Creek Indians*, 525 F. Supp. 3d 1359 (M.D. Ala. 2021).

34. Liz Gray, "Ambassador Position Created," *Muscogee Nation News*, January 15, 2019, vol. 49, issue 2, 5, Okmulgee, Oklahoma.

35. Testimony of Jonodev Osceola Chaudhuri, Ambassador to the Muscogee (Creek) Nation, Subcommittee for Indigenous Peoples of the United States, Oversight Hearing on "Reviewing the Broken Promises Report: Examining the Federal Funding Shortfalls in Indian Country," November 19, 2019, https://www.congress.gov/116/meeting/house/110246/witnesses/HHRG-116-II24-Wstate-ChaudhuriJ-20191119.pdf, accessed December 31, 2021.

36. Mvskoke History: A Short Course for Muscogee Nation Employees, Muscogee Nation website, https://sde.ok.gov/sites/ok.gov.sde/files/Mvskoke_History_Powerpoint.pdf, accessed December 31, 2021.

37. George Looney Interview by Grace Kelley, June 28, 1937, Interview 6569, 257, Weleetka, Oklahoma, Indian-Pioneer Papers, Western History Collections, University of Oklahoma, Norman.

202

Acknowledgments

For many years, I have been working, off and on, on this study about Chitto Harjo. The idea came to me in 1979, when I first taught American Indian history at Rose State College while I was in graduate school at the University of Oklahoma. I used Angie Debo's textbook, *A History of the Indians of the United States,* and she frequently quoted Crazy Snake, quotes that I underlined. Over the years, I continued to collect scraps of information and articles here and there, filing things away and collecting book titles. In the early Covid summer of 2021, it became time to start this book—or to not do it at all.

I want to thank many people who provided assistance, guidance, and information during my research. In July 2021, I returned to Oklahoma to research historic sites and archival materials. I thank John Beaver, curator of the Cultural Center and Archives for the Muscogee Nation, for our long conversation about our tribe's history while I was visiting the renovated Council House in downtown Okmulgee. I appreciate the research help and guidance, plus conversations, with Melissa Harjo-Moffer and Odette Freeman at the Muscogee National Library and Archives. I enjoyed discussing the history of Muskogee and Keetoowahs with Lorraine Sacks, operations manager at the Five Civilized Tribes Museum. I appreciate the long conversations about the local area and Mvskoke history with Deacon Wendell Wayne Harjo of Hickory Ground No. 1 Church and Deacon Levi OnTheHill of Cucharty while visiting their

ACKNOWLEDGMENTS

church grounds. Deacon Levi showed my wife and me the inside of the church. About a dozen carefully folded black shawls hung seemingly randomly over the back of the pews. We were told they marked the places where church members usually sat before they died from Covid.

While visiting the Tahlequah area, I learned a lot from my lengthy conversation with Justin Smith, museum interpreter, at the John Ross Museum. Local knowledge is important in looking for historic sites, and I appreciate the directions from the owner of the Dry Creek Café in Mounds, Oklahoma, while I was researching Isparhecher and the Green Peach War. I also appreciate help received from Crystal Murphy at the Muskogee Public Library, whose great-great-grandfather fought alongside Chitto Harjo, to whom she may have been related.

I would like to thank several Mvskokes and Semvnoles whom I never met but whose deep knowledge about traditional cultures and the Medicine Way helped guide me. I thank Rosemary McCombs Maxey, Mvskoke, for explaining the Road of Suffering; Willie Lena, Semvnole, explained the medicine ways of the Semvnoles; David Franks, a Muscogee of Hickory Ground, gave us directions; and Mēkko George Thompson gave us permission to visit Hickory Ground. It is not an easy place to find, and the half dozen churches in the vicinity are evasive clues that a ceremonial ground exists nearby. Hickory Ground rested in silence, but locked inside was a great story waiting to unfold. David said that after Chitto Harjo's house burned down, well over a hundred years ago, Hickory Ground was moved once or twice, but the current square ground remains in the same vicinity as the original ceremonial site.

Across Indian country and academic country, I wish to thank friends and colleagues, many of whom I have known for a very long time, because I have learned from their works and our conversations.

204

ACKNOWLEDGMENTS

In this listing I have included individuals whose books I have learned from. I am grateful to Gary Anderson, Kent Blansett, David Chang, Joy Chaudhuri, Blue Clark, David Edmunds, Robbie Ethridge, Steven Hahn, Joy Harjo, Tom Holm, Peter Iverson who has left us, Paul Kelton, Daniel Littlefield, Ken McIntosh, Jeff Ostler, Julie Reed, Claudio Saunt, Margaret Connell Szasz, Cliff Trafzer, Mary Jane Ward, and Terry Wilson. I am also grateful to Dr. Sharon O'Brien and Kaynaan Henry for our conversations about Mvskoke history.

When I was younger, I was influenced by a number of older scholars; I am grateful to them for their guidance and mentorship. Thank you, William Bittle, Arrell Gibson, William T. Hagan, Reginald Horsman, William Mahl Jr., H. Wayne Morgan, and Francis Paul Prucha. Among those with whom I took courses or who influenced my thinking about Chitto Harjo and Mvskoke and Semvnole histories at the University of Oklahoma, I wish to thank John Ellisor, Duane Hale, Carol Hampton, Tom Holm, Linda Parker, Gary Roberts, and Bob Winfrey. In the mid-1970s, when I was a graduate student, Angie Debo visited the University of Oklahoma to be honored. She had earned her doctorate from OU. Angie Debo was eighty-two years old and had recently published her book on Geronimo. She signed my copy of *The Road to Disappearance: A History of the Creek Indians.* On the title page Dr. Debo wrote, "I hope you will enjoy reading in this book the noble history of your ancestors. And your own writing in the years ahead will contribute an understanding of their place in the human annals. Proud to be your friend, Angie Debo." As a great admirer of Dr. Debo, I am indebted to her for helping to establish the field of American Indian history and to my mentors listed above who have shaped my scholarship.

Many people have helped me with this book. I appreciate the support from Adina Popescu, executive editor, Ann-Marie Imbornoni, senior production editor, Kristy Leonard, and Eva Skewes at Yale

ACKNOWLEDGMENTS

University Press. Adina's editorial talent helped to make the book much better. Thank you, Eliza Childs, for your superb copyediting. Thank you, Tom Jonas, for your careful work in making the maps for the book. I am grateful to President Michael Crow and the Regents of Arizona for naming me a Regents' Professor at Arizona State University, and I am appreciative of the Distinguished Foundation Professorship that I hold. Provost Nancy Gonzales, Dean Kenro Kusumi, Humanities Dean Jeffrey Cohen, and School Director Richard Amsbury have always been supportive of my work. I also appreciate the work of the SHPRS staff, who make my faculty duties and those of other professors much easier: Becky Tsang, Teri Houston, Marissa Timmerman, Yvonne Delgado, Jamise Caesar, and others, among them Ozzie and the student workers at the front desk. I am extremely grateful to my former research assistant, Travis Cook, who is now Dr. Cook, having earned his doctorate in history in summer 2021, and to my research assistants Erica Price and Audrey Casem.

During my years of research in Oklahoma, the staff at the Oklahoma Heritage Center, especially Dr. Bob Blackburn, who retired in December 2020, were very helpful. I am also grateful to the staff at the Western History Collections at the University of Oklahoma, especially Todd Fuller, curator; William Welch, professor; Lina Ortega; and John Lovett, who has since retired as curator of the photograph collections.

I am appreciative to Frank and Linda Alexander. Frank is my oldest living relative. I am grateful to my cousins Angie Butler and Judy Proctor, as well as Barney Mitchell, who left us just after the new year in 2020. Thank you for answering my questions over the years. I am also grateful to my younger relatives, whom I am still getting to know: Ramona Mitchell Ray, Bruce Mitchell, Serena Mitchell Melton, Mikal Alexander, Jared Alexander, Steven Alexander, and others.

ACKNOWLEDGMENTS

As always, I am grateful to Keytha Fixico, who wants to know more about our people, the Mvskokes. I also express appreciation for Josie the cat, who holds down the end of the sofa in my study—and my desk chair whenever I get up to retrieve a book from the other room. Most of all, I appreciate the help and support of the best researcher I know, my wife, Dr. Michelle Martin, who is on the history faculty at Northeastern State University in Tahlequah, Oklahoma. Our many conversations about her work, Chitto Harjo, and Indian Territory have inspired me to keep working on this book. Last of all, I am grateful to my parents, Virginia and John (who was a Baptist preacher most of his life and a Lighthorse later on), who are gone. I am very grateful to all my Mvskoke and Semvnole relatives, especially Echoille, Hockifke, and Tustennuck Hadjo who walked the Road of Suffering to Indian Territory, and whose courageous resilience has allowed me to write these pages.

Index

Abbott, Lyman: allotment advocacy 84–85; Dawes criticism 85
Act of the National Council (Oct. 16, 1882) 93
Africa, tribes (disappearance) 9
Ainu, attack 6
Alaska Native Reorganization Act 161
Alfred, Taiaiake 7
Allotment. *See* Land allotment
Allotment Law, passage 116–117
American Board of Commissioners for Foreign Mission: missionaries, work 31; removal argument 41–42
American Indian groups, written history (absence) 10
anhissi (my friend) (friendly town) 24
ankipaya (my enemy or opponent) (unfriendly town) 24
Arbeka Hadjo 73
Arbeka people, removal 50–51
Asbury (Methodist mission school) 33
Atkins, John D. C. 30–31

Bailey, Lorenzo A. 115, 120–121
Baker, Newton D. 160
Baptism, rite/process 27
Baptist churches 32–33, 166

Barnett, Jackson 126
Batak (Southeast Asia), extinction (cusp) 8
Bateman, Lee 149
Battle of Round Mountain (Battle of Red Fork) 63
Baum, Edward 149
Bennett, Leo 121–122
Berryhill, Martha (death) 166
Bible: missionary storytelling, impact 26–27; Mvskoke publication 31–32; preaching 76–77
Bird Creek, fight 76
Bixby, Tams 3
Blackhawk, Ned 7
Blackstone, P.N. 82
Blair, Willie 116, 131
Bland, Susan 125
Board of Indian Commissioners, resolution 78
Bob, Daniel 156; photo 101; spirit house construction 156
Boomer movement: development 95; impact 3, 79–86; population, increase 131; pressure 109
Botha (evil spirit), impact 2–3
"Bringing in the Sheaves" (singing) 69
British traders, Mvskokes contact 5

INDEX

Broker Promises Report (Chaudhuri) 168

Brown, John W. 112

Bruner, William 95–96

Bruyneel, Kevin 7

Buckner, H. F. 31

Bushyhead, D. W. 82

Busk ceremonies 18–19

Butcher, Nafa 162

Canadian River: Deep Fork 75–76; North Fork 129, 143, 153; Upper Mvskokes existence 51–52

Canton, Frank (Harjo meeting) 142

Carr, Bill 149

Carruth, E.J. 62

Carter, Jacob V. 92

Cass, Lewis 41, 43

Census Card No. 2718 3

Century of Dishonor, A (Hunt Jackson) 85

Cēpvnē (Indian story character) 72–73, 170; naming 72; old witch visit 14; plant discovery 14–15

Cēpvnvke (little boy) 72

Chaudhuri, Jean Hill 168

Chaudhuri, Jonodev Osceola 168

Chaudhuri, Joyotpaul 168

Checotah, founding 145

Checote, Samuel 74, 76–77, 87; delegates, Washington travel 77; election defeat 95–96; leadership 5; peace agreement 92–93; photo 99; resignation 93; U.S. recognition 77–78

Cheeks, Billy 133

Cherokee Commission (Jerome Commission) 127

Cherokee National Council (Smith membership) 117

Cherokees: assimilation, test 40; citizenship, entitlement 95; gold rush, '29ers (impact) 40

Chewey, Sam 164

Chickawas, land sale 68

Childers, Daniel "Goob" 91

Children, tribal language usage (prohibition) 30–31

Choctaws, land sale 68

Christian beliefs, traditional beliefs (blending) 50

Christian doctrine, promotion 124

Christianity: increase 8; intrusion 26–27; Mvskokes/Semvnoles conversion 27, 29; proliferation 33; tenets, impact 59; threat 30–32

Christian Mvskokes, number (increase) 26

Christie, Tom (leadership) 162–163

Churches 26–35, 166; Indian churches, denominations 32–33

Cimarron River (Red Fork) 62–63; camp setup 60; Lower Mvskokes existence 51–52

Civilization Fund Act 84

Clark, Clarence D. 135

Coachman, Ward 82

Cody, Buffalo Bill 156

Coke, Richard 81, 84

Coker, Charlie 150–151, 154; attack 149

Colbert, Winchester 67

Colonization process 8–9

Columbus, Christopher: *Botha,* impact 2; greed 9

Confederate States of America: Choctaws/Semvnoles, treaty (signing) 61; Indian fight, Pike bargain 60–61; Native regiments, formation 62

INDEX

Constitutional rights, test 97
Cook, Don 66, 76
Cook, Fred 152
Cooper, Douglas Hancock 62–65;
 reinforcements, need 64–65
Cooper, Whina 6
Corn, importance/cultivation
 21–22
Cotchochee (Sands leader) 79
Council House, renovation 165–166
Court of Indian Offenses 30
Court system, power (observation)
 115–116
Cox, Claude 164–165
Crazy Snake Indians/tribe 120;
 arrests 123, 128; description 131;
 detention 122; summoning
 132–133
Crazy Snake movement 5, 6–7;
 action/justice, relationship 9;
 growth 121–122; hostilities
 126–127; occurrence 8
Crazy Snake Rebellion 3, 6–7; photo
 103
Creek Indian Council, recognition
 163
Creek Nation, 1866 treaty 67–68
Crockett, Davy 41
Cruce, Lee 124
Cummins, Frederick T. 133
Curtis, Charles 110–111
Curtis Act 110–111, 119; amendment
 165; impact 134

Dance ceremonies (stomp dances)
 2, 23
Davis, Jefferson 61
Davis, John 163
Davis, Polly 153–154
Dawes, Henry Lauren 4, 83–84

Dawes Act (General Allotment Act)
 (Dawes Severalty Act) 4, 161;
 allotment proposal 118–119; impact
 126–127; discussion 166; Indian
 enrollment 115; Indian exemptions
 119; induction 114; passage 85–86;
 provisions, extension 110–111;
 territory protection 108–109;
 undoing, hope 139–140
Dawes Commission 111–117;
 agreement 123; allotment proposal
 118–119; closure 133–134; creation
 127; negotiations 117–118; photo
 100
Deloria, Jr., Vine 7
Dixon, H. B. 122
Dreams, Indian belief 25
Dunbar Ortiz, Roxane 7
Dunn, J. W. (denunciation) 78

Earth, Mvskoke reverence 9
Eastern tribes, homeland exchange
 42–43
Eastern Woodland tribes, Pontiac
 rebellion 6
ehosa (mystical being) 71
ēkvnv (earth), human/animal origins
 23–24
Emotional assistance, need 29
Enabling Act (June 16, 1906) 125
Epohfvnkv. See Medicine Way of
 Epohfvnkv
este-hvtke (este-cate) (white people)
 29, 113, 156; acting 77; becoming
 52–53, 119; Botha, impact 2;
 description 38–39; dressing 38;
 factionalism 39; identities,
 preservation 94; protection 4
Estemerketv Nene (Road of Suffering)
 (Trail of Suffering) (Path of

INDEX

Estemerketv Nene (continued)
Suffering) 44–53, 118; inhumane
treatment 53
etekvlkē (factionalism) 98; addition
132; pain 4–5
etekvlkē curse, persistence 89
Eufaula, violence (warning) 133
Eufaula Hadjo 73

Federal paternalism, impact 163
feke ofv (seventh direction) 66
fek herkv ("inner peace"), pursuit 10
Ferguson, Walter 124; attack/
bleeding 146–147
Fickinger, Paul L. 163–164
Fire, burning (locations) 18
First Nations of Indigenous groups,
Canada treaties 4
Five Civilized Tribes: Dawes Act,
provisions (extension) 110–111;
protection 85–86; territories,
Dawes Act protection 108–109
Five Nations: allotment process 98;
government dissolution, Curtis
Act (impact) 134; lands: allotments, member enrollment
111–112; retention, question 60;
white settler encroachment 39;
leaders, election (enablement)
164–165; rules exemptions 30;
sovereignty, undermining 68;
surrender agreements 67–68;
traditionalists, impact 117–124
Fixico, Fus (letter) 107
Fixico, Hotulke 115, 116
Fixico, Jonas 166
Fleming, John 31
Fort Gibson: Mvskoke arrival 50–51;
Mvskoke destination 46–47,
64–65; Sequoyah capital
selection 141

Fort Leavenworth: Crazy Snake
followers, sentencing 123, 128;
Indian arrival 63–67
Fort Row, Indian protection
(Lincoln promise) 62
Fort Scott 65–66
Fort Sill Apache Tribe 10
Fort Smith, Crazy Snake members
(detention) 123
Foster, Edwin B. 124
Four (number), observation 11
Four Mothers Society: formation 5,
139–140; letter 160; lobbying
power, absence 140; meeting 163
Four Mothers Stomp Grounds,
Keetoowah Cherokees dance
7–8
Fourth Sunday tradition 28–29
Fowler, Timothy 146–147; death
147
Freedmen: arrest 148–149; gatherings
142
Freedmen Negroes, death 151–152
Frelinghuysen, Theodore 41–42
Frisco railroad lines, towns (estab-
lishment) 86
Full-bloods 168; gatherings 142;
mixed-bloods, split 39; thefts 131

Galbreath, Robert F. 125
Gary, Walter (interview) 54
Gentry, Jeff 54–55
Geography Made Easy (Morse) 32
Ghost Dance 35–36
Glass, Dick 91
God, live (rededication) 29
Grayson, Joe 113
Grayson, Sampson 46
Great Depression 162
"Great Seal of the Muscogee
Nation I.T." 69

INDEX

Great War, Mvskoke men (drafting) 159–160
Great White Father's Court, Indian trial 122–123
Green Corn Ceremony 127–128; following 98; Medicine Way, Christianity (threat) 30; practice 23, 27
Green Corn Dances, holding 60
Green Corn Dance Tas, Cherokee/Choctaw practice 15
Green Corn Rebellion 159
Green Peach War (Spa-he-ch's War) 2, 5, 74, 75, 86–93
Guin, Jim 132–133

Habbe, Asa 92
Hadjo, Arbeka ("Fearless Person of Arbeka Town") 73
Hadjo, Eufaula ("Fearless Person of Eufaula Town") 73
Haggty, Sol (collector) 130
Hale, Salma 32
Happy Hunting Grounds 107
Harding, Warren (Four Mothers Society letter) 160
Harjo, Ahalock/Milley 72
Harjo, Ben 122
Harjo, Bill 1
Harjo, Chinnubbie. See Posey, Alexander
Harjo, Chitto (Crazy Snake): allotment resistance 113; arrest 128; birth 72; blame 152; cabin, burning 152–153; camp (Hickory Ground) (photo) 103; Canton meeting 142; capture 148; Census Card No. 2718 3; Coker assistance 154; complaints 114; concerns 30; conspiracy charge/arrest 122; council grounds, establishment

137; crime, rumor 145–146; Cusseta Treaty copy, usage 121; death 155, 156; existence 3–4; family life 129; fight 30; followers, death/capture 148–149; full-blood Mvskoke 1–2; government, maintenance (argument) 144; *henehv* (second leader) 2; home (photo) 102; hostilities 146–147; Indian condemnation 123–124; indictment 153; land allotment acceptance 117; legacy 159; loyalist, affiliation 66–67; Medicine Way preservation 79; money, collection 130; Mvskoke Roll No. 7934 3; names, alternates 1; negro followers 130; paternalism perspective 95; perception 1; photo 102, 104; property, lawmen (approach) 149–150; rebels, arrest (photo) 101; reconciliation/hybridity 10; story, parallels 6; traditionalists/freedmen, joining 120; Washington meeting 134–135; Washington trip 134; wound 154–155
Harjo, Eufaula 159–160, 166; leadership 46
Harjo, Nokeche 134
Harjo, Oktarharsars 76
Harjo, Pin 153
Harjo, Thomas 134; hanging, attempt 150–151
Harjo, Tuckabatchee 89
Harjo, Wendell Wayne 169
Harjo v. Kleepe 165
Harris, Frank 154
Harrison, Benjamin 109
Harrison, John 88–89
Haskell, Charles 130, 152
Hawkins, Lee 130, 148–149

213

INDEX

Hayes, Marie L. (meeting) 163–164

Head, Calvin Naked 162–163

hecetv 1

heleswv (medicine) 24

henehv (orator) 23

henehv (second leader) 2

Henryetta (town) 118; council grounds, establishment 137; Snakes: return 128–129; search 144; Troop A, encampment 122; whites, arrival 143

Henryetta Home Guard, action 159

Herrod, G. 31

Hesaketvmesē (Maker of Breath) 13, 75, 98; external elements, arrangement 24–25; Mvskoke prayer 49; naming 18; prayer 64; thanks, giving 13–14

Hesaketvmesē pon Hesaketvmesē, Poth key hul we lay gets cv (Maker of Breath oh Maker of Breath) 76

Heydrick, Jesse 125

Hickory Ground 127–136; council gathering, call 142; Crazy Snake camp (photo) 103; Creek Nation capital 113; Indian gathering 151; protection, Mvskoke National Council law 167; search 169; shooting, escape 155; war, approach/anticipation 145

Hickory Ground Stomp Ground, everlasting feeling 170

Hickory Stomp Ground 2; Harjo perceptions 120; Keetoowah Cherokees dance 8

Hicks, Bunner 162

History of the United States (Hale) 32

Hodge, David M. 82

Hoffman, Roy 152–153

Homestead Act (public lands availability) 80–81

hotvle rakko (tornado) 75–76

House Concurrent Resolution 108 164

House of Kings 69, 121; mixed-blood 135; replacement 165

House of Warriors 69, 121; replacement 165

House Resolution 8581, introduction 110

Hubbard, E. H. 133

Hunting claim 20–21

Hunt Jackson, Helen 85

"Hus-see O-sa Le-Cha" (Under the Rising of the Sun) 12

hvlpvtv (alligator clan) 1

Hvmmaketv 13, 57, 75, 108, 139, 159

Ida Glenn No. I oil field 125

Identity, importance 9–10

Indian allotment system, "pulverizing engine" 127

Indian Appropriation Act, passage 79–80

Indian Base Line and Meridian, authorization 127

Indian chief elections (1883/1895) 93–98

Indian churches, denominations 32–33

Indian land, allotment (goals) 82

Indian Mission Conference 77

Indian Nations: U.S. treaties/agreements 4; white citizens, tax collections 111

Indian nations, warriors (Tecumseh recruitment) 6

Indian problem, solution (need) 85

Indian Reorganization Act (IRA) 161

214

INDEX

Indians: assimilation/removal, choice 39–44; early Indians, health 12; government, maintenance (Harjo argument) 144; inhumane treatment 53; newcomers, western tribe attacks 51; non-Indian conflicts 7; offenses (Price establishment) 30; removal: Congressional legislation 41–42; hardship, description 52–53; self-determination 165; tribes, independent nation status (government nonrecognition) 80; whites, fight (Harjo avoidance) 122

Indian Territory: federal district court, establishment 95; leaders, autonomy (preservation) 140; outlaws/cattle drives, impact 143; removal parties, arrival 48; removals 5, 31; resettling 8–9; white expeditions, impact 80–81; white settlers, influx 3

Indian-white relations, problem (increase) 131

Indigenous worldviews/cultures, understanding 6–7

Inter-Tribal Council of the Five Civilized Tribes, re-emergence 163

Iowa Tribe of Oklahoma 10

Irish traders, Mvskokes contact 5

Isparhecher (Chief): defeat 88; equality/justice, stress 97; hostility, continuation 5; House of Warriors election 86; land allotment choice 97; Medicine Way preservation 7–8; open letter (public statement) 96–97; peace agreement 92–93; political leadership 2, 74; Porter pursuit 92; pursuit 91; recognition/protection request 87–88; seclusion 96; warning 111; warriors, capture 92

Isphecha, home (visit) 137

Jackson, Andrew: battle 2; *Botha,* impact 2–3; fight, McIntosh (joining) 39; greed 9; Opothleya-hola/Red Sticks, fight 47; S.102 law approval/signing 42; tribal argument 40

Jackson, Simon 47

Jackson, Sonny 153–154

Jacobs, Henry 113, 130

Jesus, story (impact) 27

Jim Crowism 143

Johnson, Grant 121, 128

Jones, Bill 1

Jones, Legus 134, 152

Jones, Salina 112, 114, 120, 134

Jones, William Frank 128, 146, 149; Porter contact 116

Jones, Wilson 1, 3, 112

Jones Davis, Polly 154

Katy railroad: depot 145; Mvskoke Nation towns, connection 59; towns, establishment 86

Kaw Medicine Way 110

Keetoowah Cherokees: Crazy Snake, relationship 133; dance 7–8

Keetoowahs, leadership 162–163

Kelley, Agnes 74, 131

Kile, William (care, providing) 66

Lake Mohonk "Lake in the Sky" meeting, Indian land allotment discussion 84–85

Land: ownership, perception 22; speculators (sand shakers): chaos, cause 48; intrusion 43

INDEX

Land, understanding 6–7
Land allotment: acceptance 111;
Choctaw/Chickasaw acceptance
118; Fixico letter 107; Harjo
acceptance 117; Harjo resistance
113; Nighthawk Keetoowah
enrollment 117; perspectives/
arguments 82–84; Porter doubts
128–129; procedures, refusal
120–121; refusal 113–114; Treaty of
Cusseta, impact 135–136; with-
drawals, Congress (impact) 134
Land Run of 1889 109
Language, understanding 6–7
Last handshake 156–157
Lee, Robert E. (surrender) 67
"Legend of Abuska, The" (Semv-
noles/Mvskokes story) 14
Leupp, Francis 144
Lewis, Saley 113
Lewis, Winey 113
Life: beginning, denotation 11–12;
elements 17
Light/dark, meeting (significance)
33–34
Lighthorse: arrests 87; patrols 32;
Porter Command 5, 79; tribal
police, creation 58
Light Horsemen 74
Likowski, John 131
Lincoln, Abraham (Hutko/
Opothleyahola question) 61–62
"Little Brother of War" (stick ball
games) 24
Long, Chester 135
Long talk 23
Looney, George 169
Loughridge, R.M. 31
Loughridge Boarding School,
opening 33

Lower Mvskokes: compliance 69;
federal funds, distribution 77–78;
problems 52
Lower towns (lower *tvlofvs*),
Mvskokes trader contacts 5
Lunar moons, Mvskoke counting
method 34

Maori: land rights recognition,
demands 6; people, New Zealand
treaty 4
Mapuche, attack 6
Mareco, Carlos 6
Marshall, Benjamin 52
Marshall, Gabriel 91
Marshell, Punch 145–146
McCumber, Porter 141
McGilbray, John 96
McIntosh, Albert Gallatin "Cheesie"
115
McIntosh, Chilly 77
McIntosh, Daniel Newman 76
McIntosh, James M. 64
McIntosh, William 38–40; *Botha,*
impact 2
McKinley, William (Mvskoke
National Council message) 109
Medicine men, songs (usage) 16
Medicine Way of *Epohfvnkv*
(Medicine Way of Life) (Medicine
Way) 1, 13, 26; balance 19, 22; tilt
98; church/school challenge 26–35;
continuation 25; dance, relation-
ship 2; inclusiveness 130–131;
maintenance, Upper Mvskokes
belief 4–5; metaphysical energy
170; positive continuum 2;
preservation, attempt 3, 7–8, 79;
support 113–114; thanks, giving 73;
Upper Mvskokes beliefs 4–5

216

INDEX

Mēkko Ho-ne-cha (Wild King), ingestion 47
mēkkvke (chiefs): appointment 163; land allotment 43
mēkkvke (town leaders), origin 24
"'Mellow Drammer' in All Its Gory Hideousness" 157
Merrick, Joe 147
Metaphysical realm, influence 25–26
Micco, Eneah (surrender) 46
Micco, Katcha 122
Micco, Lahtah 115, 116
Micco, Oktayache 122
Mixed-bloods: blame 139–140; full-bloods, split 139; traditionalists, gatherings 142
Modern Geography (Smith) 32
Moore, L. C. 139–140
Morey, W. H. 142
Morey, W. M. 152
Morse, Jedidiah 32
Mother Earth: Indian relationship 44; maternal metaphor 9; parcels, ownership 97; prayer 64; tribal understanding 22
Moving fire tradition 47–48
Muscogee (Creek) Nation v. Hodel 165
Muscogee Creek Nation of Oklahoma, name change 9
Muscogee Creeks, lawsuit (dismissal) 167
Muscogee Nation of Oklahoma, name correction 9
Muskogee Arkansas Town 140
Muskokee or Creek First Reader / Nakcokv Es Kerretv Enhvteceskv, student usage 34
Muskoki imunaitsu / Muskogee (Creek) Assistant (language book) (Fleming) 31

Mvskoke Confederacy 2, 19–20; government, centralization 58; *tvlofvs* characteristics 23
Mvskoke Constitution of 1867 93
Mvskoke country, white settlers (influx) 3
Mvskoke Nation: cattlemen, impact 70–71; devastation, war (impact) 69–70; districts, division 69; fires, danger 71; hardships, neighbors (assistance) 70; intruders, threat (growth) 132; missionary preaching, permissions 59; outlaws/trespassers 87; peoples, infusion 8–9; reservation, self-sustenance 168; war, impact 66
Mvskoke National Council message 109
Mvskoke Roll No. 7934 3
Mvskokes: assigned allotments, Dawes Commission recording 119; assimilation, Porter perspective 109; Checote leadership 5; Christianized farmer transformation 69; churches, hybrids 27–28; Civil War neutrality 61–63; clans 17; clans, leadership provision 24; culture/values, transportation 51–52; Cusseta Treaty delegates 43; dance ceremonies (stomp dances) 23; devastation/destruction/depression 71–72; election, fraud charges 88–89; Georgia settlers, hostilities 45–46; identity, distinction 9; Jackson assistance request 5; land: allotment, swindling 43; exchange 43; oil, discovery 125–126; life, threats 79–80; loyalists/confederates

INDEX

Mvskokes (continued)
59–63; Maker of Breath prayer 49;
medicine, taking 15; Medicine
Way, preservation (attempt) 3;
men, drafting (Great War)
159–160; metaphysical world belief
1–2; migration 16; moving (idea),
debates 39–40; national government, inclusiveness 130–131;
nationalism belief 5–6; Native
sovereignty, sustaining 7; new
constitution, completion 68–69;
protection 4; reconstruction,
ordeal 98; removal 31; McIntosh
approval 40; suffering/starvation
46–47; Snake whippings 131;
sovereignty, election demonstra-
tion 94; spoken word, translation
31–32; struggles 71–72; survivor
arrival 65–66; transportation, U.S.
Army negotiation 50; treaties,
signing 148; treaty rights, recovery
(request) 160
Mvskoke War of 1813–1814 47

Nakcokv esyvhiketv or *Muskogee
Hymns* (Loughridge/Winslett) 31
National Council, law passage 77
National Historic Preservation Act
167
Native American Church,
emergence 36
Native American Graves Protection
and Reparation Act 167
Native patriotism, illustration 6–7
Native regiments, formation 62
Native sovereignty, sustaining 7
Native traditionalism, criticism 156
Neal, Moses 94–95
New Deal Programs, impact 161

Nichols, R. L. 33
Nighthawk Keetoowahs, ceremony
160
Nighthawk Keetoowah Society,
formation 117
Nighthawk Society (photo) 99

Ocmulgee mound complex 121; town
leaders, meeting 57
Odom, Doc 145, 149–150, 155
Odom, Herman 149–150; death
150
Oil (black gold), discovery 124–127
Oklahoma, creation 136
Oklahoma Indian Welfare Act
(OIWA) 161–162, 165
Oklahoma Territory: population,
increase 109; statehood, approach
140
Oktarharsars 2; Medicine Way
preservation 7–8; Sands
Rebellion 5
Oktarharsars Harjo: Board of Indian
Commissioners hearing 78;
problems 77–78; Sands warriors,
Cotchochee (leadership) 79;
traditionalists (Sands) 77; treaty
amendment ratification 77–78
Opothleyahola (Old Gouge) 2;
Medicine Way preservation 7–8;
Msvkokes, joining 64; photo 105;
Red Stick 47; Road of Suffering,
tribal travels 47; Sac and Fox
agency arrival 66; treaty signing,
opposition 61; wisdom 60
Organic Act for Oklahoma District
109
Original identity, external influences
(increase) 8
Osage land, oil (discovery) 125–126

INDEX

Osage reservation, land (Foster lease) 124–125

Otoe-Missouri Tribe 10

owalvs (prophets), star watching 45

Page, John 46

Palmer, Eliza 97

Parker, Ely 78

Paternalism: federal paternalism, impact 163; Harjo perspective 95

Patriotic resistance 8

Patty, A. Y. 144–148

Payne, Frank 54

Pecan Creek, skirmishes 89–90

Perkins, John Henderson 151–152

Perryman, Cornelius 135

Perryman, Joseph M. 93–94; election winner 94

Pike, Albert 60–61

Pinehill, Leo 146, 155

Pitchlynn, Peter 67, 82

Pittman, Laurel 145–146

Poarch Band, tribal casinos (operation) 167

Pontiac Rebellion (Eastern Woodland tribes) 6

Porter, Pleasant 5, 76, 82; allotment perspective 119, 128–129; command 79; convention president 140–141; election 119; Fixico letter 107; influence 96; insurrection 90–91; Jones contact 116; photo 104; power, belief 96

Posey, Alexander 133–134; Chinnubbie Harjo (pen name) 141; secretary election 140–141

Posketv (Green Corn Ceremony) 13, 15, 19

Pow wow grounds 153

Poyvekco yekcetv Emeyuksvseko 168

Poyvekcv (Spirit) 5, 26; inclusiveness 26; spiritualism 170; tradition 19; way 168

Poyvekcv yekcetv (Spirit Power) 57, 126

Poyvfekcv em eyoksicetv seko ("Spirit Everlasting") 8, 10

Prairie fires, danger 70–71

Price, Hiram 30

Proctor, David 166–167

"Protest of the Representatives of the Indian Territory" (Indian memorial) 81–82

Public Law 91-495 164–165

Quayle, William 62

Rabbit (Mvskoke trickster) 34

Ransome, Bill 147–148

Reconstruction, Mvskoke national government inclusiveness 130–131

Redbird Smith Stomp Ground, Keetoowah Cherokees dance 7–8

Red Fork. *See* Cimarron River

Red River: lands, appropriation 81; migration 16

Red root *(mēkko-hoyvnēcv)*, ingestion/location 15–16

Red Stick 73; mother Red Stick towns 19; warriors, provocation 45–46

Red Stick War (1813–1814) 39

Religion, understanding 6

Religious Freedom Restoration Act 167

Revelation 6:13 45

Revised Statues of the United States, Section 5440 122

Roach, Ada 129

Robbins, Ascher 41

INDEX

Robinson, L. N. 78
Roosevelt, Theodore 126, 134, 141
Round Mountain, fight 76
Ryal, Larkin 27, 58, 145

Sac and Fox reservation, intruder
permissions 94–95
Sacred history, understanding 6–7
Salem Store 151
Sander, George 82
Sands Rebellion 5, 78
Sands Uprising 2, 75, 78–79
Santa Cruz River valley, Indigenous
tribes (disappearance) 8–9
Sa-Pa-Ye, surrender 149
Sawhoyamaxa community (Para-
guay), Mareco leadership 6
Schools 26–35; opening/operation 34
Scottish traders, Mvskokes contact 5
Seaman Building, Elks Lodge hall
(Congressional/Indian meeting)
134–135
Second Great Awakening 59
Second Semvnole War (1835–1842) 46
Select Committee to Investigate
Matters Connected with Affairs in
the Indian Territory 134
Self-determination: federal policy
165; insistence 120–121
Semvnoles: culture/values, transpor-
tation 51–52; land, sale 68
Sequoyah (leader) 40
Sermons, impact 29
Settlers, intrusion 43
Shoenfelt, J. B. 122
Short Sermon: Also Hymns and *Istutsi
in naktsoku* or *The Child's Book*
(Fleming) 31
Signal Corps Cowboys (Bedford
Riding Academy) 156–157

Sister stomp grounds, development
28
Sitting Bull, travels 35–36
Skaggs, Drennan C. 133–134
Sleeping Rabbit: capture 90; death
91; traditionalist alignment 89
Smith, Crosslin Fields 158
Smith, R. M. 32
Smith, Redbird 84, 117, 158; birthday,
celebration 164; death 160; photo
106
Smith, Stoke 164
Snake, Bill 1
Snakes 108; arrest 154; attack
149–150; death 147; desertion 148;
meeting: continuation 159;
shooting 146; return (Henryetta)
128–129; search (Henryetta) 144;
threat 144; tribes, combination
139–140
Snake War 139; name 142
Sofkey, making 22
Spiritual guidance, need 29
Sprague, Peleg 41
Springs, Morey 142
Square grounds (stomp dance
grounds) 23
Starr, Daniel 137
Starr, David 147
State of Sequoyah 140; convention
141; council 142; Indian Territory
name, vote 141; proposal 140
Steele, George W. 109
Stidham, Sally 46
Stock Market Crash 125
Stomp dances 69–70, 152: attendance
5–6; church-going, combination
34–35; grounds, reference 23; group
effort 55–56; holding 25; sermon/
song, focus 28; Sunday church

INDEX

service, relationship 35; tradition, birth 53; visitor welcoming 2; white boy stomp dance 54. *See also* Dance ceremonies

Stomp grounds, retention 163

Sue A. Bland No. I oil field 125

Sugar Creek, skirmishes 89–90

Sun *(hotvlē)* 16–17; rising, denotation 11–12; total eclipse 33–34

Swift, Frank 149

Tecumseh, warrior recruitment 6

Te Haua to Wellington march 6

Teller, Henry M. 30, 82–83, 94

Termination policy (1950s) 164

Thomas, Elmer 161

Thomas, John R. 123

Thomas, Robert 6

Thompson, Mēkko 167

Thompson, Myron H. 167

Tiger, George 112

Tiger, Thomas 152

Tiger Mountain, search 169

totkv (fire), creation 18

Towns *(tvlofvs)* 19–26; characteristics 20; confederation, opinions (differences) 38; function 38; leaders, annual meeting 57; men, responsibilities 20–21; red town/ white town division 24; reorganization, interest 162; women, responsibilities 20–21

Traditionalism: adherence, attempt 9–10; continuum 8–9; decrease 8; defense, interpretation 6; Medicine Way 166

Traditionalists, churchgoing Indians (reconciliation) 167

Treaty of 1832 (Treaty of Cusseta) (Cusseta Treaty) 42, 52; agreement

4; Article 14, impact 43–44; changes 135–136; legal rights protection 115–116; Mvskoke delegates 43

Treaty of 1866 67–72; agreement 4; amendment: National Council ratification 77–78; negotiation 77–78

Treaty of Indian Springs (McIntosh treaty), signing 39–40

Treaty of Waitangi (1840) 4

Tribal government, dissolution (opposition) 163–164

Tribal language, child usage (prohibition) 30–31

Tribal sovereignty, government hostility 79–80

Tuckabatchee Council House, sacred plates (carrying) 48–49

Tufts, Jonathan Q. 87, 91, 94

Tulahassee Wvkokaye ceremonial ground, *mēkko* 166

Tustenugee, Yarteen 86

uewv (water for life), need 18

Unappropriated Lands, white settlers (impact) 80

Unassigned Lands 108–109

Union loyalists, McIntosh attack 65

Upper Mvskokes: constitution acceptance 69; traditionalists 79

Valentine, Robert G. 144

Ward, LeRoy 114

War of 1812 6

Watie, Stand 67; photo 105

Watkins, Arthur 164

Watson, Oscar V. 151–152

White, Hugh 41

INDEX

White man's war 2, 57
Whites: racial bigotry, promotion 142–143; settlers, influx 3
White Stick (Ehvtkecvlke) 1, 73, 122; Cēpvnē, relationship 72; mother towns 19
Wick, John S. 125
Wiley, Mose 48
Willhite, Andrew 129–130, 143
Wilson, Thomas 128
Wind (Hesaketvmesē) 18
Wind (spirit) 16–17

Wind Creek Casino and Resort (Wetumpka) 167
Winslett, David 31
Wisest ones (owalvs), warnings 19
Witgen, Michael 7
Women's National Indian Association, allotment argument 85
Writ Hastings, William 141
Written history, absence 10

Yahola, Hotulke 115, 116